# THE BRUTAL TRUTH

# THE BRUTAL TRUTH

## THE INSIDE STORY
## OF A GANGLAND LEGEND

### ERIC MASON

MAINSTREAM
PUBLISHING

EDINBURGH AND LONDON

## ACKNOWLEDGEMENTS

I could not have written my autobiography without the invaluable help of the following people, to whom I am very much indebted: Eileen Copus, Roy Copus, Jimmy Donnelly, Maxine Doyle, John Nash, Linda Nash, Louise Norris, Mixie Walsh.

I'd like to thank the many friends who have provided me with additional photographs and allowed me to use their names in my book.

First published in Great Britain in 2000 by
MAINSTREAM PUBLISHING COMPANY (EDINBURGH) LTD
7 Albany Street
Edinburgh EH1 3UG

ISBN 1 84018 362 4

A catalogue record for this book is available from the British Library

Typeset in Berkeley Book and Trixie Plain
Printed and bound in Great Britain by Butler & Tanner Ltd, Frome and London

# CONTENTS

# PREFACE

There are many reasons for writing my autobiography. One of them was that I wanted to put the record straight.

In March of 1993, I received a letter, out of the blue, from the authorities at Broadmoor Hospital, requesting permission from myself for Ronnie Kray to telephone me. He started to call me, sometimes every day for a week or so, then I wouldn't hear from him for a while. Then it would begin again. This went on for about two years, during which time he told me many things about himself and his brother, Reggie Kray. I would visit Reggie quite often at this time and would discuss many things from the past, the present and our hopes for the future. I'm afraid, though, that Reggie had too many hangers-on trying to get him to endorse various schemes and he seemed to have lost touch with the reality of life. In the end, I gave up my visits, but I wish him well all the same.

Meanwhile, Ronnie was continuing to phone me and because he seemed to realise he was very ill, he wanted to tell me things and get them off his mind. He gave me the reason he had killed George Cornell and why he had asked Reggie to get me to see him where he was hiding out. It seemed that he knew he was going to die and that he wanted to put the record straight. Within a matter of days, he was taken back to the hospital, where he died.

Some years prior to this, I had moved to a different part of the country and had changed my life completely. I had lost touch with all the faces from the past. Then came Ronnie's funeral. Everyone there was rekindling old friendships and catching up with what had been going on in the underworld. It was a time of reflection for me and I became privy to many things to do with major crime incidents that had happened in the past few years.

Since then, I have read many books by notorious characters who have been involved in some way with the underworld and I find that, with very few exceptions, they have all been 'ghost-written' – which explains why they all seem to contradict each other.

In one book currently available, an incident is mentioned where I am supposed to have visited John Bloom's club, the Phone Box, with the intention of getting a 'pension' from there. I have never been to that club and only ever met one person in my life who was involved with John Bloom, 'Scouse Norman' Johnson, who was a good friend of mine. As for the chap I was supposed to have been with, a cousin of the Kray twins, I can't ever remember going to any club at any point with him.

Another story by the same author concerns my fall-out with Frank Fraser and the Richardson brothers. The only people who left town after that fracas were Fraser and the rest of them. They went to Southport, where they were involved in setting about a tiny little waiter known as the 'Greek Midget'. Their 'bubble' really burst that night and they all left town again.

Some inaccuracies are not worth getting annoyed about, they are laughable; other blatant lies, though, have to be addressed.

*The Brutal Truth* is a true account of one man's life in the underworld. It recalls the people I have had dealings with – inside and outside some of the harshest prisons in the British penal system. It describes how I was the last man to be flogged with the cat-o'-nine-tails. I have been involved in some of London' s most notorious gang wars – and lived to tell the tale.

# FOREWORD

I have known Eric Mason for about forty years (though I shouldn't really say how many, as it tends to shop your age). Having said that, I don't know where the years have gone. But what I do know is that as hard a life as Eric has had, it certainly hasn't blunted his memory. That, and the fact he still hasn't lost his scruples, makes Eric one of the most respected men in the country with anyone connected with the underworld.

I have read a rough proof of *The Brutal Truth* and it's a no-holds-barred book of fact. A good part of it covers a very difficult era, different from today in many ways and I am looking forward to reading the finished article. I'm sure it will be a winner and be hard to put down.

You certainly can't say anything better of anyone, than that he is a good friend – they are very hard to come by. Eric is such a person and anyone who knows him, or who is close to him, can count themselves lucky.

I wish the book every success – as I've said, it will be a winner! And it couldn't happen to a better man.

*Johnny Nash*
*April 2000*

# 1.

## My Introduction to the Penal System

By the time I arrived at the strongbox, I was barely conscious. I had been dragged to the punishment block, the blows raining down on me while the screws pulling me along happily smashed my head against the iron stanchions. The last thing I remember was a screw jumping on me while the baton-wielders were beating my testicles. I was beyond fighting back – all I could do was try to protect my body from the worst of their attacks. Eventually I must have passed out.

I woke up in the strongbox, strapped into a body belt. It felt as though every bone in my body was broken. My mouth was full of blood, the same blood that covered my whole body. In the dim light I could make out that I had no clothes on. I must have lain like that for hours – I was freezing cold and the pain was unbearable. At that point I was beyond caring whether I lived or died.

The next morning, about sixteen hours later, the screws came in and dragged me to the strongbox next door while the cleaner came down to mop up the blood. I was still caked in it and could hardly move when they told me to stand for adjudication. I just spat the blood out of my mouth as the governor arrived with the chief and stood in the doorway looking down at me, as I lay naked on the floor.

Then off they went leaving me there. Later that day, someone came in with a bucket of water and washed me down like an animal, then dragged me back into the cell I'd been in while the cleaner cleaned up the other one. I knew that I had broken bones in my hands. I had a severe pain in the lower part of my body and back which took many months to subside.

After two days with nothing to eat, they finally brought a mess of goulash on a papier maché plate and a cup of prison tea. My hands were still cuffed in the body belt so I couldn' t use them. Instead I was forced to eat from the plate off the floor like an animal. I realised that a tooth had broken when I went to pick the cup up with my teeth to tilt it. Although feeling more than a little depressed, I was more determined than ever that I was going to beat them.

For about two weeks, I was not allowed any access to a toilet. And not being able to use my hands, I had to perform my bodily functions where I lay. The screws dragged me from cell to cell, their cleaner following to clear up after me.

Eventually, eight screws came into the strongbox with a pair of slippers, trousers and a jacket about two sizes too big for me. They pulled the trousers on and tied them round with a piece of mailbag rope, then wrapped the jacket right around me, buttoned it up and said, 'Visiting magistrates'.

Everyone was locked in their own cells while I was taken to the boardroom. They didn' t seem to mind the magistrates seeing me but they didn't want the other cons to witness my condition. The trial was farcical like they always were – a typical kangaroo court. After about five minutes, I was taken back into the boardroom and told by the chairman, 'Your punishment has been sent for recommendation to the Home Office.'

At midday about two weeks later, after everyone had been fed except me, the door of my cell was thrown open and about twelve screws stood outside. 'Take this prisoner to the laundry,' the chief said. When I got to the laundry there stood the governor and the doctor with their henchmen. The governor wasted no time.

'The Home Office has confirmed your punishment. You will receive twelve strokes of the cat-o'-nine-tails and loss of six months' remission. Remove the prisoner's upper clothing and proceed to the frame.'

I was taken to the back section of the laundry. There stood a large wooden frame in the shape of a triangle. Next to this frame was an ordinary wooden table. On the table I saw a large square of lint smeared with ointment, then a large canvas belt, which I discovered was to protect my kidneys, a collar of soft material to protect my neck and a long rectangular box which presumably held the cat-o'-nine-tails.

I had just taken all this in when my ankles were shackled to the legs of the frame and my wrists cuffed to two pulleys. My head was pushed through a slit in the canvas sheet attached to the frame and a cover was buckled over my head to stop me looking around to see who was flogging me. The pulleys were then pulled by two screws who took pains to avoid looking at me – perhaps they were squeamish. I could look to my right side where my 'friend' the doctor stood so that he could see both my face and back.

I heard the footsteps of the screw who was to administer the punishment. He came to the table. I could hear him open the box and take the whip out of it and I could hear the swish of the strands as he sorted and separated them. It seemed as though everyone was holding their breath. It was so quiet. I started to think about what Gibbsy had said to me, when he knew I was going to have the 'pussy'. 'The first one hurts so much that it numbs your back and after that you can hardly feel anything.' It was some comfort.

So there I was in an atmosphere of silence and hatred, despairing and frustrated. I knew I had to take my punishment without a murmur to help me through my own private war against the system, a struggle that had started at the age of 13, when I was sent to an approved school. I was now 24 years old and a 'hardened criminal'. Sometimes I wondered how I had come to this . . .

I was born in St Mary's Hospital, Paddington, on 27 July 1930, the second of five brothers. Dennis was two years older than me, Fred and Brian two and five years younger respectively. Our youngest brother Raymond was not born until 1951.

My mother was a gentle person and I believe I was a bit of a favourite with her, although she loved all her boys and was proud of us all. For years she was convinced that I only got into trouble through taking the blame for other people – a belief that started during the war. My brother Fred, up to mischief again, had started a small fire in an air-raid shelter. When the police came to investigate they were told that one of the Masons had done it. I said it was me rather than see my kid brother get into trouble – though everyone knew Fred was the culprit.

Unlike my mother, my father was a strict disciplinarian. My earliest memories of him are of being beaten with his thick leather belt. He was an ambitious man, proud of the fact that he was the chauffeur to the then Prime Minister, Ramsay MacDonald. He was also a good amateur boxer and it was through his interest in boxing that he met my mother, whose father Jack and my great uncle Nick Foy were both professional fighters. Nick Foy was well known as 'The Marylebone Cyclone'. My father taught us to look after ourselves and to always fight fair. He would put boxing gloves on us and, kneeling on the floor, he would make us try to hit him. Having to accept his counter-punches in return left quite an impression on us children.

But one event left an even greater impression on me. I remember being in the house one time and hearing my mum screaming. Terrified, I ran downstairs, to see my father hitting her. I don't think I have ever got over witnessing that sight. My life has been violent at times but I have never hit any of the women I've had relationships with.

It was when I was about seven years old that I first became aware of how important boxing was in my family. My brother Dennis and I were allowed to get up at 3 a.m. to listen on the radio to the heavyweight Tommy Farr fighting Louis. I remember how excited my father was when he thought Farr had won, only to hear the commentator declare Louis the winner and still champion of the world.

The arguments about who should have won seemed to be the only topic of conversation when anyone came to the house. (I was later to meet both of those great gladiators and tell them of my early memories.) About a year later, I was to listen to another fight, between Eric Boon and Arthur Danahar, which was reputed to be the greatest lightweight battle of all time. Many years afterwards I met Eric Boon, who had something of a colourful life outside the ring. So it was no wonder that when my brothers and I used to put the boxing gloves on to spar with each other, the sessions seemed to turn into a war of attrition, with both of us adopting the names of our current personal heroes.

It was later during the war when my older brother Dennis joined the Sea Cadets and began to box for them, that I became interested enough to do anything other than roam the streets and get into mischief. So I joined the Sea Cadets with my brother and we both boxed in the annual championships at Edgware Drill Hall, where our prizes were given to us by Admiral Sir Roger Keyes. We were so proud when we showed Mother what we had won – a gold-plated bosun's pipe. I think she'd have been happier if it had been a joint of meat, but our mother, like many other mothers during the war years, had to put on a bold front and somehow succeed in bringing up a large family on a pittance.

I look back on those days with a certain nostalgia, although they were probably hard times for my mother. I remember how she used to get me to go to the grocer to ask for three pennyworth of bacon bones so that we could always have a pot of bacon-bone soup simmering on the stove during the cold winters. She would send me because the grocer used to come to the amateur shows and sponsored some of the bouts – so he would always give me extra bones.

When the war started, my father joined the Royal Army Service Corps as a driver and was quickly made a staff sergeant. With him no longer living at home and rarely being able to visit us, life seemed a lot freer. Before the war we had moved from Marylebone into a council house a little way from where we had first grown up. I missed my grandparents and my cousins, who all lived near each other. My grandfather used to teach me to punch correctly, to cover up, move and build up my stamina, which was to stand me in good stead in later years. I was forever disappearing back to my grandparents and my mother got used to me not being around for days on end. I also loved to roam around on my own. I used to go on the tube, buy a three-halfpence return ticket to the next station, then travel all over the tube network for hours before returning home.

By 1941, the war was at its height with bombing most nights and fighter planes having dog-fights in the clear skies over London during the day. By the time the air-raid sirens sounded their warning after dark, most people would already be in the shelters or be getting ready to go down for the night. But I was usually to be found wandering around looking for good pieces of shrapnel to swap at school the next day or on my way to my grandmother's where I sometimes arrived around midnight before going to the shelter that had been dug between the blocks of flats. If it was the weekend, there was invariably a party going on, with plenty of beer for the adults and lemonade for the kids and plenty of cockney songs.

One night, on my way to my grandmother's, there was an air-raid and I heard a bomb go off about a mile in front of me. I felt the deep tremor of the blast and when I got to where the bomb had dropped in the middle of the main road, the emergency services were helping people from the damaged flats. One constable asked if I was from one of the flats. 'No, I was bombed out further up the road and I'm going to my gran's,' I said. So he helped me by-pass the bomb crater and let me take a large tin of biscuits from a grocer shop that had had its front blown in. By the time I got to the shelter in Marylebone, I was a welcome guest with my tin.

I wasn't always allowed to get away with it, however. Christmas 1941 saw me travelling on the tube for most of the day. I hadn't been home for a couple of days and when I arrived at Kennington Station, the guard came and told us all to change as it was the last train. As I stepped on to the platform everyone by this time had claimed their pitch for the night and had already laid out their bed rolls. As it was Christmas, there were plenty of party hats, lemonade, mouth organs, accordions and singing. I thought, 'This will do for me', so I just stood there looking sorry for myself until somebody asked me: 'What's up, son?'

'I've been bombed out and I'm on my way to my gran's, but the trains have stopped,' I replied.

Everyone rallied around. 'Poor little sod, give him something to eat and drink.' I'd been enjoying myself, bursting with lemonade and cakes, when the old special constable came around.

'Poor sod, he's been bombed out, all his family killed,' they told him.

'What's your name, son?' he asked paternally.

'Eric Mason,' I replied.

'Are you from Edgware Road?' he asked suspiciously.

'Yes,' I said, before it occurred to me to wonder how he could know that.

It wasn't long before I was enlightened with a crack around the ear and both myself and all the people who had been kind and sympathetic to me were to learn that half the police in London had been looking for me, once again worrying the life out of my mother by going missing. I was taken to the local nick, given plenty of verbal abuse and a few clouts around the head before being taken home. After an inquest at home, it was decided that I would go to live in Marylebone with my grandparents. It was okay there, but the school was no good for me. I was always fighting as I was deemed an outsider and there was only one way that kids settled their differences in that school. Eventually I was slung out of the school and had to go back to my mum's.

Luckily I found new friends: Arthur Holland, Eddie Sullivan, John Cooney and the Milsons. The Sullivan and Cooney families lived next door to each other, directly across the street from us. They always seemed to be feuding and it was the normal thing for everyone to come out to the street whenever a row broke out between the two families. We were lucky to have a ringside view as our house was nearest to the flats where these two Irish families lived. One would frequently hear the cry, 'The Sullivans and Cooneys are at it' and in no time the street would be full of spectators, each supporting their particular family. I had no decision to make as my two best mates were Eddie and John. Those two got on very well and as a trio we went everywhere and did everything together.

By this time, I was always breaking into and stealing from shops – mostly sweets and chocolates. It sounds bad but lots of kids from our background did the same. Then one day Arthur Holland told me that his mum's lodger, Tom, had hundreds of pounds in the house.

'Perhaps we should take some? He won't miss any if we only take a few,' Arthur suggested.

So it was arranged that I would go round to Arthur's house when Tom took Hilda out for a drink to the Stag. When the time came, I went straight to Tom's room with Arthur and there it was in a drawer – more money than I'd seen in my life. I took a handful – which turned out to be £124 – and considering the average wage of a man was under £2 per week in those days, you can imagine how enormous the amount seemed when we got it to our den and counted it.

'Just give me one pound and you keep the rest,' Arthur said.

There was an old kettle in my dad's shed at home so I put £100 in that and the remaining £23 into my pocket. I couldn't wait for the morning to come to dash off to school.

I gathered all of the gang around me in the playground, gave them all a ten-bob note apiece and said we'd all meet in George's Café at dinnertime. It was tea and pies all round.

'Who's paying?' demanded George when we placed our order.

'Don't worry, George, I'm paying,' I said grandly.

The bill for 12 teas and pies was about four shillings and eight pence, so I put a nicker on the counter and said, 'Keep the change.'

George was quick to catch on. He soon came around the counter. 'Do you want to buy this?' he said, lowering his voice.

'This' was a small metal box, which when one opened the front revealed a figure of Jane from the cartoon strip, with her little dog. As you turned the cog at the side of the box, a man came towards Jane with no clothes on. George was the first porn peddler I was to meet. I gave him a nicker for it and took it back to school.

With the next day came a more realistic sexual encounter. We were all playing on and around the air-raid shelters at school when a girl called Mary, who was 16 and who knew my elder brother, came along. 'Tell Denny I'll see him at the arcade tonight,' she said.

I called her over and said, 'Look what I've got.' I showed her my little mechanical gadget and about £15, which I had in my pocket.

'Where did you get all that?' she asked, pointing at the cash.

'I've got hundreds,' I said, with plenty of bravado, as all my mates were there.

'Give me some,' she said.

'I'll give you some if you come down the shelter with me'

'No, don't be so rude. I'll tell your brother what you said.'

'I don't care,' I shrugged.

But as she walked away she called me over and said quietly, 'I'll meet you after school but don't tell any of your friends.'

I made solemn promises then went and promptly told all my mates as soon as she had gone.

After school had finished, she came by with a loaf of bread under her arm as if she had just been shopping. I'd told my friends to pretend they knew nothing, but asked them all to come as soon as we went into the shelter.

'Don't leave me on my own with her,' I had begged them all.

'Grab the loaf and run down the shelter because I think all your friends know something,' she said.

Which I did. She came trotting after me into the shelter but then my bottle went and I didn't know what to do. My pals, who couldn't contain themselves any longer, came dashing in after us, which certainly saved my face. It was then that the instructions started to come from out of the darkness.

'Lift her jumper up.'

'Lay her down.'

'No, you'll have to pay a shilling for a kiss and half a crown to touch anywhere,' she said swiftly.

Then she did her great actress bit by informing us that she was fainting and didn't know what was going on and couldn't feel anything happening to her. But she still had the presence of mind to keep taking money from me, as the boys commented on what was revealed.

'Look at the size of her tits,' an awed voice said from behind me.

I was certainly growing up quickly. Some days after this and following other similar incidents, the police came to the school and interviewed about twenty kids. Eventually I was charged with stealing the money and about seventeen others for receiving part of it. In the course of being interviewed, one of our neighbours enlightened the police about where most of the money was spent or given away, namely on the girl called Mary and at George's Café. Both ended up in court; I believe George was sent to prison for a few months and the girl was sent away somewhere. I was fined ten shillings and my friends were each fined five shillings. I didn't worry too much as no one knew about the rest of the money left in the drum. But it certainly helped us through some pretty bleak days of food rationing and such.

By late 1943, Hitler had decided to bomb London out of existence and we had to endure a continual bombardment of his V-1 and V-2 rockets. The V-1s, which became known as 'doodlebugs', seemed to fascinate more than frighten us. As they were droning overhead we used to look at them and hope they would drop on the local sweet shop or somewhere else that would supplement our meagre rations. One day our dream came true when one landed on Kays toy factory off Edgware Road. I think just about every kid living within a mile radius descended on the factory. I remember my brother Fred and I were among the first to arrive, only to find a special constable minding the building. However, we soon realised he was, like most of the specials, a pre-war ex-policeman recruited to replace the younger and more nimble men who had been called up into the forces. We spent nearly all day nipping in and out of Kays, dodging the bumbling attempts of the lumbering 'special' to lay his hands on us and, in the meantime, getting plenty of games and other things to sell at school.

One of the most lucrative operations we had during the war, came about as a result of the decision to get rid of the trams and remove the tram lines to use in the munitions factories. Once the workmen arrived, they ripped up the tar blocks – blocks of wood set into tar to stabilise the tram lines – and piled the blocks at the side of the road before taking the tram lines away. The next day a lorry would come for the tar blocks but not before we got our hands on them. Every kid in Britain used to have a home-made trolley consisting of a plank of wood with two wooden axles and ballbearing wheels with an orange box screwed on the back and guide rope attached to the front axle. So we would make a few trips to the pile of tar blocks during the evening and take them back to the house, where we would spend hours chopping them into sticks, then into neat bundles. We would spend most of the weekend going around the houses to sell our firewood for a couple of coppers per bundle.

Less than a year later, at the age of 14, I was arrested again, for breaking into a Home Guard ammunition store and stealing four boxes of hand grenades, detonators and bullets. One of the Milson brothers and I had decided to wag school one day. We took our trolleys with us, intending to load them with any ill-gotten gains we could find. We found a Home Guard store which was secured with an inadequate padlock. It wasn't long before we had the door open and discovered to our surprise that the place was packed with dozens of boxes of ammunition. We had seen enough newsreel films to know how to arm the hand grenades, so we packed as many as we could, together with their detonators, on to our trolleys and made our way back home. As my friend wouldn't risk taking any to his house in case his father found them, I deposited the load in my dad's shed. Later, when the coast was clear, I took a couple of grenades and a tin of detonators to my bedroom and began the simple task of arming the grenades. This involved unscrewing the base of the grenades, inserting a detonator into the small holes inside and then screwing the base back on again. I couldn't wait for the next day to arrive so that I could show my friends what I'd got.

Next day, after debating what we should do with the grenades, it was decided that we would blow up the headmaster's office. As the evening began to close in we made our way to the park at the rear of the school. Right outside the head's office was a line of air-raid shelters. We crouched behind them and myself and one of my friends each took a grenade. We drew the pins simultaneously, threw in approved military style towards the school, then quickly ducked back. The explosion brought us all back to our senses immediately. Luckily, both grenades had missed the target and had fallen against the school wall. We did not have time to check what damage had been done as the explosion had alerted the Air Raid Precaution warden. He immediately began to give chase but we were able to outstrip him easily and make our escape.

However, it was only a matter of time before the police arrived at my house. They frightened the life out of my mother when they told her that there were enough explosives in the shed to blow up the whole street. They also told her that it would only have taken the heat of one's hand to set off the detonators. I don't know whether that statement was true, but it certainly had the desired effect upon my mother and she didn't argue when they took me away to the police station. For this crime I was sent to St Vincent's Approved School.

# 2.

## THE GERMAN PRISONERS
## WERE OUR ONLY FRIENDS

Although it is easy to be wise in retrospect, I think that St Vincent's decided the course my life was to take. The bullying, the physical and mental cruelty I suffered there at the hands of those in charge, gave me a hatred of authority and a determination not to be beaten by their tactics that was to last all my life.

I was 13 when I was sent to St Vincent's, an approved school run by monks that took in boys from the ages of 10 to 18. The school had been evacuated in the early years of the war and was now located in a camp belonging to the Forestry Commission, which looked like an Army barracks. My heart sank when I saw it and the reception committee did nothing to reassure me. The first thing they did was give me a number to be used instead of my name. My clothes were also stamped with this number and my peg in the shower room, on which I was to hang my clothes, was similarly marked. In fact, each person was better remembered by their number than by their name, so those whose names I recall, had some special reason to stand out. Mostly it was because they became good friends or they were characters who stuck in my memory for acts of bravado or bullies whom I will never forget. There were a few who went through such misery without saying a word. It amazed me how they could keep on taking it.

My introduction to the brutality came the first week I was there. Shortly after I arrived, I was allocated to one of the eight dormitories, which slept 16. There was a rule which said that after eight in the evening there was to be no talking in the dormitories and I was caught whispering to the boy in the next bed by the dormitory leader, who was the oldest and biggest boy in the dorm. He could talk to his cronies as long as he liked, but us new boys were ruled with an iron fist. I was told to stop talking and when I said, 'You're talking yourself,' it was as if I'd brought all the wrath of the gods down upon myself. No one would dare answer back to a dormitory leader. The next thing I knew I was being dragged from under the covers and ordered to stand at the end of the bed in my nightshirt, until the brother came around to put the gas lamp out. I was freezing cold and I thought in my innocence that when he came in, he would see I was shivering and feel sorry for me. What a rude awakening I was to get.

'What are you standing out for?' he bellowed.

'You'd better ask him,' I said, pointing to the leader 'He's made me stand here in the cold just because I spoke a few words.'

With this the brother punched me full in the face and split my eye. I dropped to the floor with the force of the blow. I'd never been hit so hard in my life. I was then ordered to stand up. I did. I couldn't believe what had just happened. I thought, he will now realise what he's done and feel sorry for me.

When I got to my feet he flattened me again and said, 'If I find you standing out again when I come around you will be birched.' I had a lot to learn.

I was soon to learn there was no mercy in that place. I had never had to worry about physical violence before. I could look after myself. Boxing gloves were very familiar to me as I had used them from an early age and even when we were kids we settled our disputes with our fists. If you got beaten there were no lasting grudges. But St Vincent's changed all that. Firstly, when you fight as a boy at school it is generally with a boy of your own age and size. But not at St Vincent's. The older, bigger boys were encouraged by the staff to discipline the younger, smaller inmates. This gave the bullies licence to engage in the most brutal violence and perversions. Obviously, there were only three options for the victims of these attacks: to fight back against impossible odds, to suffer without a murmur or to run away and then, when you were brought back, get twice as much violence from the staff. I can only talk with conviction about how I felt after I had tasted the first acts of brutality and how I decided I would face the next few years in St Vincent's. I knew I had to hold my head up high and never let them see the slightest sign that I was going to give in.

The most traumatic experience in my early days at St Vincent's was coming to terms with the sexual abuse. Like most small boys, I had discovered the delights of masturbation and the pleasure of discovering what boys and girls did with each other before I was sent away. But I had never heard the word homosexuality and I had never met anyone who was a homosexual. I was soon to learn how rife it was in such institutions as St Vincent's. I've seen sexual abuse by people who were in a position of authority and took advantage of that position either to bribe their way to gratify their own lust or, in quite a lot of cases, to force young boys who were too terrified to do anything about it. But I think the worst type of bullying and abuse came from the older boys against the younger ones. Whilst I was in St Vincent's, every night after lights out, I would hear the sounds of the bigger boys forcing themselves on to the younger ones, the cries of resistance and then the prolonged sobbing of the victim. I spent the first year of my existence in St Vincent's lying awake until I just dropped off with sheer exhaustion. I think I had made it clear to any would-be molester that I was going to fight until I dropped, rather than be bullied or abused. Obviously, I had the odd approach in the ordinary way but was never tempted. The worst type of abuse came about when boys discovered that some poor little sod was a practising 'homo' and was in fact enjoying himself. They would form a gang and subject that person to all kinds of abuses and perversions.

I had a very miserable few years there, but through all of the misery and pain, there were the odd light moments and memories of the mates that I had the good fortune to meet, some of whom I still see today. One of my best pals was Joey Mayo, a great character who sadly died of cancer many years ago. Joe and I had some terrible hidings in that place when we were young boys. Joe would do anything for a smoke and, as smoking was not allowed, it was the cause of quite a lot of grief for Joe – and for myself being his mate, I found myself involved on many occasions. One such incident was to get us one of the most severe beatings we ever had.

The lights had been out for about two hours when Joe came to my bedside and whispered, 'Meet me outside by the toilet.' I went out and found Joe standing there with a bootlace in his hand.

'Eric, I'm dying for a smoke,' he said desperately. 'I've managed to get some dog-ends from the staff room.'

He had risked a beating by going into the staff quarters to collect a few dog-ends from the ashtrays. Unfortunately, he didn't have a light. He asked would I come with him to the church, where the sanctuary lamp was always burning, as he needed to climb on my shoulders to reach the lamp to light the bootlace. Once lit, it would then smoulder for hours. I agreed and off we crept to the church, hoping that no terrible curse would come down upon us. Everything was going according to plan and Joe was kneeling on my shoulders, putting the lace into the lamp, when I felt the most violent kick up my backside. I staggered forward while Joe came tumbling off my shoulders and landed on the altar. We were dragged out of the church and given a terrible beating. Unfortunately we hadn't realised that it was the practice of a few of the brothers to go to the church at night and sit in the darkness to pray. Worse was to come.

The next morning everyone in the school was assembled in the recreation room to watch Joe and me be punished for sacrilege. We were both given a pair of skin-tight cotton shorts and told to take all our clothes off and put the shorts on. We were then put on the stage at one end of the recreation room and beaten on our backsides until blood ran down our legs. Those beatings were so severe that it took months for the wounds to heal. I had as many public beatings as anyone in the years that I was there – some even overlapping. On occasions I hadn't even recovered from one beating before I was given another. There was a flagpost outside the head's office and on more than one occasion Joe and I were tied to it and given a beating and subsequently left for several hours as an example for everyone to see. I've been back recently and photographed what remains of that place and, although it's razed and obliterated, the post still stands – a symbol of all that was evil about that establishment.

Poor Gypsy Bennet, I think he suffered more than anyone. Here was a guy who wanted nothing more than to go into the woods surrounding the school and befriend the animal life that was there in abundance. He was always arriving back with a young rabbit or a bird that couldn't fly. Unfortunately for him, he was always late for the count before meals and regardless of the weather, the rest of us would have to stand to attention until such time as he returned. As we were standing waiting, the brothers would be inciting the boys with words like, 'Bennet needs a good hiding for keeping everyone from their meals' and 'There will be no privileges this week, unless he's taught a lesson'. So by the time the poor sod came out of the woods, usually clutching some unfortunate bird with a broken wing, the whole school would be baying for his blood. The brothers just stood around as he was beaten up and left to attend to his own broken bones.

The only real kindness that I ever found while I was at St Vincent's came from a strange quarter. At about the time the war was coming to the end, we were all assembled and told that inmates from a German prisoner of war camp were coming on a courtesy visit. None of us knew what to expect as we had grown up with stories about what terrible people the Germans were. At that time, my father was with the British Army on the Rhine and I had visions of him fighting hand-to-hand against these people we were supposed to make welcome and entertain with a display of sport, gymnastics, boxing and football. This was the face we were supposed to portray to our visitors – one big happy family that had been taken from the back streets of the big cities and made into gentle sports-loving people. Whatever we expected, it wasn't the sight of these smart-looking men with smiling faces and every one

THE BRUTAL TRUTH

24

of them with a present to give to us. In no time at all it was as if we'd recognised that we were kindred spirits, each of us missing our respective home lives. Treasured family photographs were eagerly exchanged and the language barrier did not exist in such a situation; family life was the same whatever the country. Their photographs were mainly of wives and children. Most of the Germans had children of our age. Nostalgic times for everyone. The German prisoners started to come every weekend and we eagerly looked forward to their visits. They used to get a football team to play against us and some of them had played for top teams in Germany before the war. Some were musicians who would bring violins and such and play beautiful music.

Of course, you could not hide all the physical signs of what people like Joe and myself were going through. I remember the German prisoners started to get concerned about our treatment after Joe and I had been whipped for one of our escapades. The usual thing: Joe had been down to the boiler house to light his bootlace and noticed that one of the kitchen windows was open. We always seemed to be starving hungry and the thought of finding some extra food was more than we could resist. We couldn't believe our eyes when we got into the kitchen, for there was a big currant duff and two big tureens of custard. This must have been a Saturday night as we only had a sweet on Sundays. Joe and I did no more than pull big chunks off the duff and while I was filling my shirt with big lumps of the stuff, Joe had his head stuck right into the bowl of custard. We got back to the dormitory and woke up a couple of mates and gave them each a lump of duff then went to sleep. The next morning we were all tipped out of our beds and told to stand by them without moving. The brothers came straight up to our bed-spaces. It was then that I saw all the crumbs on the floor – at the same time that they did. They looked in disbelief at Joe, who had a big yellow ring of dried custard around his face. There were no words spoken, only the usual assembly and public beating. Later that day the Germans came for a football match and the whole place seemed more gloomy than ever. A few of them were looking at Joe and me with compassion in their eyes but when they saw the heavy weals and blood on the backs of our legs their mood changed to anger. I don't know if they ever complained about our treatment. We never saw them again. We never knew why their visits suddenly stopped, but I suspect they were aware that we were being ill treated. Without their visits life seemed much duller.

During the week there were classes. Brother Charles, the only brother who seemed to show some compassion, ran a class for those who were illiterate. As I had a smattering of education I was put into Brother George's class. It was his habit to prowl the classroom with an ebony ruler in his hand ready to rap your knuckles at the smallest excuse. There was a certain incentive to be moved up to Brother Raymond's class, where all one had to contend with was his sarcasm and ridicule. Unfortunately, once you had shown that you had a fair smattering of the three Rs you were sent to the Dickensian workshops. I seemed to spend all my days sandpapering planks of wood until my hands were sore. The instructor was a crack shot with wooden missiles that he would throw at anyone not working hard enough.

We had an hour of recreation time in the evening and in the summer we'd play football and other games on an adjoining field. We were free on the weekends, once we'd done such chores as scrubbing the dormitory, cleaning the windows and tidying-up outside. On Sundays, of course, we went to church twice – once in the morning and again in the afternoon. I don't think much of this religion rubbed off on us though.

As the years went by, I grew bigger and fitter. The war was nearing its end and I was spending nearly all of my time training and had been picked, along with a couple of other boys, to represent the school in the Home Office Boxing Championships. My personal suffering seemed to abate a little. I was beginning to rebel a bit and there were a lot of easier pickings for the bullies and staff. My rebellion was sparked off when the inspector in the wood shop hit me with one of the missiles he was so fond of throwing. I'd finally had enough and for the first time I hit back, hurling a sanding block at him. He came running towards me, throwing punches. I started to trade blows with him and although he was bigger and stronger than myself, I could see that I had shocked him. I was severely flogged for this but he never threw anything at me again.

One boy I became very friendly with in those days was Joe King. He was a very good boxer, though after he left St Vincent's, it was as a singer that he made a living. His brother, Peter King, was to fight Peter Waterman, the brother of Dennis Waterman, for the British welterweight title. I went on to win my weight division in the Home Office Boxing Championships at Chelsea Barracks, where I was to meet a boy from another school with whom I became very friendly years later. His name was Jimmy Lynas – 'The Coventry Iron Man'. He was later to become the first man to beat Dick Tiger, who went on to become the middleweight champion of the world.

I seemed to get a new status after my return from Chelsea Barracks and I didn't have to join in the forced route marches the boys had to endure. I hated those marches, as we were expected to walk about ten miles through country lanes in boots which were ill-fitting and sometimes without laces. There was absolutely no reason for these marches and I can only presume that it was enforced purely to gratify the sadism of the people who ran the home. At the end of the 'walks' there would be the ritual of bursting blisters or bathing bleeding feet.

It was at this time that I had my first full sexual experience that put my encounter with my eldest brother's girlfriend to shame. It came about when, as one of the more senior boys, I was allowed to go to the local carnival with the gym team. It was at a village three miles from the school and we were to give a gymnastics exhibition for the locals. As soon as the exhibition ended we were allowed to mingle with the villagers and, to my surprise, I found myself being invited to walk into a field next to the one in which the carnival was being held. In no time at all I was indulging in the kind of things that I had only been able to dream about until then. When I got back to the school I was soon telling my pals about the beautiful girl that I'd met and the things that we'd done. As soon as I'd finished describing her they all said, 'Yeah, we know her, every older boy in the school has had the pleasure.' That certainly gave my ego a jolt – I thought I was her first lover!

# 3.

## SOHO, THE SNAKE PIT
## AND ALL THAT JAZZ

I was discharged from St Vincent's in 1946 and given a train warrant back to London. I thought I'd get a job, settle down, join a good boxing club and live happily ever after. My dad was back from the Army, Dennis was in the Navy and Fred and Brian were at school. I expected to get a job and contribute towards my keep. I didn't ever fancy going through the type of life I'd had for the last three years. So it was with great expectation that I went looking for my first job. But like all best-laid plans there was a pitfall. The first came with the question, 'Where did you work before?'

As everyone from our walk of life left school at 14 and went immediately into a job, the fact that I was 16 and hadn't worked needed explaining. I had no option but to tell people that I'd been in an approved school for three years. After the interviewers had obtained all the details from me, they'd either tell me straight out that there wasn't any work or they'd let me know in more subtle ways. The end result was always the same.

At the time of leaving St Vincent's, I was approaching 16 years of age. The war had ended and there was an air of happiness and relief. Everyone seemed to smile at each other, money seemed to be plentiful and, with the American servicemen still in this country, the West End of London was the place to be – even prostitutes didn't mind the amateurs encroaching on their 'pitch'. They would often take a young 'brass' under their wing and show them the ropes.

I was soon to make my mark in the West End. I had just spent three years of the toughest education any boy could have. You fought for everything –

food, a place near the fire for warmth, brutality, tobacco and, most of all, against the perverts and paedophiles (although in those days, I had never heard of the word paedophile). The people who ran the approved school were just dirty old men who would use every method there was to seduce young boys. They would create great misery in those places.

And so, on being released from that kind of environment, it was pretty easy to face the hardest of problems. All you had to do was evade getting nicked by the police. When I see homeless people selling magazines like *The Big Issue* today, it reminds me of those days after being released from St Vincent's. I suppose it was convenient for me to forget the cold winter nights because I just want to remember the good times.

There were some great characters around Soho in those days. My friend, Charlie Dice, who I still see these days at the ex-boxers' reunions, was a tough little guy around both the East End and the West End. There was 'Chick' Joyce, who was later to get a life sentence for killing a guardsman during a fight in Piccadilly.

With nothing better to do, I took to sitting around in well-known cafés in Soho – Queenie's, the Little Hut and the Snake Pit. Most of the girls who frequented these places were prostitutes and I always remember them with fondness. I'd invariably have a meal or a cup of tea sent over to me whenever any of them came in and, in due course, I felt protective towards them, although some were old enough to be my mother. There would be some sort of incident each day. Either a punter would arrive screaming that a girl had 'rolled' him and left him with no trousers while she made off with his money or one of their ponces would come in pissed and demand money for more booze. I would always 'make one' and rarely had any difficulty in knocking these individuals out, so I became a great favourite with the girls around the West End.

At this time I was meeting all kinds of villains. Jack Spot was the 'name' both in the East End and the West End. Jack had made quite a name for himself by championing the Jews against Oswald Mosley's Black Shirts and by this time was a pretty well-respected and well-organised villain. I used to see Jack and several of his 'firm' in those days. Many had girlfriends who were 'brasses', so I got the odd 'bung' from a few faces.

Jack made a fortune from the many rackets that he ran – one of the most lucrative was the 'bookmaker's sponge'. It was so very simple and yet so financially rewarding. It worked like this. As each bookmaker set up his pitch, for which he was licensed, he would erect his blackboard and list the various horses running in each race. As the prices fluctuated throughout the betting, the bookie would rub out the old odds and replace them with the new. At the 'off', the boards would be wiped clean ready for the next race. Jack decided that he would supply the bookmakers with their sponges – at an exorbitant price of course. If any bookie refused to take one of Jack's sponges, he would find himself trying to carry on conducting his business while a gang of hard men fought around his pitch. On many such occasions, the bookie would be knocked down in the mock battle along with all of his equipment.

When it became known that Jack was making plenty of money from the tracks around London, the organised gangs from the North and the Midlands wanted to get in on the act. So Jack became the guardian angel of all of the southern bookies who went to the race tracks up and down the country. During the '30s and '40s the racecourse fights between underworld gangs made the headlines with the razor slashings and general violence getting out of hand. It all culminated in a famous battle at Brighton where the Sabini brothers, a well-known Italian family, became involved. There were a number of arrests and plenty of hard labour dished out to all concerned, but Jack Spot came through it all to be acknowledged as the 'Governor'. He set himself up as London's very first gang leader. He had a lifestyle to match: big cars, expensive suits and attractive women. He eventually set up his headquarters in a hotel at Marble Arch, where he could be seen every night holding court with his right-hand men, Moisha Blue Ball and Sonny the Yank, and there was always plenty of coming and going. The waiters who worked there in those days were getting more money in tips than the manager of the hotel earned in salary.

It all came to an end for Jack after his fight in Frith Street, Soho, with Albert Dimes – Italian Albert. They ended up cutting lumps out of each other and were both arrested for an affray. But it became known as the fight that never was after a retired vicar arrived at the Old Bailey with an entirely different story from the one given by the prosecution and the case was dismissed. If any member of the jury had gone to the bar in Jack's hotel that evening they would have seen the vicar swallowing plenty of champagne and brandy with guys from Jack's firm. But from then on it was all downhill for Jack. He was accused of slashing a guy, but he had been set up. The victim had his arm slashed by his own friends and then gave evidence that Jack had done it.

The last time I saw Jack was in a club in Bayswater in '66. As I rang the doorbell, I could see someone looking through a slit in the door and could hear several bolts being pulled. It was a fortress. Jack had been attacked just prior to this and had given evidence against the perpetrators, who were sentenced to long terms of imprisonment. It spelled the end of Jack Spot's reign as the underworld boss. For a feared and respected villain, the code of the underworld is such that you would never give evidence against another villain, regardless of how serious the crime. A criminal boss would be expected to avenge a crime, using method, rather than enlist the help of the Police. Jack had forgotten the old maxim – if you live by the sword, you die by it.

Soho in the late '40s and early '50s was a unique and fascinating part of London. In the summer evenings people would sit outside the open doors of their premises and everyone seemed to know each other. The girls who worked the streets would click up and down on their stiletto heels, greeting everyone with a cheery 'hello' and 'I've got to get a few quid tonight as the rent's due tomorrow'. You would see the buskers pull up in their cars and stroll down to Leicester Square to do the soft-shoe shuffle or mimic the sand dancers in the middle of the road. The one-man bands and street singers all added to the attractive atmosphere. One great character who used to stroll through Soho, if he wasn't at a race meeting, would be Prince Monolulu. He was an imposing black man who always wore flowing robes and a feathered head-dress. As he walked, he would chant his cry, 'I've gotta horse!'

One of the greatest characters I have known for over thirty years is Charlie Dice. Charlie, who used to train in the East End, was a very fit and strong man. He made his living in the illegal 'speilers' (gaming clubs) or in the street dice games, which were a feature of London right up to the '60s.

People would travel for miles to play dice in the street. I've seen men win fortunes in a couple of hours crouching down outside the Little Hut Café in Greek Street, Soho. When Billy Gardner and Charlie ran the games in Soho, the police tried in every way possible to catch them, but their look-out system was too good. The police couldn't get within a hundred yards before the warning was given and the gamblers either dispersed or were discovered sitting innocently in the Little Hut having a cup of tea.

But the police scored a victory one night.

There was a big game on at the time and nobody took any notice of the council dust cart trundling down the street. If anyone had looked harder they would have noticed that there were twice as many dustmen as usual. But no, everyone was used to seeing the dust cart at 3 a.m. so the look-outs were relaxed as the vehicle pulled up alongside. The dustmen, who were all from Savile Row Police Station, pounced and grabbed the dice and what money they could and nicked most of the guys involved. Everyone appeared at Marlborough Street Magistrates' Court the next morning and were fined sums from £2 up to £5 for the organisers.

In fact, if you were feeling bored and in need of cheering up, all you had to do was go to any of the courts within a mile of Soho for some free amusement. There were three of them working flat out and you would see the same old faces day after day. The girls would turn up in all their furs and finery, say good morning to the magistrate, who would reply, 'Good morning, Sonia' – or whatever the girl's name was – and immediately give them the maximum fine for prostitution.

Then there were the fly pitchers, the guys who sold gear out of a suitcase on the pavement in Oxford Street. This was much more serious than prostitution and would involve a £5 fine. There was a lot of good humour in the courts and after their appearance, everyone would meet in Queenie's Café, in Rupert Court, for breakfast before going home to bed to get ready for the evening's work.

The place that I enjoyed the most in those days was the Club 11. I was to see all the great jazz men of the day playing there: Ronnie Scott, Tubby Hayes, Lennie Bush. I could name dozens of great musicians who played the old Club 11 and I watched a lot of them become famous, seeing them years later in Ronnie Scott's place in Gerrard Street and Frith Street. I had some good times with Tony Crombie and Alan Haven when they used to tour with Wee Willie Harris and there was always some place to go after the show for a drink.

It was in the Club 11 that I first heard of drugs. The place was packed with happy jazz fans one evening, when our numbers were suddenly swelled by hordes of policemen. I noticed everyone around me was throwing little paper packages on to the floor. We were all rounded up and taken down to the local nick and searched. It didn't matter whether you had anything on you or not, because the police had picked up all of the packets from the floor – which contained marijuana, sometimes called Indian hemp – and if there was someone there who didn't have any, they would soon see that they were suitably 'fitted up' with some. Those of us who were in our teens were given a ticking off and asked for our names and addresses, which we all quickly supplied – giving them fictitious ones – before being allowed to go. But sadly some of our heroes were sent to prison for three years.

I was also training quite regularly. Every day I would go to Kline's gym in Fitzroy Square but on the odd occasion I would go down to Jack Solomon's gym where I could pick up a few quid for sparring with the Americans who came to fight British boxers. Most of the great American fighters who came to this country would train at Solomon's in Windmill Street, except for Sugar Ray Robinson. When he came to the UK to fight Randolph Turpin he trained at Windsor. Most of these guys from the States had pretty large contingents of followers, managers, trainers and sparring partners who would always be on the bill. Robinson went overboard with his own hairdresser, manicurist and valet – he even had a 'midget'. He had over fourteen people in his entourage but it didn't help him. He still lost the middleweight title in the epic fight at Earls Court. It was a great day for British boxing when they held Turpin's hand up after the fight. Freddie Mills had lost the light heavyweight title to Joey Maxim earlier the same year and so it made Turpin's win that extra bit special.

But I was still looking for the cloud with the silver lining. It didn't matter how many rounds I sparred or boxed, I wasn't going to get the type of money that I needed. I was looking for more. And chance showed me how to find it.

On my way home from Jack Solomon's gym I'd sometimes pop into the snooker hall on the first floor of the same building for a cup of tea or a soft drink. It was a popular haunt for smash-and-grab raiders who would meet their 'fences' there. A 'fence' is a buyer or receiver of stolen goods. I'd watch these guys with their wads of money bet heavily on the games of snooker. The word soon got out and every hustler in London seemed to find his way to the Windmill snooker hall. A lot of these raiders knew that I used the gym upstairs. It suited them to have a fit person on the team – and I let it be known that I was willing to join them.

I first became aware of the Messina Brothers in early '47. Eugene was a thickset, affable type of guy whom I had seen on numerous occasions strolling around Soho with his camel-hair coat draped over his shoulders, a big smile would greet anyone he thought was a 'face'.

I had just knocked-out a known fighting man around this time, so I was honoured by the big grin. Eugene seemed to be the top jolly among the 'Malts', as all of the Mediterranean ponces were referred to. The Messinas were going through a bit of a vendetta with another gang of Malts, namely the Vasallos. Carmelo Vasallo was the top jolly among his 'family' and so when Eugene Messina cut Vasallo's fingers off, it gave the Messinas a certain glamour among the twilight world that Soho had become.

The Messinas first came to London in the 1930s. Joe Messina, the father, had grown up in Sicily – all Sicilians have the reputation of being Mafia, so this added to their glamour and mystique. I met all of the family at sometime or other. They all assumed English names. Alfredo, when arrested in his smart suburban house in Wembley was charged as Raymond Maynard. I think only two of the brothers had been born in Malta: Salvatore and Alfredo. The others were born in Alexandria, Egypt, where Guiseppi 'Joe' Messina opened a brothel at the beginning of the century, with his Maltese wife as the Madam. If the Messinas were operating today, the chances are that they would never have seen the inside of a prison. Because of their immense wealth and the modern technology, the police wouldn't have been able to 'fit them up' the way they did in the early '50s.

I had good personal knowledge of the police methods of ensuring that they had many successful results that kept them in the public eye, so ensuring their promotion. I remember sitting with a few old friends in Coventry Street Corner House (an old meeting place for all the 'chaps') and we all fell about laughing at the article in the evening paper relating how Alfredo Messina had been arrested for living on immoral earnings and charged with attempting to bribe the police superintendent who arrested him with a couple of hundred quid. Everyone in my company knew full well that practically every copper on the Vice Squad was bent and the amazing thing that everybody else seemed to miss was that a chief superintendent found it necessary to be present when arresting a man for a charge that the maximum sentence was two years' imprisonment.

I was later with Alfredo in Wandsworth Prison and he told me that the first thing the 'Top Old Bill' said was, 'Open your safe'. He then looked at the big stack of notes and said, 'I'll leave you some of that as I'm not as hard as some of my men.' It was blatant robbery and until the days when Robert Mark came down from Manchester as Commissioner, the Old Bill had a complete licence to do exactly what they wanted to do. But it was never entirely stamped out. It was a fact that most of the bent coppers had retired and bought pubs and guest houses and lived the comfortable life, that those days afforded; but today, I see many ex-coppers on the Costa Del Sol with their flash little villas, with some little 'toe-rag' in tow who had once been their informer.

When Attillo Messina was arrested in the late '50s, he came to Wandsworth Prison where I was still serving a sentence and awaiting transportation to Dartmoor. At about this time, Reggie Kray got a short sentence for demanding money with menaces. Reggie, being of the old school, wondered why I would want to talk to a 'mackerel' (the common slang for someone who lived off the earnings of a prostitute). But when I had explained to Reggie about the way the Old Bill had fitted him up, in the same way as they had previously fitted his brother up, Reg wanted to talk to him. And so we arranged a little get-together in one of the few places that cons could have a little head-to-head without being overheard – that was the famous Wandsworth Chapel. I think a lot of things were discussed during that initial meeting. Subsequent meetings between the two were to have quite a lot of influence on Reggie's thinking in future years. Reggie and Ronnie never got involved in vice or drugs, but I think a lot of their organising and thinking came from meeting with people like the Messinas, Billy Hill, Jack Spot and Peter Rachman.

All of the Messinas eventually left London and you would hear stories of them in other European cities. I remember Eugene being involved in a jewellery business, but later getting seven years' imprisonment in Belgium. Certainly, while they were in London, everyone was aware of them. They were also pioneers for hundreds of other Mediterranean villains – vice barons, gamblers, conmen and gunmen, who certainly kept newspaper reporters happy and the police unhappy – unless, of course, you happened to be a bent copper. But for any common crook or grafter, there was a certain glamour about the West End in those days in the '50s and '60s. Everyone would greet each other. Everyone seemed to know what everyone else was up to until someone got shot or maimed. Then everyone would go quiet and hurry past each other or there would be a big exodus when the Old Bill walked into a bar. The Great Train Robbery was a great boost to the morale of the underworld. It was like carnival time.

I had opened a couple of clubs in Soho around that time and it seemed that every customer of mine either had a relation or knew somebody who was involved in the robbery. One of my best customers in those days was Jim Barnett. His best friend was Tommy Smithson. They were earning a good living from the Maltese club owners, blatantly putting the fear of God into them by telling them they would be looked after and no terrible people would come into their premises and cause trouble, whether it was a drinking club, a clip joint, a striptease place or an ordinary sex-cum-book shop. Tommy and Jim would look after them all for a few quid. But Tommy Smithson's downfall came when he decided to carve up a man called Slip Sullivan, who had been giving George Caruana some problems. George was something of a boss to all the Maltese 'faces' after the demise of the Messinas and he paid Tommy Smithson a fair good wage to look after him. So Tommy decided to give 'Slip' Sullivan some treatment. Sullivan was badly cut and marked, but he was well connected. There was a council of war called and this was before Billy Hill and Jack Spot had fallen out with each other, so the firm that sat down to decide Tommy Smithson's fate was pretty formidable. Tommy was lured to Mornington Crescent where he was captured by a mob of about ten handed. He was dragged into a large van and cut to pieces and dumped in Regents Park. He survived and a few people started to worry as he got better and began to get fit again. He was a very tough boy, so when he asked for a few quid to open his own club, he was given it. Tommy was soon back to his old self and, after a short time, was earning a couple of grand a week along with his old mate Jim Barnett. It wasn't long before Billy Hill and Jack Spot were falling out. Jack Spot was attacked outside his house in Marylebone. Later seven men were sentenced to terms of imprisonment of up to seven years for this attack. The day or so after that case was over, Tommy Smithson was gunned down in the flat he shared with Fay Richardson, a girl from Stockport who became quite infamous herself.

Three men were charged with killing Tommy Smithson. They were all Maltese: 'Little Joe' Zammit, Philip Ellul and another Malt. Joe and his mate were cleared of the murder, but Philip Ellul was found guilty and sentenced to life imprisonment. I was soon working with Philip in the stone quarry at Dartmoor Prison, where he told me all about how he was offered a large sum of money to get rid of Tommy. He was given a key to Tommy's flat in Maida Vale. Tommy was in the bedroom, just getting ready for the day's stroll around Soho. He glanced up as Philip and his friend walked into the room and grabbed a pair of scissors. But he was gunned down before he could use them.

Fay Richardson went under many names: Fay Smithson and Fay Sadler were other names she used, but there were two other men in her life who died tragically. One was Jimmy Neil, who owned the Cabinet Club in Gerard

Street, Soho. Jimmy was gunned down in the famous Pen Club shooting where another old friend of mine was shot in the stomach but survived to become a very successful businessman. Another old friend of mine, Jack Rosa, died in an accident whilst being associated with Fay. No wonder the mob refer to her as the 'Kiss of Death'. Fay was quite friendly with a girl that I knew quite well. Her name was Zoe Progul, known by the press as 'Zippy Zoe' after her escape from Holloway Prison. Jimmy Barnett and myself came back together recently at the funeral of Zoe, whom we all referred to as 'Mickey'. After the funeral, we all went to Mistress P's, a pub at Clapham Common, where I was to meet Mickey's daughter, who seems to have been blessed with all the nice attributes of her mother.

After the death of Tommy Smithson – which highlighted the various ways people were earning big money – there was enough money around to have anyone bumped off and it was his case that brought to prominence names that had not been mentioned in any way before, except by the people who were 'connected' in Soho. George Caruana was fairly well known as a guy who ran a couple of illegal spielers. He was also alleged to have ran a few girls and other minor vice operations. But then the names of Bernie Silver, who was an old East End face, along with his partner 'Big Frank' Mifsud, a Maltese, took over the reins of everything that the Messinas had left behind, added a few ideas themselves and ended up with an estimated weekly income of £100,000. They could afford to pay people to do whatever they wanted done. They were, in fact, accused of the murder of Tommy Smithson. Later on, Bernie Silver was actually found guilty of this and was sentenced to life imprisonment, but he was later released after a successful appeal. Frank Mifsud used to come to my club quite often. He would buy drinks for everyone in the bar all night and tip the bar staff and doorman with a £100 left behind the bar for them all. Frank told me that he and Bernie were paying various senior police and other people in various departments £10,000 per week in bribes. They could get a licence for anything they wanted and immunity from any prosecution. They were always tipped off about any impending raids and so they would always have a down-and-out stooge with a rent book of the various premises that would be raided. The stooge would then appear in court and plead guilty to running either an illegal gaming club or other vice activities. He would then tell the court it was his first offence and be fined the minimum fine and told to be a good boy in the future.

The Bernie Silver/Frank Mifsud trial was unbelievable for the amount of witnesses the prosecution brought into court. Here was a case of seven men in all being tried for various crimes like renting flats to prostitutes, selling 'dirty' books and running striptease shows. The prosecution's own witnesses were stating in court that when police raids became a problem, there would be a man from the Home Office who would put a stop to the raids and, although the prosecution witness, Frank Dyer, made these allegations, no one thought to investigate this evidence. Another witness, Joe Mantini, accused the defence counsel, Michael Havers, of being a ponce, saying that he had been aware that people had tried to buy him off with £10,000 and he would die if he went into the witness box. But after all the evidence had been given and the men in the wigs gave their summing up, the only things that were stressed to the jury were the deeds of the terrible men in the dock. A brief mention was made about the cretins the prosecution had produced as their witnesses, who had made a good living with the accused and the allegations of bribery and verbal evidence being manufactured. Bernie Silver was given a six-year imprisonment. No enquiry was ordered pertaining to the allegation of police or government figures being investigated, but immediately after the trial, Bernie Silver and Mifsud were investigated for *ordering* the murder of Tommy Smithson. They even went to the expense of bringing another ponce from Malta to give evidence against him – a guy named Spampinato. He said he had been given a message that the 'punk' (meaning Smithson) had got to be exterminated and alleged that when Philip Ellul shot Smithson, he recalled the sight of thick blood coming out of Smithson's mouth.

It wasn't long before I started to learn the ropes. It was simple. Smash-and-grab raids on jewellers' shops were the most popular way of making easy money in those days. Without unbreakable glass, all the jewellers' shops were at the mercy of the daring raider. 'Ringing' cars was as commonplace then as joyriding is today, so there was always a car available with false plates.

All we would have to do was look for a window display where the pads of rings were easily accessible, then drive the car up to the shop, pointing the front right into the doorway with the engine running. Moving fast we'd take our 'lump hammer', make a hole at the bottom of the window, reach in with a long bar we called the 'cane' and then cane the 'burnt' – burnt cinder being rhyming slang for window. The 'burnt' would come out with a crash on to the pavement below, leaving us to pull as many pads out as we could, stuffing them into a canvas bag we took with us. Everything we did was at top speed, adrenaline pumping, hurrying each other along, ears straining for the sound of police whistles. In less than a minute we'd be off, driving to the nearest tube station if we hadn't been followed. We'd dump the car round the corner and get on the first train, regardless of where it was going. At that point we'd be high with excitement, relief making us laugh at anything.

The more windows you smashed, the more expert you got at it. Eventually, you could take a window out without covering all the jewels with broken glass, or as I'd done on many occasions previously, spending an hour or so afterwards taking slivers of glass from your head. We loved to read the papers after we'd had a particularly exhilarating chase with the police and managed to evade capture. The headlines used to read 'WIZARD OF THE WHEEL' and then go on to describe a dramatic chase across London after an especially daring raid on a jewellers.

I was now starting to pal about with different West End faces. One was Chic Joyce who was later to get a life sentence for a fight where a guardsman died. Most of the guys wanted to go to the dance halls like the Lyceum, Hammersmith Palais, the Royal or the Paramount in Tottenham Court Road. It was in the Paramount that I made a bit of a name for myself. I was 17 at the time and I felt that a guy was paying too much attention to my girlfriend. An argument broke out and I hooked him to the chin. He went down as if he had been pole-axed. I was to read later in the paper that the Empire featherweight champion had been knocked out in the Paramount dance hall.

It was a strange life for a teenager to live and I loved the danger and the excitement, the feeling that we were pitting our wits against the law and winning. I was also enjoying a new independence, having moved out of my parents' house to a flat in Frith Street. But every so often my brother Fred would search me out in the West End with the message that the 'old lady' was worried about me, so I'd go home for a short visit. I tried to keep what I was doing from her, otherwise she really would have been worried!

It was about this time that I started to break into places like cigarette shops, milk depots and bakers' depots, usually with an accomplice. One of my best friends was a guy called Teddy Bright, a well-known tea-leaf and a lovable rogue. He lived in the next street to my parents and we were forever getting up to some kind of villainy. We used to sit in Ted's house and plan our future moneymaking schemes, with a little bit of encouragement from Ted's mother. They made a great team. Ted, who took everything in his stride, looked on crime as an ordinary occupation, as normal as working in a factory. And his mum had the same attitude. If he needed to get up early to do a break-in she would wake him up in time and have his gloves and jemmy all ready for him.

One particular day I was telling Ted something that I had overheard my father talking about. My father had gone into business, with a partner, in the fruit and veg trade. They had a pitch next to the local fish shop whose owner was running a football pontoon scheme. All of the local traders were putting money into it and it had now gone about seven weeks without there being a winner. My father reckoned that if he won it, there would be a few hundred quid to collect.

Ted and I deduced that all this money would have to be in the office of the fish shop and we decided it would have to be 'done' before someone won it. We decided to break in that very moment, a Sunday lunchtime. We had no trouble getting into the place as there was an iron staircase leading to a verandah and once on the verandah, it only took us a minute to get through the window into the office. To our disappointment, we found a small safe. We searched the rest of the place but no money came to light, so it had to be in the safe. Ted and I knew nothing about opening safes, in those days, but we thought if we could get it safely away we would be able to force it open. First we would need a car and we knew that the local Catholic priest had one in his little lock-up garage which he never used on a Sunday. We decided to borrow it. We soon had the priest's car rolling towards the back of the fish shop, where we left it and went back inside the office. We had a bit of a job lifting the small safe through the window and on to the verandah, but once there, we quickly moved it across the verandah to the top of the iron stairs and pushed. It made a terrible racket as it bounced down and we hurriedly manhandled it into the boot of the car. We couldn't close the boot lid so we decided to get away from the shop in case someone came to see what all the noise was about. Ted was driving as we came out on to the Edgware Road and passed a queue outside the picture house. We knew practically everyone in that queue and we could see them all pointing at the back of the priest's car where the safe was sticking out. We lost no time in turning off into a side-street where we tied the boot down over the safe with the laces from my shoes.

We eventually arrived at a place which was a lover's lane at night but in the daytime was nearly always deserted and set about the back of the safe using the railings torn from the park fence and a tyre lever. But we couldn't open it and so decided to leave it hidden in the bushes and go for some more sensible tools. We obtained a jemmy, a lump hammer and a big chisel from the builder's yard at the back of Ted's house and went back to our task. It wasn't long before we had the back off the safe and after that, the inner casing was easy. We were soon lifting the money. We were lucky, not only the football money but the shop takings from Friday evening and all day Saturday were inside. We took the money back to Ted's house, where his mother helped us count it. We gave her all of the silver and coppers and split the notes between ourselves, then returned the priest's car and got tidied up ready to get down the West End to see the bright lights.

The next day my father was fuming. He came in from work saying some villains had broken into the fish shop and nicked all of the football money. He described what he would do if only he could get his hands on them, which worried me more than the police finding out. I started to think of all the people who had been queueing for the pictures and wondered uneasily how long it would be before they put two and two together and started gossiping. But strangely nothing ever came of it, although I know my father did suspect Teddy Bright, as he said to my mum one evening, 'That young Brighty had something to do with that break-in at the fish shop. His mother's been in the Stag every evening this week and I know she always gets a share of his ill-gotten gains.'

Shortly after this, Ted and I went our separate ways and I wasn't to see him until I met him in Dartmoor where he was doing seven years for sticking up a bank. His accomplice was his girlfriend. The papers called them the modern Bonnie and Clyde.

# 4.

# BREAD AND WATER
# AND THE STRAITJACKET

Perhaps because I was so young, I never worried about being caught. I was enjoying life and saw no reason why I shouldn't carry on stealing and living it up with the proceeds. I was to have a rude awakening. I was finally arrested for breaking into a store and stealing cigarettes, spirits and cash to the value of £3,000 and remanded to Wormwood Scrubs. That was my first look into a prison and it was a pretty horrendous experience. The first thing that struck me, like a physical blow to the stomach, was the terrible stench of urine and excreta that permeated the whole prison, lingering even in your clothes. I never got entirely used to it. The cons would empty their slop buckets out of their cell windows and the contents would linger in the yard until the screws detailed someone to clean it up. As for the toilets, it was necessary to take a deep breath before entering them otherwise the smell would make you vomit. The screws spoke to the prisoners as if they were the scum of the earth. You were not allowed to talk to anyone and if you answered the screws back, you would soon find yourself on bread and water.

After being sentenced to three years' borstal, I was immediately taken back to Wormwood Scrubs Prison to await allocation to whatever Borstal I was to serve my time at. I had already had my card marked as to the reception I was going to get if I was sentenced because of my verbal run-ins with a few of the screws whilst on remand. They had to be a bit careful until I had been sentenced. It wouldn't do for me to go to court with the marks of a beating all over me, so they settled for verbal abuse and general harassment, putting me on report for the most trivial of offences – and there were hundreds of ways they could do that even though you were locked in your cell for 23 hours a day.

I was, therefore, expecting to have problems when I got back into Wormwood Scrubs, but I was still surprised by the way it happened. Trouble came the first morning after being sentenced. When they brought the breakfast to the cells – a cup of watery tea, a cob of bread and a plate of porridge – we would also get a spoonful of sugar, which we normally kept to eke out between our breakfast and cocoa later on. This time the screw just pulled my door shut without giving me any sugar, so I yanked the bar that rang the bell. I could hear them shouting, 'Who's ringing that bell?' though they could see who it was, as the tally outside your door would drop down when you pulled the bell bar. They ignored me until everyone had been served then three or four of them came to my cell and said, 'What are you ringing that bell for?'

'I've not had any sugar,' I replied.

The screw who'd shut the door said, 'You put it in your tea.'

'You know that I was never given any,' I said.

With that, he lashed out with his fist. That was the signal for them all to jump on me. I was taken, still struggling, to the strongbox at the end of the wing and thrown inside. As the doors shut behind me I looked around. There were a few tiny panes of unbreakable glass set high up in the wall which allowed in a little light from the gas lamp set behind them. A grill over the door allowed in some air. The only furniture was a bed made up of a board set in concrete. There were no blankets.

When the two reinforced doors leading into the strongbox were shut, it was almost entirely sound-proof. Sometimes you would hear the reverberation of doors slamming elsewhere in the prison, but that was the only other sign of life.

I was left alone until dinnertime, when the sharp grating of the key in the lock of the outer door announced the arrival of the screws. I braced myself, remembering the threats they had uttered before shutting me in – threats it would be all too easy for them to carry out in this isolated cell. It took six of them to bring me my dinner, which was contained in a can about eight inches tall and about five inches in diameter. The contents appeared to be some watery soup with something that looked like rubber floating in it. This was the well-known 'floating duff' which was served in all prisons at that time.

I was also given a charge sheet that said I would be accused of gross personal violence against a prison officer. As I read it I knew that no one was ever found not guilty of any charge, so with nothing to lose, I thought I might just as well let them see that I wasn't so easily beaten. Without warning, I flattened one of the screws who had given me the trumped-up charge. Within a very short time I was feeling very sore and was securely strapped into a straitjacket – for what was to be the first of many times.

I was eventually sentenced to 15 days No. 1 diet and 42 days No. 2 diet, for my alleged attack on a prison officer and taken back to the strongbox. The No. 1 diet was served as three days on bread and water with one day off until you'd served your 15 days. Then you'd start your No. 2 diet when your bread and water would be supplemented with porridge and two potatoes. This would be seven days on and three days off until you'd served your 42 days. There would be no furniture in your cell, just three boards of wood set in concrete and they would give you a papier-maché receptacle to put your drinking water in. During all this time I had not been allowed to wash, so when the governor came around, I asked him if I could have permission to clean myself. He ordered: 'Get this man washed up.'

A little later a screw came in with a couple of his friends and said, 'I've got a present for you; it's a bar of soap, compliments of the governor.'

With that he dropped the bar of carbolic soap into my drinking water and left, saying, 'Get cleaned up.'

I have recently read in the newspapers about the brutality at Wormwood Scrubs Prison in west London that has, at last, been made public. One paper describes the prison officers as waging a reign of terror on inmates, but why haven't the prison officers been charged in exactly the same way as if a prisoner attacked a member of staff? Why also are the POA (Prison Officers' Association) so up-in-arms that some of their colleagues have been caught out? Why doesn't somebody at the Home Office tell the POA to get their men back to running the prisons and let the courts decide who's guilty and who isn't? Perhaps it's time that the Home Office decided to let the management run the prisons and use the type of resettlement method that has already been successful elsewhere, without the disruptive actions employed by the POA.

After about three or four months of complete misery in that place, I was told I'd been allocated to Portland Borstal. This I expected, as it had the reputation of being the hardest place in the British penal system. I was soon to find out that nothing had been exaggerated.

Portland Borstal was situated on a peninsula off the coast of Dorset and it had been in the past one of the most notorious prisons in the old days of penal servitude and hard labour. It was where Charlie Peace, one of the more infamous characters in Madame Tussaud's House of Horrors, did his time with a ball and chain around his ankle.

The punishment block had been used to house the old lags in years gone by. It still had an atmosphere of gloom and despair. I was to spend a few months in that block whilst I was in Portland. The ordinary time spent in Portland was bad enough, with the spartan regime and the hard work, but the punishment block was something else. If you were sentenced to a period in the 'block', as it was known, your day went as follows. At 6 a.m. you would fold your bed neatly and, on being unlocked, you would take your bedding to a rack at the end of the block. Then you would fill a bucket full with cold water and, taking carbolic soap and a scrubbing brush, scrub every inch of your cell. You would then clean the bucket and put it back where you got it from. Next you would line up and be marched out into the yard at the back of the block – regardless of what the weather was like – where you would do half an hour of physical training. This would be repeated five times during the day, only interrupted by the job of sawing railway sleepers into logs for chopping into sticks for the screws' fires. By 4.30 p.m., you would be back in your cell to be given a couple of pairs of handcuffs that had been lying in water for a couple of days to make them rusty. It would be your job to polish them until they shone. When you had finished and they were gleaming, they would be put back into the water to start the process over again. At eight o'clock you would be allowed to go and get your bedding and take it back to your cell.

This spartan regime was equally monotonous except for the weekends which were very good if you liked sport. I looked forward to the weekends with great anticipation. We indulged in most sports but they limited boxing to the odd bout between two guys from different houses who had the reputation of being the best in the place. With these official fights, everyone would go down to the gym to see the outcome, but most of the differences were settled in a cell or in the toilets. I met some pretty tough people whilst I was there.

The worst part of being in Portland, the thing that I still think of with horror, was the Burma Road. That was our place of work and it was just as hard as the name implies. The idea behind the Burma Road was a good one. The aim was to turn the barren land nearby into sports fields and, before I arrived, the old quarry had been converted into the stadium. It was one of the best sports grounds that I had seen. However, I could vividly imagine the suffering that had occurred whilst the quarry had been transformed into the pride and joy of the Home Office. Visitors were invariably taken to see the stadium to show what the borstal boys had created for their own recreation. But no one was ever told of the real feelings of the boys involved. Those who had to work with blistered and bleeding hands whilst the screw stood in close attendance to ensure that the rocks were removed and the earth thrown at the riddles. Absolute silence was the principal rule and the screws made sure that nobody talked.

There were many men who couldn't face another day on the Burma Road and they would inflict injuries on themselves. Some that couldn't do it to themselves would ask their mates to do it. It was nothing to walk into the wash-house and see some poor individual having his arm broken. I remember a guy having a pickaxe put through his foot. He was crippled for life.

The team that I worked with there were a pretty hard bunch. There were four of us: Alfie Burns from Manchester, Ronnie Smith from Battersea, Tam McGory from Glasgow and myself. Alfie was a very big guy with a mop of blond hair, who was always in trouble with the authorities and the house captain for refusing to get his hair cut. He loved his sport and although he wasn't the fastest athlete in the world he was like a brick wall in defence at football. We would play a game called 'murder ball' which involved no rules whatsoever. Alfie Burns loved that game. Two teams, consisting of anything from six to 12 players on each side, would endeavour, at the whistle, to get a medicine ball over the opposing team's defensive line starting from a spot mid-way between the two dead-ball lines. You could use any method to achieve this objective. A favourite ploy would be for one of the team to wrap himself around the ball whilst the rest of the team tried to drag him over the opponents' line. Meanwhile the other team would try to drag the guy the other way. Murder ball was a real test of physical endurance.

It wasn't long after Alfie Burns had been released from Portland that he was charged with murder, together with another Mancunian named Devlin. It became known as the Burns/Devlin case and they were the last two people to be hanged at Walton Prison in Liverpool.

Ronnie Smith was a very tough guy indeed. I later met his brother Les whilst in Wandsworth Prison and by that time other members of the family were becoming well known. Tam, the other member of the quartet, had been sent to Portland following a riot in the top Borstal in Scotland. He arrived with a very big reputation but he turned out to be quiet. It soon became clear, however, that his quietness was not because he feared what Portland had to offer. His theory was that if you left people alone, you would not be bothered by anyone yourself. Unfortunately for him, things didn't work that way. There was always someone ready to test the water. The first guy who wanted to test Tam's strength was called 'The Bull'. He was a big rough-looking man who would eat about a gallon of porridge every morning. He was absolutely despicable in every way, stank of BO and never washed. But the day he tried his hand with Tam was the biggest mistake of his life. Tam gave him a real beating and then dumped him in the shower – which I think hurt The Bull even more. This event was just one of the many small interruptions in our normal life, which was dominated by the back-breaking tasks on the Burma Road.

It was after a particularly hard day at this work that Tommy Williams approached me with a plan to escape. It wasn't much of a plan but I think I would have taken any chance to break away from the hardship and monotony. Tommy had worked in the fitter's shop and whilst there had made a key which would start most cars. It looked like an old Lucas key, made from a flat piece of metal shaped like a spade. It was normal practice every weekend for the boys to be taken to the sports field, situated outside the rear wall of the institution, to participate in some inter-house sporting activity. We all looked forward eagerly to these events and the screws would 'psych' the boys to fever pitch to ensure that their own house won as many tournaments as possible. There were five houses named after great naval heroes and I guess any boy who passed through Portland just after the war will recall those confrontations between the various houses until his dying day.

Now, to fall in with Tommy's plan, I had to feign an injury in order to exclude myself from taking an active part in the forthcoming weekend sporting events. Tommy had spotted a car which was parked outside the old quarrymaster's house at the top of the sports field. The idea was that, given a fair bit of luck, we should be able to slip over the fence and make it to the car whilst everyone's attention was directed towards the inter-house tug-of-war contests. Tommy thought that if we were able to get a couple of minutes' start we could get to the car and drive down to Chesil Beach. If our luck held and we were off Portland Bill before the screws could phone the police, who would then close the roads, we could have had a good chance of getting away. It was well known that the only possible escape was via the road over Chesil Beach. There had been numerous attempts by boys to swim away, but many of these had ended in near-disaster due to the treacherous local currents.

As the time approached for us to make our break, we walked slowly towards the quarry at the top of the sports field, while everyone else's attention was focused on the tug-of-war teams. As soon as we heard the referee shout, 'Take the strain, heave', Tommy and I went over the fence and ran towards the parked car.

To our dismay we heard the screws shout, 'Two away' and we were chased immediately. But we got to the car before the screws crossed the quarry and the engine fired into life at the first pull on the starter.

We were away. It now became a matter of urgency to get across Chesil Beach before the police were notified and closed the road. As we drove down the steep hill towards Weymouth, we saw one of the off-duty screws trudging up the hill. With freedom so close, we gave him a cheery wave. He was just about to respond when he realised that it was two escapees. He nearly had a fit, shaking his fist and stamping his feet.

Tommy and I were in a very buoyant mood when we got to Chesil Beach and found that there were no roadblocks. We went flying through Weymouth and nearly mowed down a group of people waiting at a bus stop. Then we made a very fundamental mistake. We tried to drive straight through to Dorchester instead of abandoning the car where it would not be found for some time and then lying low until darkness. Not long out of Weymouth, we heard the familiar ringing bell of the old Wolseley police car. Turning round, I reported that we had a couple on our tail.

We both waved in a fit of bravado.

'Right,' I said briskly to Tommy, 'let's lose them.'

He speeded up. But we couldn't shake them off. We soon decided we would have more chance on foot, so we abandoned the car and struck off across the fields. The chase began and we were clearly out-distancing the pursuers. We were just starting to feel hopeful again, when looking up, we saw another posse up ahead cutting off our escape. We were soon captured and returned to the Borstal. As soon as the police departed we knew what to expect and were not surprised to see the off-duty screw we had passed earlier during our drive down the hill, come in to take part in the chastisement which was meted out to us in the punishment block.

I never saw or heard anything of Tommy after I left Portland. I would think that the two months spent in the punishment block probably decided his future for him. As for myself, I was becoming more bitter as the months passed by.

Whenever I think of my days at Portland, I only seem to remember the violence and the continual bullying that went on. Not only the staff but the inmates allowed themselves to be used and corrupted by the system. Each house had six groups and a group leader was appointed for each. In addition, a house captain, usually one of the toughest guys in the house, was also created. A new inmate would be introduced to the house captain as soon as he was allocated to a particular house. The house rules and regulations would then be spelt out by the captain and any of the group leaders who were present. The first thing that would happen to the new inmate would be the haircut, when all of his hair would be shaved off.

On my arrival, I didn't fancy my hair being shaved by another inmate. My attitude led to my first confrontation with the house captain. He decided he was going to let me know who was 'governor' straightaway. However, it soon became clear to him that I wasn't just another push-over and he had to call on the help of his group leaders. I remember that not a day passed without me being involved in at least one fight, until the other inmates realised that I wasn't going to conform to their ways of running the house. Having established this understanding, I was then ignored by most of the leaders. I was later offered the job of being the next leader, which I turned down. I never wished to be used as a tool of the authorities. I suppose I could have made life a lot easier for myself if I had conformed, but I don't think it would have done anything for my mental attitude.

Just before I was due to be discharged, I was called before the governor and told that I would be given the papers appertaining to my National Service on the day of my release.

# 5.

## 'YOU'RE IN THE ARMY NOW'

So here I was, 20 years old, just released from three years of imprisonment, being told to report immediately to 1st Battalion REME at Blandford Camp, Dorset. I wasn't very happy with the fact that I didn't get a chance to go home first, but I thought they'd let me go home once they knew that I'd not seen anyone there for three years. I should have known better.

'You're in the army now, go and get kitted out,' I was told.

The next day, after getting our kit, we were told to assemble in the gymnasium, where we were met by a couple of guys in red-and-black-striped jerseys. They were PTIs.

'Line up,' the first jersey said. 'Do we have any sportsmen here?'

Most of the recruits put their hands up and declared they'd participated in various sports. Then he said, 'You, the bloke with the funny hair cut' – borstal style – 'can you do anything? Play football, box or run?'

'Yes, a bit of each,' I replied.

'Oh, a superman, eh?' he sneered. 'Well, let's see how you are with the gloves on.'

Putting a pair on himself he then gave me a hook to the body. That was the first and last blow he threw. All the hate and frustration came boiling out of me and I just gave him a fusillade of punches that left him flat on the floor.

He wasn't very talented himself, but I did meet one or two very good boxers while I was at Blandford. I also met one of the fastest fighters I ever sparred with. His name was Darkie Hughes from Cardiff and he was the current ABA Champion. He eventually went on to fight for the professional title.

I was to meet many fighters at Blandford. One of the fittest and best looking was Mickey O'Sullivan, one of three brothers who were professional fighters (the other two being Dickie and Danny.) Mickey O'Sullivan is the grandfather of the ex-world champion snooker player. I last saw Mickey in 1998 at a meeting of the London Ex-Boxers at St Pancras. It was nice to meet him again with a couple of old pals of mine, Terry Spinks and Charlie Dice.

I couldn't settle into anything at this period of my life and it wasn't very long before I was going AWOL from Blandford. After a short period, I was brought back to the camp to be charged and it was then that I met Mick Emmett-Dunne, the provost-sergeant. He was apparently a legend in that camp and was certainly a striking-looking guy, well over six foot with a proportionate build. I was to meet Mick again several years later in Dartmoor. I was going through a pretty rough time and had to have an operation. The authorities wouldn't let me go to Freedom Fields Hospital in Plymouth which was only 15 miles away and I was taken 200 miles to London's Wormwood Scrubs Prison, where they had the facilities to operate. After my operation, I was put into the ordinary wing to await a transfer back to Dartmoor. It was while I was in the hospital that I got some old papers and read that Mick had gone to Germany with his unit after I had left Blandford Camp for a 'better life'. Whilst there, he had been accused of killing another soldier with a karate blow during a row about the other soldier's wife. Mick had married the girl after the burial of her husband and had settled down. The coroner had apparently concluded that the guy had hanged himself, but after some pretty strong rumours, it was decided to exhume the body. Mick was charged and sentenced to life imprisonment for his murder.

It was while I was going into church, after being put into the ordinary wing from the hospital, that I first saw Mick in the Scrubs. He was handing out the hymn books. He had his eyes cast downwards and as I clutched the book without taking it, he looked up blankly at first, then with recognition; his eyes came alight. I was to remind him of his words to me all those years before. 'If you don't get rid of that hatred, you'll spend many years in prison.'

It was at that same time that I got another surprise. I was standing in the doorway of my cell when I saw a familiar face walking past me with a chamber pot in his hand on his way to slopping out. The last time I had seen that face was in the gym when he was training for the British light-heavyweight title. His name, George Walker, later became well known in the city with his company, Brent Walker. Many great pundits of the boxing game still rate George's title fight at the Liverpool Stadium with Dennis Powell as the greatest light-heavyweight title fight this country has ever seen. It was sad to see him walking along that landing. He told me later that he was in for taking a lorry-load out of the docks and that he had been given two years. It didn't seem to do him any harm, for the next time I was to meet George, years later at the Log Cabin Club in Wardour Street, Soho, he was well on the way to making his first million.

I decided that there was no way I was ever going to finish off my National Service. I'd just spent three years at Portland Borstal and then I was expected to go straight into the Army without a break. I wanted to see some of the bright lights, so when I was released from the guardroom, I wasted no time. I ran off and made my way back to London. It didn't take me long to find some of my old pals. A few of the girls I knew were still working around the West End, but by then they had gone a little up-market. It wasn't the Soho cafés they frequented, but the Lyons Corner Houses. There was one in Coventry Street that everyone used in the daytime and the one in the Strand was open all night, so that was a popular meeting place after hours. You could always expect to see certain faces in the Corner House in those days.

But back to my life on the run from the army. We still carried identification cards in those days, unless you were in the Army when you had your pay book. I had to be a bit careful so I'd sometimes borrow my friends' ID cards. One particular ID caused me some awkward moments as it was in the name of Angus McKenzie with an address in Glasgow. So on the odd occasion I got 'pulled' by the law for my ID card I had to adopt a Glaswegian accent. I must be the worst mimic in the world, but for some unknown reason it was never questioned.

Years later, when I was in Dartmoor, I heard of a pop singer called Karl Denver. He had a few big hits in the '50s and '60s. Then I saw a photograph of him and realised that he was my old pal Angus McKenzie. Sadly, Angus died quite recently.

Whilst on the run from the Army I was in a very mixed-up frame of mind. My hatred for anyone in authority had built up in me since my early days in St Vincent's, but I still had my sense of fair play. Consequently, I was a bit choosy about the guys I knocked around with. It was obvious to me that, having a record, I was going to have to obtain my living as a criminal, but there were certain things that I would never have done, such as pushing drugs or living off immoral earnings. Luckily I've kept to those principles throughout my life.

There seemed to be a different atmosphere of violence creeping into the underworld at this time. Perhaps I noticed it more from having been out of circulation for a while. It was more sinister than the odd punch-up, razor slashing and the gang wars. That was a kind of accepted violence that didn't affect the ordinary public. But now we had crimes like the 'Antiques Murder', where a gang of smash-and-grab bandits, including one of the Jenkins brothers, gunned down a motorcyclist who 'had a go' and were later hanged at Wandsworth. There were so many of these types of incidents that it seemed that the ordinary criminal was getting more desperate.

I was hanging out in the Corner House with guys like Curly King and forever looking for ways to make some easy money. Curly was one of the nicer people I came across in those days and we got into a few scrapes together. I was also seeing a girl who I'd met before I was sent to Portland. She was a very attractive girl, but I wasn't looking for a steady relationship. However, she became pregnant and we had a son, a beautiful boy, Jeff. I thought I should try to do the responsible thing so we married in a registry office and got a tiny flat together. She hated my way of life and moved back home. I realised even then that a lot of what she said made good sense, but I kept looking for ways to make my fortune. I loved her in many ways and would keep going back to her with the intention of fulfilling my responsibilities, but my good intentions would never last. We had two more daughters, born between prison sentences. To my everlasting regret I never got to know my children very well but I know my ex-wife was a good mother. Jeff has become a musician and my eldest daughter went to university and has done well for herself, despite not having a father about.

I eventually ended up working with a team of guys who specialised in stealing lorries. In those days lorry drivers used to park their wagons up in transport café car parks and leave them overnight. There were none of the sophisticated anti-theft devices that they have now, so it was simply a matter of going out and looking for the right wagon. Once found, our driver would be inside the cabin and driving it away within minutes. We used to take pot-luck in the early days, we'd just hope there was a worthwhile load and we often got more rubbish than good gear. But we had our odd tickle and the champagne would flow. We used to take all of our stuff to a guy in Commercial Road. Whenever we'd pull up he'd say, 'Have you hit the jackpot yet?' Then we'd tell him we didn't know what was in it yet and he would groan. He used to say, 'Why don't you check it out first? I've still got all those tin-openers you brought me.'

Who is a typical 'fence' (a buyer of stolen goods)? Well, they come in all shapes and sizes and you couldn't pick one out by looking at him. But they've all got one thing in common, however, and that is that they are probably the brightest of all the criminal fraternity. People think of a fence as a guy who looks and acts like Fagin in *Oliver Twist*. Well, they may not all look like him, but most of those I've known act like him. So did Abe Tee, the man who bought thousands of tin openers from us – and had them for a long time afterwards. He knew from experience that we were a professional team and after he'd met our driver, Jock from Kilmarnock, he knew that we would eventually come up with the goods.

Jock had just finished his National Service and there was nothing he didn't know about lorries. Whatever the size, he could handle them as though each one was a Mini Cooper – which wasn't always to our advantage. We had all met through a mutual friend who had known Jock in the Army. Jock didn't want to go back to Kilmarnock until he'd made a few quid, so he was quite prepared to lend his expertise to us until he'd made enough to go back north in style. Unfortunately, we were all a bit green at the beginning and the first wagons that Jock pulled away were full of rubbish; hence our man Abe giving us a reminder about the tin openers. Mind you, he did have a problem at the time as they were a new design and he couldn't send a team of demonstrators around the markets while he was the only bloke in the whole country to have them 'in stock'.

We learned from our experiences. By checking out the lorries beforehand, we started to get a few sensible loads and some good 'tickles'. So Abe decided to invest in a new 'slaughter' (a place to change over and store stolen goods). He bought a small-holding in the country with a big barn and we were taken down to familiarise ourselves with the terrain. We were a bit disappointed about the narrow country roads we would have to traverse – apart from Jock, who was overjoyed. When he saw some of the hairpin bends he couldn't wait to tackle them with a big articulated lorry.

The first disaster came, not through Jock's driving, but through Abe failing to test the drive into the farmyard, which was just a cinder track. With the first truck we took in, Jock was told by Abe to run around to the side of the barn and then to get rid of the unit. Jock let the legs down on the trailer and went on his merry way to dump the unit on the other side of London. The rest of us went into the house to look at the delivery note and do our business with Abe. When we came out again we saw, to our horror, that the legs had sunk about two feet into the ground. We spent hours getting the stuff unloaded and then 'our man' said he was going to dismantle the trailer as he had a bloke in Oxfordshire who was going to buy the axles, wheels and other spare parts.

From then on, I saw two very lucrative businesses built up, but they were not without a few headaches. The most serious of these came when Jock, who was bringing in a load of carpets, rounded a bend at about sixty miles per hour and simply turned the wagon onto its side. There were carpets everywhere and the road was completely blocked. But more seriously, it was only about half a mile from the slaughter. The only thing we could do was leave the carpets decorating the road and pick up Jock, who was a bit dazed, and drive him down to the slaughter to let our man know. There was a bit of a panic about all of the spare parts laying around in the barn and there was no time to move them. But amazingly, the Old Bill came to remove the carpets but never paid a visit to any of the premises in the area.

It was while we were waiting to see how that little episode was going to work out that Jock decided to go to Scotland and take all of his clan on a

THE BRUTAL TRUTH

week-long binge. They looked forward to his periodic visits, as he always took a stack of money up there with him and stayed until it was all gone. When Jock returned to London, we were still giving the slaughter a miss, but we had a friend with a coal yard in south London and for a few quid, we could always use it at a pinch. So Jock, who was skint again, decided to go out and do a quick bit of moonlighting. He phoned me at about 1.30 a.m. to say he had a load and could I meet him. By about 2.30 a.m. I was with him and the lorry which he had parked in a square in a quiet part of London. We opened the back and found it was loaded with apples. I looked at Jock and said with exasperation: 'Where do you think we're going to sell this lot? Why didn't you check the load first?' I remembered a guy I knew who had a couple of fruit shops and rang him from a phone box. He wasn't very pleased at being woken up at 3 a.m., as he normally got up about 5 a.m. to go to the market.

'What kind of apples are they?' he asked.

'I don't know,' I said, surprised at the question. All apples were the same to me.

'Go and have a look. If they're Golden Delicious I can probably place them for you,' he said.

I went back to Jock. 'Open that wagon again, I might have found a buyer,' I said.

I couldn't believe my eyes when I read on the boxes: 'French Golden Delicious'.

I went back to the phone and told my man, who was delighted. I then phoned the coalman and told him I needed his yard and, as it was so late, I told him he'd get an extra few bob. We found there were 1,200 cases in the wagon and my man gave us 10 shillings a case for them. £600 was a pretty good earner in those days, as one could have bought a house for that sort of money.

Everyone had a good day and so it was off to the West End for a day out: the coalman, the fruiterer, Jock and I.

We had some pretty good days to follow and things seemed to go without too many hiccups until the Old Bill decided to do something about our little enterprise. We were surrounded just as we were about to drive a lorry away from a yard in Hertfordshire. Three of us were sent to Hertfordshire Assizes where Mr Justice Croom-Johnson gave us five years' imprisonment each.

# 6.

## THE CAT-O'-NINE-TAILS
## SCARS FOREVER

I was taken to Pentonville to start my sentence. From the moment I stepped inside the prison, I knew it was going to start all over again, the same as Wormwood Scrubs, the same as Portland. There was a reception of six screws waiting for me. Eyeing the group of new inmates, the spokesman demanded: 'Which one is Mason?'

'Me,' I replied.

'Right, come with us.'

I was taken straight to the punishment block and told, 'This is where you'll do all your bird if you once get out of line. We've checked your record out and we don't like people like you. The governor will see you tomorrow.'

The same old intimidation routine. I thought, I'm not going to have five years of this and I told them so. I also told every one of them, that if anyone laid a finger on me I would eventually do the same to him. Then it started.

On my first day in the mailbag shop, where there was a 'no talking' rule, one of the discipline screws suddenly said to me: 'Stop talking or you'll be put on report.' As I hadn't opened my mouth, I knew that this was a confrontation. I knew that I could not stop what was going to happen. So I just swore at him and said, 'Get on with what you've got in mind.'

He made a signal to the screw in the observation box, who promptly rang the alarm bell. Almost immediately, as if they had been waiting outside, the door of the workshop was flung open and the heavy mob came flooding in – about a dozen of them. The discipline screw pointed at me and declared,

'He threatened me.' Seconds later I was being dragged to the door, struggling and lashing out as best as I could. The other cons started to boo the screws and it seemed that an eruption of violence was just a knife-edge away. Then we were through the door, which slammed shut behind us. Out of sight of the cons, the screws seemed to go mad. 'He tried to start a riot,' they shouted as they began smashing me with their batons.

It came as no surprise when I was charged with an unprovoked attack on a screw. After a couple of months in the punishment block on a bread-and-water-diet and loss of a few months' remission, I was sent to Wandsworth, where I believe they thought they would be better equipped for dealing with someone who wouldn't lie down to them. They were certainly better equipped, but I still wasn't going to give in. I spent the next year in and out of the punishment block – more in than out.

By this time I was going through plenty of aggravation with the authorities. The governor of Wandsworth at that time was a man called Lawton. He was the harshest, most pitiless person I ever met in my life. I think the day he presided over me being flogged with the cat-o'-nine-tails was the happiest day of his life, but I can tell you that one of the unhappiest days for him was the day I humiliated him in the brush shop.

During one of my breaks from the punishment cells, I was determined to get one over on him for what he'd put me through over the past few months. I put a bucket in the toilet and told everyone that I knew to use it. They started to go one after the other – the discipline screws must have thought there was something in the food with so many needing to use the toilet.

After about a dozen blokes had used the bucket it wasn't a pretty sight – it stank to high heaven. Lawton, regular as clockwork, came through that shop at about 11 a.m. along with his henchman. He had all of the screws terrified of him and as soon as he walked in, they would all leap to attention and salute and shout, 'All correct, sir.' He loved it, the pompous little sod. But I soon took the sneer off his face when I dumped the contents of the bucket over his head and threw the residue over his henchman, who had the grace to vomit. I got a terrible beating for that but it was worth it – an extra air of lightness was added to the atmosphere in the prison for quite some time.

I was to have one or two more run-ins with the prison staff in later months which resulted in me spending more time in the strongbox. When I came out of the punishment block I was put into D-Wing and given a job in the tailor's shop, although I was still supposed to sew mailbags. Only the privileged few did any tailoring and that was restricted to making prisoners' shirts. It wasn't unusual to get a shirt that had one sleeve six inches longer than the other, or a collar that joined somewhere beneath the ear. As soon as I got into the workshop, I knew there would be trouble as the discipline screw sitting with the alarm bell at his elbow was an old enemy of mine. He never took his eyes off me from the minute I got in the shop – as we both knew that he'd been in on a few of the kickings I had received whilst in the punishment block. If the struggle was to go on, I had to beat him.

When the dinner break came at noon, we were 'rubbed down' (searched) and sent back into our cells. Then I realised why I'd been put into the tailor's shop. It was because the workshop was right next to the wing I was in and also adjacent to the punishment block. They were ready for me. I had my suspicions confirmed when I came out into the exercise yard after dinner. There was the discipline screw talking to another officer who was supposed to be their hard man. Both were giving me the once over. I noticed there were more screws on duty than usual and I knew then that they had taken me seriously when, lying in a pool of blood in the strongbox, I warned them I would be back at them. As I walked into the workshop that afternoon I made up my mind that I was going to 'do' the discipline screw no matter what the consequences were. I sat on my stool glancing casually around and I saw that he had been joined in the shop by three fellow screws. I knew it wasn't going to be easy, but I also knew that this was the time for confrontation and I had to do it. I stood up and said, looking straight at him, 'I'm going for a shit.'

'Sit down. You don't do anything without permission,' he said.

But by this time I was up close to him and his momentary hesitation was all I needed. I leaped on to his high seat and hooked him to the chin, then dragged him out of the box and with a quick fusillade of punches, flattened him. I looked around to see their hard man bearing down on me but I could read the fear in his eyes and as he reached out to grab me, I moved inside and 'nutted' him. He went down as if poleaxed and his massive frame cringed away, trying to cover up. The other two were just rooted to the floor but I saw the principal officer in his office with the old-fashioned telephone to his ear. I dived in, took the phone from him and hit him on the head with it. He just rolled up like a ball in the corner of the office. I ran quickly back towards the door and noticed that one of the other discipline screws was ringing the alarm bell. I knew I didn't have a lot of time, as it was guaranteed that the heavy mob would be waiting for the bell to ring. I started to grab the sewing machines and throw them in front of the door. I heard Wally Probyn say ruefully, 'Fuck me! I've waited nine months to get this machine, now look at it.'

But I was too late. In no time at all, the screws were crashing the door in and were swarming all over me. They hauled me through the door and threw me down the steps leading into D-Wing. I was back on my feet before they could reach me and was able to get inside the door. I nutted the screw in the doorway and grabbed his stick and started to belt the others as they came in. But I couldn't hold out for long; I was soon forced to the floor with ten or a dozen sticks thudding down on me. They then proceeded to beat me the length of D-Wing, over the centre and down into the punishment block, the screws dragging me along, deliberately smashing my head against the iron stanchions holding up the landing above.

By the time I arrived at the strongbox I was barely conscious. The last thing I remember was a screw jumping on me while the baton wielders were beating my testicles. I was beyond fighting back . . .

When the first stroke came, it hurt a fair bit, but having steeled myself for the anticipated pain, I was able to stand it pretty well. The governor counted, 'One', and in the quiet, I again heard the screw sorting out the strands of the whip.

The next stroke came, but this time it was twice as bad. It seemed to land right in the same place as the first, as did the rest of the strokes. They seemed to get progressively harder, slicing into my bruised skin. The governor counted slowly as the sweat poured down my face. It probably only took about twenty minutes but it seemed never-ending. It was only after they released me from the frame that my back started to go numb and I realised that Gibbsy had got his time-scale entirely wrong.

It wasn't till I got back to the cell that the numbness started to go. It was replaced by a deep throbbing that was getting progressively more painful. I knew that the screws were looking through the spy-hole to see my reaction, which steeled me against showing any emotion. I felt what I thought was sweat running down my body under my arm, but when I looked it was blood. I looked at the right side of my chest and I could see where one of the strokes had cut deep into my flesh.

That was the closest I ever came to giving in.

# 7.

## THE CONDEMNED, THE MAD AXEMAN AND JACK THE HAT

The first few days after having the cat-o'-nine-tails were a strange time for me. I was still recovering from the beating I had taken and my back was extremely sore. It was a few weeks before I could lie on it properly and when I went back to the workshop I had a few well-meaning mates to welcome me back from the punishment block – giving me a slap on the back without thinking! The screw who had to rub down everyone as they returned to the wing after work nearly had a heart attack when I screamed at him to take his hands off me.

The atmosphere in Wandsworth was tense and getting worse.

Of the 1,500 or so men, there were only a handful fighting back, either physically or by trying to smuggle out word of what was happening within the prison. But when news got around that someone was being beaten in the punishment block, all the cons showed their solidarity in the only way they could. I'll never forget the menacing, awesome sound of over a thousand prisoners banging their pots and plates on the metal-clad doors and chanting for the blood of the people who had been tormenting them for years. What with the brutality in the punishment block and the number of hangings in Wandsworth at that time, the prison was like a cauldron waiting to boil over.

The condemned cells, which always seemed to be occupied, were right above the punishment block and at the opposite end to the strongbox. When you had finished the first part of your sentence, you were moved from

THE BRUTAL TRUTH

61

the strongbox to the other end of the block to finish off your 'confined to cell' stint, commonly known as 'CC'. So it turned out that over the various times I was in Wandsworth, I was often unfortunate enough to be located underneath the condemned cell and adjacent to the cell the body would drop into. I hated the moment when, on the day before execution, the hangman came into the prison and while the condemned man was on exercise, tested the trap door. It dropped with a dreadful sound of finality that reverberated around the wing.

Some hangings affected us more than others.

There was a guy called Whiteway who must have been a complete lunatic. He was the infamous tow-path murderer and he thought he was Tarzan. He used to do the Tarzan call frequently and everyone would shout, 'Hurry up and hang the bastard.'

Then there was a guy called Burgess. I think he did a murder in a hotel in Croydon. I remember him because he was very quiet for the three weeks he was waiting to hang, but on the morning he was due to 'go', he cracked and set about the two screws who were with him in the condemned cell. I could hear the thuds and shouts above me and the insistent ringing of the alarm bell. Then I heard the heavy mob arrive and the beating seemed to go on for ages with the condemned man screaming his head off. After some time everything went quiet and they came to take us for our exercise. When we came back from the yard, I saw a pile of clothes outside the PO's office. They were all ripped and covered in blood. I knew they had belonged to Burgess, as they had no buttons on; only tapes to keep them together.

But the incident that upset the whole prison more than any other was the hanging of Derek Bentley. Derek, who was eighteen at the time, had been sentenced to death for being with a chap called Chris Craig, when the latter shot a policeman, notwithstanding the fact that Bentley was already in police custody when Craig shot the copper. Arguments have gone on for many years about whether he was guilty or not. Like many people, I believe it was a revenge execution, because the boy Chris Craig, who did the actual murder, was legally too young to hang. The evidence against Bentley, that he told Craig to 'Let him have it', was interpreted as an instruction to shoot the policeman, when he could have meant that Craig should hand over the gun. In fact there is now even some doubt about whether Bentley said those words at all.

I was right under his cell for the whole of the time he was waiting to be hanged and I used to look out of the window each day and see his mother and sister come to the back of the condemned cell and climb the iron staircase into the cell next to it to visit him. They both seemed to age so much in the space of a few weeks. It was terrible to see, because they, like many people, believed he was innocent of any murder. We all thought Bentley was certain to get a reprieve and they must have kidded him right up to the last minute. The day before his execution I watched the hangman, who on this occasion was Pierrepoint's assistant Harry Allen, come down the path with a big grin on his face to test the trap-door. In some ways he looked more sinister, dressed in his everyday bowler hat and dark suit than Pierrepoint himself did in his trilby. They had taken Bentley for his exercise at the side of the hospital while they tried the trap-door, which banged down into the cell next to mine and shook the dividing wall. I was in that cell many a time when people were hanged but I still have very clear memories of Derek Bentley playing a tune on a comb and a piece of toilet paper the night before he died. There was a very strained atmosphere that day in Wandsworth and it was a long time before it lifted.

It was while in Wandsworth at this time, that I first met Jack 'The Hat' McVitie and Frank Mitchell, 'The Mad Axeman'. Frank had gone to Portland after I'd left and I often heard stories about this young man there with super-human strength who was always championing the little and weak guys. When I met him, I understood why he impressed people so much. He was very good looking and a perfect physical specimen, about 6ft 2in in height and weighing about sixteen stone – all of which was muscle. He was probably the strongest man I ever met and he would exercise at every opportunity. His presence in the prison reassured quite a lot of men, as he was against all kinds of bullying. Although he had been nicknamed 'The Mad Axeman', he was never mad and would never have hit anyone with an axe. He was a victim of the system: a big, gentle giant who hated to see people weaker than himself being treated like dirt.

Frank loved a good laugh. Being a fitness fanatic he used to do a couple of hundred press-ups and sit-ups every day. Once most of his problems in prison had been sorted out, Frank was left mostly to his own devices – until the arrival of a zealous, new chief officer.

Frank had found a very thick manhole cover, the type with concrete and steel, which he used as a weight to build up his body. He had no problem pressing it over his head twenty or thirty times. The new chief officer, walking round the yard, saw the manhole cover lying on the ground. He asked the screw walking with him, 'What's that doing there?'

'That's Mitchell's training weight,' said the screw.

The new chief had obviously been filled in about Frank, but for some reason, he decided to test the water himself.

'I want this object removed to the building yard,' he ordered.

The screw bent down but he couldn't budge it. Looking sheepishly at his chief he said, 'It's too heavy, sir.'

'Well go and get some help,' yelled the chief.

It took the screw some time before he found a volunteer willing to give him a hand, as it seemed that no one fancied going down to the yard to take

Frank's weight away, especially as the exercise period was about to start. Sure enough, just as the two screws were struggling towards the building yard with the manhole cover, Frank came out of the wing.

'What are you doing with my weight?' he asked quite mildly.

'It's not our fault Frank, the new chief ordered us to take it away.'

With this, Frank took it from them and – with absolutely no effort whatsoever – strolled back to the end of the yard. Over his shoulder he said, 'You'd better tell the chief to come and get it himself.' Then as Frank started to smile, the whole prison yard fell about laughing. I believe the prison governor must have had a word with the chief, as from then on, whenever he passed Frank, he used to say, 'Good morning, Mitchell. How's the training going?'

Although outwardly tough, Frank was very kind-hearted, as his actions showed. He never smoked and in the later days of his sentence, when he was allowed to buy sweets or tobacco with his earnings, he would send the money instead to under-privileged kids. He was a very good friend to me and I will always cherish his memory.

Jack McVitie was a different guy to Frank. He was above average height with a thick mop of black hair (which fell out later in life) and he took to always wearing a hat even in a night club or restaurant. He had piercing blue eyes that always seemed to be laughing. There were many times when he and I were recovering from a beating and I'd look at Jack who, with a twinkle in his eye, would remark something like, 'I'll be all right when I get out of here, some birds like guys with battered features.'

Jack had been what they termed a 'Borstal failure', which meant that they couldn't beat him into submission, so he was sent to the punishment block in Reading Prison. That's where I first started to hear about him and I knew he had to be a bit special because there were quite a few blokes in those days who were not taking it lying down. Although I got to know many such men as the years went by, my friendship with Frank and Jack was very close. During one period, when we were all out of the punishment block, we managed to snatch a few words together. We knew that the prison staff at Wandsworth were determined to break us and we decided that if we were to have any chance we'd stick together as much as we could, so if one was taken to the punishment block the other two would follow. For instance, one afternoon I was working in the brush shop. Among the screws in the shop that day was a member of the Wandsworth heavy mob. He was always boasting about his prowess as a hard man, but he would forget to mention that he never had less than half a dozen other screws with him when he beat a prisoner up. He used to strut around the workshop being sarcastic and generally making everyone's life a misery. He had already told me that he was going to have his eyes on me and at the first chance I gave him, he would

Frank 'the Mad Axeman'
Mitchell, captured
after his escape from
Broadmoor.

Jack 'the Hat' McVitie.

Myself, third from the left, in the forefront,
working in the quarry at Dartmoor in the early
'50s. The Pony Patrol, 'Pedaller Palmer', is
riding shotgun at the top of the quarry face.

The gravestone of
Ted Richards,
'the Arab', at
St Michael's
Church, Dartmoor.

The entrance to the quarry at Dartmoor Prison.

Top: At one of Christine Keeler's parties. Second
from left, standing, Charlie Dice; sixth from
left, myself; on my right, 'Scouse Norman'
Johnson; far right, Reggie Kray; seated, with
back to camera, Limehouse Willy, the twins'
uncle.

Above: Left to right: Joey Pyle, Reggie Kray, Joe
Louis (Heavyweight Champion of the World), Alex
Stein (Promoter), Joe 'Diamond' Marlow and
friend, Ronnie Kray, Ronnie Cowley.

Pellicci's Café where I used to meet the Kray twins in the '50s.

Seated around the table from left: Mickey Forsyth, Billy Daniels, Reggie Kray, Johnny Squibb, Johnny Davies, a guy called Peter, myself and Ronnie Kray.

Top: Myself and Johnny Nash in the Cumberland
Hotel.

Above: Left to right: Myself, Chris Ellison
(Burnside of *The Bill*), Roy 'Polly' Pollard and
Barry Noonan in Nosher Powell's old pub.

Myself and Ronnie
Knight in Mijas,
Costa del Sol.

Left to right: Myself, Jimmy the Weed, Mixie Walsh.

The Strangeways Riot, 1990.

break me. One day he obviously decided that the time had come to see how much I had left in me. I asked permission to go to the toilet, which we had to do. But he kept letting other people go in front of me – the usual sort of petty behaviour that eventually drives you to the end of your tether. I'd had enough, so I got up to walk to the toilet. He signalled to the screw in the box to ring the alarm bell and took my arm to guide me away, knowing full well that the heavy mob were racing to the workshop.

'Just try something and you're dead,' he said, goading me.

Something inside me snapped and I lost control, flattening him and the two other screws. By the time reinforcements arrived, the three officers had barricaded themselves in the storeroom, but there was no escape for me.

I was subsequently dragged and beaten back to the punishment block and into one of the two strongboxes which were in E-Wing. I had been there for about two hours, feeling a bit sore, when I heard the sound of a beating going on in the next strongbox. Then Frank's voice called my name. I let him know that I could hear him.

'I heard they'd done you again. Don't worry, we'll win in the end. I've done a few in the centre,' he said.

Frank had come in from the pouch shop, learned that I'd had trouble and had run down to my cell. Seeing that it was empty, he went straight back to the centre where all the senior staff were assembled and demanded to see me. They tried to get rid of him but he stood his ground. They tried to jump him but he was too strong for them. He put four or five of them down before they overpowered him and got him into the strongbox next to mine.

The next morning, just before adjudication, we could hear the usual sounds of the heavy mob and their batons going to town and the unmistakable voice of Jack McVitie, shouting our names and saying, 'Stick together and we'll beat these bastards yet.'

It's a great feeling to know that you've got people who will stick with you, even though the odds make it nearly impossible to win. I tried to express how I felt in a letter to Frank and Jack. In fact it was written on a long piece of toilet paper – which was the usual way of passing messages. We used to call these notes 'stiffs'. Jack, Frank and I would send a couple of stiffs to each other every week. Frank would write about his little sister Linda, whom he thought the world of. He told me that he worried about her so much it would kill him if anything happened to her. Jack would go on about the screws, whom he hated even more than I did, but he would also write reams about his girlfriend, Anne, whom he loved very much and later married.

It was nearly a year before we were to come out of the punishment block, only to be split up. Frank went to Parkhurst. I don't remember where Jack went, but I was to meet them both again years later. I was told that I was going to Dartmoor and was moved over to Pentonville, to await the national draft that went to the 'Moor' every month.

During my life, I have spent over thirteen years inside Dartmoor Prison on three separate occasions, initially going there when I was 24 years of age. Therefore, the 'Moor' has had a major impact upon my life and features strongly in my story.

Recently I returned to Princetown. As I walked around the environs of the prison, many of my experiences of the place and of my former fellow inmates came flooding back. Though I have recalled many of my experiences in my story, there are so many others which have been left untold.

Whilst visiting St Michael's Church, I read a brief history of the place which was displayed for public interest. I reproduce the significant points, abstracted from this document, by way of giving some background to this institution.

## PRINCETOWN – MAY 1803.

Owing to the battles between the Napoleonic armies and the English, it was decided to put French prisoners of war into hulks docked at Plymouth. Thomas Tyerwitt said this was an opportunity to build up Princetown as a prison, as it was far enough away for safety, yet within marching distance and near enough to obtain military assistance in times of trouble.

The foundation stone was laid in 1806 and on 24th May 1809, the first 2,500 prisoners marched from Plymouth to the new prison. It was built to house 5,000 prisoners, but for a long period it housed 9,000. Soon Princetown grew as warders required accommodation and a daily market brought trade to the area.

In 1810, the French prisoners began to erect the church of St Michael, using the granite they had quarried. They were paid 6d a day and it took four years to build.

In 1812, America, incensed by the seizure of American ships during the British blockade of the French, declared war and the first 250 American prisoners of war reached Princetown on 3rd April 1813. On 28th May in the same year, a further 250 arrived and were housed with the French prisoners. Scuffles often occurred and during August of that year, smallpox broke out and the already high mortality increased tenfold.

On 31st March 1814, Paris was occupied by the Allies and on 11th April, Napoleon abdicated and by 20th June, the last of the French prisoners had gone.

On 24th December 1814, peace was declared between England and America at the Treaty of Ghent. However, transport was not immediately available and on 23rd April 1815, the prisoners mutinied. Seven of them were shot dead and many more wounded.

By February 1816, the last of the sick prisoners were sent home, the prison was closed and the church was locked up. Princetown fell into decay.

The prison was later reopened and in 1865, Captain Stopford, the then prison governor, caused the bodies of the 218 Americans and the many Frenchmen to be exhumed from a field where they had been buried. They were reburied in two separate graves, just outside the prison wall. Two granite obelisks were erected over them bearing the inscription – '*Dulce et Decorum Est Pro Patria Mori*' – 'It is sweet to die for one's country'.

When I first went to Dartmoor in the early 1950s and was sent to the quarry to work, the American graveyard was pointed out to me. It is a tree-lined, fairly neat area of ground lying to the right as you came out of the gate to the east of the prison. When I asked where the French graveyard was, I was told that the prison farm had been built where that was located. Apparently, it is quite usual for human bones and the odd skull to be dug up by the pigs as they root around.

Whilst I was in Dartmoor, a section of the garden working party was detailed each year to spend a couple of days tidying up and putting potted flowers around the American graveyard, prior to a delegation arriving to hold a brief memorial service. The flowers would be removed the moment the Americans left.

# 8.

## DARTMOOR - DARK, DANK AND DAMP

Dartmoor was commonly regarded as one of the world's grimmest prisons, housing some of Britain's most violent and notorious villains. Entering, you felt that beneath the surface was a smouldering fire of hatred waiting to explode into a terrible conflict that would be impossible to stop if it ever started. In my view the prison authorities had created their own dilemma by persistently sending to Dartmoor anyone who had been violent in any other prison. A prisoner needed only one other qualification – to be doing a sentence of five years or more. The man in question could turn out to be a homicidal maniac, a psychopath or just another one of those prisoners who had taken enough knocks and had decided to fight back.

There was an induction of new prisoners each month, all of whom would be collected from Pentonville Prison in London, the day before they were taken to the 'Moor'. They would come from Horfield in Bristol, Winson Green in Birmingham, Walton in Liverpool, Strangeways in Manchester and Armley in Leeds. But you could guarantee one thing: each of these men, wherever they came from, would be the toughest nuts from their respective towns. However, once inside Dartmoor, you were not a Geordie or a Scouse or Cockney or anything else. It was a 'them' and 'us' situation. By the time I arrived in Dartmoor, I had already been on many charges for attacking prison staff and my fight with the authorities had been going on for quite some time. Now I was only one amongst many who had decided to fight back against what we perceived to be a brutal regime, so we were all treated alike.

We were taken in chains and under heavy guard to Paddington Station. After arriving at Tavistock we boarded a coach to Princetown where we immediately started to feel the gloom – the place always seemed to be shrouded in a damp, cold mist. We were driven through the gates with their inscription in French. Referring to the French prisoners of war who were first housed in Dartmoor, the inscription read: 'Pity the Vanquished.'

I was not to see pity for anything for many years.

The coach drove directly to the punishment block which looked and smelled medieval and dank. We were each placed in a cell where all of our kit was already deposited and told to put our own property in a brown cardboard box. The first thing that new arrivals noticed was not the cold, but the damp. Your bedding was damp, the walls were damp and even had moss growing on them. It was a grim feeling to know that you had years of this. The attitude of the screws showed that they had the situation pretty well taped and that it was going to be a hard struggle just to keep your sanity.

The next morning we each saw the governor who spoke to us through bars just like a cage in a zoo. I suppose he thought we were the animals. It was then decided which wing each of us would be allocated to and what job we were to be given. I was sent to D-1 and given a job on the quarry. There were A-1, A-2, B-1, B-2, D-1 and D-2 wings but no C-Wing as that had been destroyed during the mutiny in the 1930s. One of the leaders of that mutiny, who was to become a good friend years later, was called 'Ruby' Sparkes. He was a great character who ended up as a publican in north London.

The Home Secretary has declared in Parliament that as a result of the Strangeways riot, the government is going to bring in a charge of mutiny as a 'new' deterrent. They have been charging people for mutiny in British prisons before he or his father were born. They have got to do a lot more constructive talking and thinking, followed by effective action, before they stop people cracking up in our present system. There is a worryingly high suicide rate in British prisons. 'Where there is life there is hope.' But some people can never see any hope for themselves and are consequently driven to extremes.

My first day on the quarry brought back dark memories. As soon as I saw it, I was immediately reminded of my days at Portland on the dreaded Burma Road. A typical day's routine went as follows. We were first lined up at the tally point, counted and then taken to a gate at the back end of the prison. Two large doors were opened and as we went through them we were met by the pony patrol who were armed with shotguns. We were then marched past the American Prisoners of War graveyard, up a steep hill until we came to a tunnel under the road that led us into the quarry proper. As we walked, the biting wind would hit us, freezing our faces and hands until they were so numb with the cold you could stick a needle in them without feeling it. By the time we got into the quarry we would be feeling pretty miserable!

As new blokes we were taken to a shed next to the stone crusher and given a 14lb hammer and told by the wizened old quarry master that he would show us how to break rocks. I thought all you had to do was whack them, but I was soon to find out it wasn't as easy as that. I was shown that rocks had a grain to them and our job was to break the rocks that had been blown from the cliff face at the weekend, smashing them into handy sizes to be thrown into a bogie. When it was filled, the rocks would go down to the crusher to be made small enough for road chippings and breeze blocks. We were watched all the time by a screw in the gun turret near the entrance to the quarry and from a sentry-box above us.

I was lucky to have three good friends among the 50 or so cons who were working in the quarry. Benny Stewart and Willie O'Dare were two Glaswegians who had been among the leaders of one of the most violent riots that had ever erupted in Wandsworth Prison. Benny and Willie were two of the last five who had held out in a store room until they were finally forced out by the screws. Their hatred for the authorities was etched in their faces. The third of the trio was Ronnie Everett, who was a giant of a man and one of the most respected people in the prison. He was quiet and intelligent but everyone knew that he was someone you didn't mess around with. He is currently in 'exile' on Spain's Costa del Sol, wanted for questioning about his alleged involvement in a £6 million robbery from Security Express. Our little quartet got on with our time in our own way and any contraband that was obtained was split equally among the four of us.

There was a small spring of the most delicious cold water about 50 yards from where we worked and each day one of us would take time to go and fill an old dinner can from the spring. The screws would turn a blind eye when we did this, but if some other poor sod, who was doing his time, did the same thing, he would find himself on report for leaving his place of work without permission. It was whilst one of us was getting the water that the wild strawberry bush was discovered. We were as excited as if we had found gold. There was the bush just above our heads, growing amongst the craggy rocks. On the bush were twelve small strawberries, not quite ripe enough for eating. We decided we would wait until they were fully ripe before having a feast, as three strawberries each was a treat to look forward to. Every morning when we arrived at the quarry we would collect our hammers, then make straight for the strawberry bush on the way to the rock face. It became something of a pilgrimage. Each day we would see that the strawberries were ripening and we would discuss how long we should leave them once they had turned completely red.

Then one morning, when we turned up at the bush, to our horror there

THE BRUTAL TRUTH

were the strawberries looking healthy and nearly ripe – but two were missing. We counted them over and over again but there was no mistake. We all started to look at each other with suspicion and trudged on to work with not a word said between us. There was a very strained atmosphere all day and rocks were being smashed with more venom than usual. It seemed that everyone in the quarry sensed there was something wrong, as there was a strange silence only broken by the ringing of hammers on rock.

The next morning, the day we should have been picking our strawberries, we made our way without speaking towards the bush. I heard Ronnie mutter under his breath, 'I don't believe it. Is someone mucking about?'

We all looked. Two more strawberries had gone. By now we were openly glaring at each other. Willie O'Dare was the first to crack. He said excitedly, 'Don't look at me, I've not nicked the fucking strawberries, I've only been out of sight of everyone when I've used the khazi. I've not been near the fucking bush.'

And then Benny asked, 'Who got the water yesterday?'

I had. And all three stared hard at me though no open accusations were made. I knew I hadn't done it and said so. It then became a case of if we can't trust each other, who can we trust? It soon became apparent that there was some very bad feeling building up between us and all of the other cons started to work further along the rock face, isolating us in case something terrible happened.

Just when we were on the verge of explosion Willie suddenly shouted, 'Look!' and pointed to the bush. We all turned to see a blackbird pecking away at a strawberry. Instantly we felt the tension lift and started to smile at each other while a low murmuring of relieved conversation began growing around the quarry. Even the screw in the gun turret came out to banter with the screw below. We all swore our great friendship with each other and then went over to pick a strawberry each, leaving two on the bush for the bird.

There was always something going on in the quarry. No two days were alike. You would think that such a humdrum job as breaking rocks under the glare of some sadistic gaoler would be the most dreaded of tasks, but it is amazing how resilient the human body and mind can be. Some guys, my friend Mixie Walsh among them, couldn't wait to get the hammer into their hands and smash rocks. It seemed as if they were purging themselves of all the hatred that had built up inside. Then there were the little survivors who always managed to get enough rocks together to fill the bogie that took their quota to the crushing machine. Another group were the moaners, who were always writing petitions to the Home Office about how their health was deteriorating – though even they must have realised that those petitions never found their destination. The answer was always the same: 'The Home Secretary has looked into your complaint and can find no grounds to take any action.' But the fact that they had written seemed to sustain them through their ordeal. The ones we gave a wide berth to were the silent brooders who no one could get to the bottom of. Now and again they would crack and try to attack everyone within reach. Even that was a welcome break in the monotony of our routine.

And there were the animal lovers who would collect anything from insects and mice to the odd rabbit that had strayed into the quarry. The guy with the most status amongst this group had actually hatched a jackdaw under his own armpit. The bird survived and would go everywhere with him. It was uncanny the way the bird, which was left on the window ledge when this guy went out to work, would quickly fly to the quarry, find him and land on his head or shoulder. Dartmoor had more than its fair share of jackdaws. They woke us up in the morning with their racket as they fought over the pieces of bread some cons left on the window ledges.

Most cons would, at some time, leave a scrap of hard bread outside for the birds, but one night after doing so, I had the most shocking experience. There were hundreds of wild ponies on Dartmoor and in the hard bleak winters, many would descend from the moor into Princetown, scavenging for food. They would knock the dustbins over in the screws' quarters and eat anything that was chewable. The main wall around the prison, which had been built a couple of hundred years before, would occasionally disintegrate in large sections and a big hole would appear. On one such occasion I was lying on my bed asleep when there was a terrible clattering against the window. I woke up to see the head of a pony staring at me through the window. He had come through a hole in the wall and had been around all of the window ledges collecting scraps of bread. When the doors opened in the morning all the cons were whispering to each other about the shock they got being awakened in the middle of the night by a pony knocking on the window.

One of the most amusing incidents that ever happened on the quarry whilst I was working there was Dillon's great escape. Dillon was about six and a half feet tall and built like a rugby player. But because we did not have a high opinion of his intelligence, the boys started to ask him about his plan.

'I'm going to go up the rock face and disappear over the top and if the screw at the top tries to stop me, I'm just going to knock him out and make a dash for it,' he replied.

'Why don't you make a dash before you come into the quarry? It will save you the time of climbing the rock face,' we suggested sensibly.

'No, I've got a plan to hide somewhere where they'll never find me until the three-day search is over. Then I'll make my way at night to freedom,' he replied.

This was a reference to the three days when the police would block the roads leading from the prison, leaving the hazards of the moor to ensure that no one got away.

Now, the day before Dillon was planning to escape happened to be the day we got our meat ration. Everyone would get a slice of beef with their lunch – a treat which we all looked forward to. So when Dillon asked us to give him some morsel of food to sustain him while he spent the days hiding on the moors, we all reluctantly decided to bring our meagre slice of meat folded inside a cob of bread. We tightened our belts and handed over our offerings to Dillon, who stuffed them into his shirt.

When the time came for Dillon to go, everyone set about trying to distract the screws. One of our group went for water to the spring and another team rolled the bogie down to the crushing shed. Meanwhile a couple of the guys tried to use the toilet at the same time and distracted the screw who was telling one of them to get back to where he was working, until the other one had finished. In the meantime, Dillon was proceeding up the rock face. It only took him a couple of minutes to climb to the top and over, but even so it was incredible that not one of the screws noticed him. Yet every con in the quarry watched his every move as he disappeared over the top. It seemed as if the sun had come out, as everyone had a smile on his face and the rocks were getting cracked with extra application. We realised that Dillon had a two-hour start and that if he made tracks, he could be beyond the area of the road blocks before he was reported missing.

About an hour later, the pony patrol screw came into the quarry and asked the screw in charge, 'Is everything all right?'

'Yes, 58 and all correct, sir,' the other screw replied.

'Are you sure you've got 58 prisoners?' the pony screw enquired.

'Yes, sir,' came the confident reply.

'Well, you'd better count them! We've got one of yours in the punishment block. We found him sitting outside the front gate eating meat rolls,' the pony screw said.

No one will ever know what went through all the cons' minds. But most were pretty upset by the fact that they'd missed the best meal of the week for some guy who had no intention of escaping.

I was soon to find out that nearly everyone in Dartmoor Prison carried a knife or some concealed weapon. I never felt that I needed one and certainly would not have used it, so why carry it? But many did, for protection rather than because they wanted to start a fight. And of course the carrying of weapons meant that any fight was more likely to have lethal consequences, as I found out. It wasn't long after I arrived at Dartmoor that I got involved with a guy who was doing twelve years for cutting off a bloke's hand. He had a big reputation and I was known to have a reputation as well. He considered he was number one, so he didn't like it when I pulled him up for talking to a screw. Things just developed from there and we had a fight during which I knocked him out. The immediate cause was not really important – we would have had to have fought at some time because that was the way things worked.

Of course, he was out for revenge but he made the mistake of telling people he was going to kill me and even saying when and where. There was a shed in the quarry, out of sight of the gun turret, where we could wash our hands. This was where he was going to get me. The day after I'd heard this, I left the rock face and casually strolled in the direction of the shed, as if I was going to the toilet. Once the building hid me from view I quickly dropped behind the wall of the lean-to. I saw my attacker approaching, pulling out a 12-inch knife as he got to the shed door. I picked up a coupling pin that was lying on the floor and hit him on the shoulder with it. He dropped the knife but before he could make another move I hit him over the head, leaving him unconscious on the floor. I threw the coupling pin in some nearby water and was back with my team on the rock face before anyone saw me. Even so, I was charged with attempted murder and tried at Winchester Assizes where I was found not guilty and sent back to Dartmoor.

This sort of incident was happening all the time and, as I started to get to know a lot of the notorious people who were in the prison, I realised we were sitting on a powder keg waiting to explode. The quietest prisoners seemed to be the 'lifers', but one soon realised that in those days the real killers were hanged. So the only lifers then were the domestic lifers, or ones who had good mitigating circumstances and were therefore reprieved. Donald Hulme was tried for the murder of Stanley Setty and found not guilty of murder, but guilty of being an accessory. He was sentenced to 12 years for that. When he came out he told the press how he'd killed Setty then cut up his body and dropped it from a plane after an argument over money for gun-running escapades in the Middle East. He was later alleged to have killed a bank manager outside London and imprisoned in Switzerland following the murder of a taxi driver, although he was sent back to England to finish the sentence. To say that he was a pretty menacing chap would be a gross understatement.

But the place was full of guys who were unpredictable. Take Frankie Bond. At the age of 17, he killed a man in Walton Prison over an argument about his week's wages, which were three old pennies. He escaped the gallows because the death penalty had been suspended for five years as a trial period. He worked right above me in the quarry. I was breaking rocks while he and another prisoner were drilling holes for the gelignite when I heard them arguing about a game of chess. The next thing I knew, there was a thud and a guy's body was lying beside me. Frank had hit him with a 14lb hammer. He looked down and said in a matter-of-fact way, 'You heard him keep arguing all of the time.' Frank was later to cut another prisoner's throat in the church for arguing with him. (This guy was luckier – he survived.)

There were hundreds of similar incidents, but one prisoner working in the mail-bag shop took the prize for holding a grudge the longest. He accused the inmate working in front of him of stealing one of his mail bags. The guy didn't like being accused and so he turned around and punched his accuser and was placed on report. He got the usual three days' bread and water for assaulting another prisoner. He then returned and sat in his old place of work. Now in the workshop they used to stencil 'Post Office' on all of the mail bags and would collect a small drop of white spirit each day to dilute the stencil ink. The guy who had been punched collected a little drop each day and put it into a sauce bottle. When he had filled it up, he calmly poured it over the chap in front of him – and set light to it.

Not everyone was homicidal. The nicest people I met in Dartmoor in those days were the old London Airport robbery gang, Jimmy and George Woods, Sammy Ross and others. They had attempted the biggest robbery of the time but got caught and were sentenced to twelve and 14 years, even though no one got hurt. They did their sentence and just smiled their way through it.

But the prison, with its violence and brutality, was beating so many people. The child molesters probably suffered more than anyone. In those days there was no rule 43, whereby a prisoner can ask to be kept segregated from the rest of the prisoners. Even worse, every prisoner had a card which was placed outside the cell door on a wooden board. Roman Catholics would have a red card, Church of England a white card and Jews would have a blue card. At that time they were the only religions considered. If a chap came through the reception and was asked, 'What's your religion?' and replied 'Muslim,' he'd get remarks like 'Oh! We've got a clever one here guv, give him a blue card so he can pray with his mates.' On each card was written what sentence you were doing and where you were sentenced. On the back of the card was written your offence. If you were a child molester, the screws always turned the card around when you were allocated to your cell to make sure that when the prisoners surfaced to slop out, they would all see it. From that day on your life would be hell. Child molesters were considered the lowest form of human life and the screws encouraged the other cons to give them plenty of treatment.

In Dartmoor, two cells on the ground floor of each wing were used as a library, where you could change your books once a week. The average con would pick out three or four easy-to-read novels. But the child molesters used to pick the thickest books they could find and put them into their waistband to make it harder for prisoners to stick knives in them as they were passing on the landing.

In those days, there never seemed to be any shortage of places to put mentally disturbed people, so if a man or woman went to court for any type of offence and there was a doubt about his or her sanity, the judge would remand them for a psychiatric report. They would go to the hospital, within the prison and after a couple of weeks, go back to the courts to be sentenced. If they had to have treatment or be kept away to protect society, then that would follow. There was no delay. It was also the case that people who had been driven to insanity whilst in prison could always be found a place. Nowadays, the government is spending millions of pounds on building new prisons, but they've closed lots of hospitals and psychiatric wards, which has put some people, in my view, out into society who cannot cope. These people are ending up in prison and may cause much of the violence and destruction within the prisons.

When I first went to Dartmoor there was a doctor who seemed to have no trouble finding places for mentally disturbed prisoners. There always seemed to be someone on the way to a secure mental home each week. Unfortunately, it was this same doctor who caused so many people to break down. If you had some reason for seeing him, you would report sick to your landing screw first thing in the morning. Then when everyone else went to work you would stay in your cell. The doctor would start his rounds in the company of one of the medical screws and an orderly who carried a bottle of liquid aspirin. These would be typical remarks between the prisoner and the doctor – it would be funny if it wasn't so tragic.

'What's wrong with you?'

'I can't sleep, doctor.'

'Right, get this man's mattress out of his cell if he can't sleep on it and give him some medicine.'

Or, to a prisoner with alopecia, 'What's wrong with you?'

'My hair is falling out, doctor.'

'Right, give him an envelope to keep his hair in and give him some medicine.'

If any prisoner mentioned anything wrong internally, he was immediately put on a water diet. This kind of treatment would invariably cause the prisoner to end up in the punishment block for shouting some abuse at the doctor. It was a vicious circle that caused men to break down completely.

After coming out of the Dartmoor quarry, one of the jobs I had was with No. 3 party, responsible for a variety of tasks inside the prison walls. It was made up of a motley crew of murderers, armed robbers and con-men. In fact in the year or so I was on it, there was practically every type of crook and villain, from every part of the British Isles, working on that party. Charles Dickens would have painted a beautiful picture of the characters. We had the task of emptying the rubbish bins from the cell blocks, the kitchen, the hospital and offices. We were also responsible for conveying food from the victualling stores to the kitchen. Consequently, we had plenty of chances to convey more than just legitimate goods. We were, in fact, the unofficial means of conveying all types of contraband from messages to betting slips plus the stakes, which was always tobacco, the universal currency of all prisoners. We worked on a commission from the prison bookmaker. We always knew of any impending transfers or any other 'classified' information concerning the prison through our own 'artful dodger', Paddy Wormsley, who had the useful ability of reading a piece of paper upside-down.

Every Friday we would take the hard-tack food from the stores to the kitchen where we would be given a can of tea – the real stuff not the gnat's pee that was usually served in the cell blocks. Friday was also the day when the kitchen staff made the jam tarts for the Sunday sweet. They were made in trays about two feet long and 18 inches wide and then left to cool down before being dissected into about 50 portions and put into a shelved trolley until Sunday.

One Friday we decided to pinch one of the newly cooked jam tarts that lay cooling by the side of the ovens. Paddy elected to do the deed while we kept the kitchen screw otherwise occupied. Paddy folded the large jam tart in half and put it down the front part of his overalls, buckled the bib back over and pulled his jacket around so that the tart was hidden from view. We then made our way hastily from the kitchen to the safety of our shed. But on the way Paddy began to look very uncomfortable and his face gradually contorted into an expression of extreme pain until he could no longer control himself and he let out a yelp. The tart that he'd put down his overalls had only just come out of the oven and the jam was still baking hot and had started to run down his body. Paddy, who didn't wear underpants, was being burnt in some very tender places indeed. By the time we got to the safety of our shed, Paddy had sustained some pretty severe burns. It was clear that he would have to have some medical treatment, but it would be difficult to report sick. So we decided to pick the rubbish up from the hospital and see if we could get something from the orderly. He said he would get some stuff and even offered to apply it to Paddy's tender parts. Paddy quickly declined the offer and said he would put it on himself. We then went back to get rid of the evidence, which we did by eating the lot. Paddy was in pain for a few days but it wasn't long before he was back to his chirpy self again.

Some of the other characters on this particular party had made a name for themselves for one reason or another. One was Jimmy Essex, a tiny little chap who didn't weigh eight stone, but was one of the most feared men in prison at this time. He had already killed two men and had attacked another, an ex-heavyweight boxer, whilst in Parkhurst Prison. As a result he had been transferred to Dartmoor. Jimmy always seemed to be angry about something but I could never take him seriously. He was always muttering to himself, 'I'm going to do him one day,' whenever someone upset him. I would smile and sometimes start laughing. He would demand to know why I was laughing at him and I would try to explain that I was just tickled by the thought of a little guy like him beating up a giant. This must have played on his mind because he was to prove himself dramatically.

One day he was grumbling about the new screw who had been put on his landing, 'He keeps digging me out.' We had all seen the new screw in Jimmy's wing, who was well over six foot and proportionately built. I said jokingly, 'Are you going to set about him, Jim?' Sure enough, next morning, Jimmy never turned up for work. He was in the punishment block for putting the screw in hospital – he nearly lost his sight. It was a long time before we saw Jimmy again.

Then there was Harry Rose, a great little character, who had a wonderful sense of humour and was always telling us some story or another about his days in Liverpool. I asked him one day how he got his teeth knocked out, and he told me the most amazing tale. He said that he was going through a particularly hard time and had no money when a mate of his told him they could get a bite to eat or a bowl of soup at a certain church mission. So Harry went along with his friend and got right to the front pew so that they would be first up for the grub. But Harry's mate had forgotten to warn him that they were expected to sing a few hymns and say a few prayers before they got their meal. The service was going on and on and Harry's stomach was beginning to rumble, so he piped up and said, 'Could we have some grub before we sing any more hymns?'

He was immediately told to 'shush' by the vicar, whereupon Harry said indignantly, 'This is a con,' and demanded a bowl of soup. At this, the vicar came down from the altar and nutted Harry in the mouth. Harry told us that he'd never been hit so hard in his life. We asked him what happened next, knowing that he was a fearless fighting man. But Harry said, 'What could I do?' You can't chin a vicar, can you?' That summed up Harry for me. He was a great chap.

One of the first real friends I met after getting settled into Dartmoor, was a man called 'Mixie' Walsh. Michael Walsh, at the time of our first meeting, had already become a legend in Blackpool at the age of 21. Mixie had just come from the heats of a Mr Great Britain competition and his then wife, Betty, who was a very attractive girl, decided to go to a coffee bar on the way home. Unfortunately, there were a few yobs (yes, there were even yobs in those days) who decided to make some derisory remarks about the pretty boy with the big muscles and even worse still, they made remarks about 'the girl clinging to him'. This was to change Mixie's whole life. He is now 70 years of age and he is already more than a legend; also a real gentleman.

That evening saw Mixie retaliate to verbal insults with one of the most controlled assaults on a few scum, plus an uncontrolled riot on half a dozen police who were sent to arrest him, that anyone who witnessed it had ever seen.

I like to think of Mixie as one of my all-time friends. I named my youngest son after him, Michael, who is now 15. If he grows up with all of Mixie's gentlemanly attributes, I shall be very proud of him. Go to any bar in Blackpool and ask for Mixie Walsh and you will see the looks of genuine fondness from everyone. The man is Mr Blackpool. Still a very tough man, I recently saw him at our very good friend Billy Grimwood's funeral in Liverpool. It was great to see him still looking so well.

I met so many old friends at Billy's funeral. Although it was a sad occasion, it was nice to see Johnny Nash and his brother Roy come up from London with Joey Pyle and a few friends to pay their last respects to another Liverpool legend. It was great to see old Dartmoor ex-residents such as 'Beech' Keatley, Bonner Dunn, Ginger Smith and Davie Wilson, who I joined along with Doctor Ken McGill, another great character, and Terry McHale. There were so many of the old faces and, at the benefit night afterwards at the St George's Hotel, organised by that nice guy Joe Beech, it felt great to have so many good friends around me in Lancashire – a reunion meeting of the old Dartmoor fraternity.

# 9.

## WILL CRIME PAY?

I finished that sentence at Dartmoor with more bitterness than when I started. By now 26 or 27, I decided that I was going to make plenty of money and have some good times. I'd met some pretty experienced law-breakers whilst I was in the Moor and I came out with the intention of putting a few things I'd learned into practice.

One of the first blokes I teamed up with was Bobby Connolly. He was just a little older than myself and he had a good team around him. Bob was a pretty good 'peterman' (safe-cracker) and in those days the old Hobbs, Banhams and Chubbs were a push-over. It took a quarter of an hour to blow a safe and we had some pretty rich pickings. It wasn't long before I was banging a few peters myself.

Then I found a new life opening up in the nightclubs in London and Paris. It would cost about £20 for a return flight to Paris and I started to discover the delights of places like the Lido on the Champs-Elysées, the Moulin Rouge, the Lucky Stripe and some of the wonderful bars in Le Place Pigalle in Montmartre. Whenever I came back to London I'd see old pals like Jack the Hat and tell him about the good time we were having in Paris, but I could never talk him into coming. I don't think he fancied flying.

Of course, the good times cost money and as soon as the coffers were empty, we'd look around for a new safe to rob. Usually this took a certain amount of preparation but sometimes it all seemed so easy. I remember we were all at a party over Christmas. Myself, Jack and Bob were having a nice drink when we were interrupted by a guy anxious to tell us about a peter in a place less than a mile away. At first we were not interested – we had no gelignite and, anyway, we were enjoying ourselves. Eventually his enthusiasm and persistence began to get to us so we decided to go and have a look. As soon as we got to the place where the peter was supposed to be Jack and I went around the back to break in. In no time we were looking at an old Reliance 5cwt. 'box peter', one of the easiest to open. Jack and I decided we'd put it in the motor and take it back to the party, which was in a flat above a sweetshop in Stratford.

First we had to negotiate the peter down a stairway. Jack got his hands under the bottom while I held the top. He had only taken a couple of the stairs when I felt the safe slipping from my grip. I yelled a warning and he flung himself aside just in time, as the safe went hurtling down the stairs. He would have been dead had it hit him. Bob came running to tell us to keep the noise down but within two minutes the safe was in the motor and we were on our way back to the party. We put it in the cellar under the sweetshop and carried on having a drink.

The guy who told us about the safe couldn't keep still. He kept begging, 'There's thousands in it, can't we open it now?' We told him to be patient and wait until the morning. We all got our heads down for what was left of the night and went down to the cellar the next morning. The first thing we saw down there was the guy with the information sitting on the safe, too excited to sleep. We realised why when we opened it. It was one of the biggest tickles we had ever had and it gave me the chance to relax and look up some of my old friends.

I had recently started to use the Barry Club in Marylebone. The proprietor was Dave Barry, an old friend from my schooldays. The clientele was a mixed bag of villains, con-men, solicitors, actors and a few well-known press people. One of the latter was Eddie Chapman, who worked for a Sunday paper called *Reynolds News*. Eddie Chapman had a fascinating and dangerous life and his story was later portrayed in a film called *The Triple Cross*.

He originated from the north-east and came to London as a youngster. He graduated from a petty thief to become an accomplished safe-cracker. After doing a few stretches in prison, he even became very selective about the type of safes he was doing. He went over to Jersey on a job but was arrested and sentenced to three years' hard labour. This was just after the start of the Second World War and Eddie was stuck in prison when the Germans invaded the Channel Islands. Being clever he devised a plan to get back home. In the course of talking to a German commandant who had taken over the prison, he let it be known how much he hated the British government and admired the Third Reich. He impressed the Germans so much that he was interviewed by the Gestapo and taken back to Germany. He was asked to work as a saboteur for Germany and to let the Germans know of troop movements and the locations of any important targets. He was also encouraged to use his expertise as a peterman to gather potentially useful information. He agreed and was put through a training course, given equipment, explosives and a radio.

However, the Germans, being careful, decided to test Eddie first. They pretended to drop him over East Anglia. Instead, they went to great lengths to set up an area in France with all the trappings of the English countryside. They dropped Eddie over this area and observed him. Luckily Eddie spotted something that caused him to guess that he was in German-occupied territory, so he carried on as he was supposed to.

The Germans were satisfied that they had a good man for the job and sent him out on a real mission – to sabotage the munitions factory at Enfield. He was dropped at night over Norfolk and immediately got in touch with the authorities to tell them of his amazing and unbelievable tale. It took a little time to convince the authorities that the story was true, as his record showed he was supposed to be in prison in Jersey. Once they were convinced – and seeing how valuable a British man trusted by the enemy was – they asked him if he would be prepared to work for British Intelligence. He agreed. His first question, however, was: 'What about the factory at Enfield?' He was told that an explosion would be arranged and an appropriate news bulletin would report that saboteurs were being blamed. Eddie successfully worked as a double agent until he was captured by the Russians near the end of the war and was interned in a Russian prison camp. He subsequently escaped and made it back to the British sector. He came back to England a hero.

Eddie was a frequent visitor to the Barry Club, as was a guy called Sir Sidney Cain. 'Sir Sid' was a con-man of some repute. He was a fascinating chap who had all the trappings of the landed gentry but was, in fact, the son of a Liverpool house-painter. He spoke beautifully and looked the business in his cashmere and vicuna overcoats, a carnation ever present in his lapel.

Sidney used to entertain us with stories of his successful attempts to con some of the more gullible titled and wealthy people in the country. One of his favourites was the saga of how he nearly married the Wills Tobacco heiress. It was only because he was exposed by the *Sunday People* that he failed to accomplish his plan. He told us about the time he took his man to stay at the Wills's mansion for the weekend. His personal servant happened to be one of the best jewel thieves in London at that time. When Sir Sid went down for breakfast the next morning, his future bride informed him that the butler had observed his man wandering around the house in the middle of the night checking all the windows and doors. Sir Sidney immediately told her that he was always the same, being extremely security conscious. Pretending to be embarrassed, Sir Sidney assured her he would have a word and tell his valet that security in the Wills's house was impregnable.

When I knew Sir Sidney, he was married to an heiress from Alderney who was also a marquesa.

Eddie Chapman was writing a book entitled *The Gentlemen of Crime*. Sir Sidney was featured in it, so we spent hours going around together while Eddie elicited stories from Sir Sidney. We must have seemed a strange combination, Eddie, David Barry, Sir Sidney and myself. It wasn't long before the Old Bill became intrigued enough to put a friendly 'eye' on our tail, but as we were using some of London's more up-market watering-holes, the Old Bill stood out more than we did. They must have hated that particular job as Sir Sidney would immediately inform the licensee and clientele, 'These gentlemen from Scotland Yard are only here to protect everyone. I must apologise for their heavy boots on this nice carpet.' But he always sent a drink over to them and it wasn't long before they realised there was nothing criminal in four odd fellows meeting each day.

I took my friends over to the East End one evening to meet a guy called Bulla Ward, with whom I had become very friendly. He was the proprietor of the Bentley Club in Aldgate, in partnership with a guy called Roy Stafford, who had been the borough surveyor. A more incongruous pair it would be hard to imagine. Bulla was a heavy-set tough-looking guy with a large razor scar running the length of his face, compliments of Ronnie Kray after an argument. 'Staffy' on the other hand, was slightly built, quiet and sophisticated. But they seemed to hit it off very well together.

The Bentley Club was in Artillery Row, right in the middle of the original 'Jack the Ripper' territory. When I first took my friends to the club I could see the looks of concern passing between them until we actually got inside. The Bentley had become one of the more popular clubs that had sprouted up in the East End in those days. The clientele was the usual mixture of celebrities, gangsters and sportsmen. I had started to use the club regularly and I'd found that Roy Stafford seemed to enjoy the company of the more ambitious criminals who frequented the place. In talking to him one evening I learned that he had more than just a passing interest in crime. He held a very definite view that the average criminal never set his sights high enough and that with more planning and common sense, most of the criminals who used his club would be able to retire in a very short time. He suggested that they should put more effort into looking at the larger movements of money and valuables, rather than into the ordinary targets of banks and post offices. But it still came as a surprise to me when, shortly afterwards, the KLM bullion robbery was pulled off with absolute precision and the minimum of force. The thieves got away with £750,000 in gold bars. I read shortly after this that Staffy had been arrested as the Mr Big behind the robbery when he stepped off a plane in Switzerland.

I think the most unusual chap I met in the Bentley Club was Sidney Proud. He was the boss of a travel agency and Bulla introduced me to him one evening. I failed to see why Bulla found him so fascinating as he looked so out of place in the club, with his foppish clothes and bow tie. He kept suggesting to Bulla, 'You must bring Eric up to the office to meet my friends.'

'What's his game? Is he the other way?' I asked Bulla suspiciously.

'No, he just likes having tough guys around him. You'll be surprised when we go to his office tomorrow,' he replied.

I couldn't wait and so we arranged to meet the next day. Bulla called for me about noon and we went to Piccadilly Circus where Sid Proud had the Spanish Travel Bureau. It was a very well-appointed block of offices and appeared to be doing plenty of business. To my surprise I was then introduced to two members of his staff. They were Max and Alex Mosley, the sons of the well-known fascist, Oswald Mosley. Alex was a giant of a young man; Max a little shorter than his brother. They were both very polite and seemed nice company. It was arranged that we should all go to Soho for a drink as there were plenty of afternoon members clubs open throughout the day. Sid insisted that we should go to Aggie Hill's club. Now Aggie's was a notorious club because Aggie had been married to gangster Billy Hill. When we arrived, it was packed with the usual motley crew of entertainers and criminals. But there was one guy sitting at the bar next to Aggie who was a well-known Member of Parliament. The minute he set eyes upon Sidney he became very abusive. I couldn't allow this to carry on as Sidney was in my company, so I told the MP to button his lip. With that a big hefty guy stood up from a seat at the bar and started to remonstrate with me. I flattened him, which had an immediate effect upon the honourable member and everything went quiet. Aggie ordered a taxi for the VIP and we settled down to a good drinking session. When the guy got off the floor he was told to leave. Sidney was overjoyed.

Later that evening, we all retired to Sidney's house in Kensington. I couldn't believe my eyes when I saw photographs all over the lounge of Sidney with Adolf Hitler and other Nazi Party bigwigs. There were also pictures of Sidney with the sons and daughters of the Nazi 'firm' and also of Mussolini's kids. He certainly moved in some very strong company. A little later in the evening, he invited me into his office, a room inside the house and gave me £500.

'That's for knocking that guy out this afternoon. I think I could do with you about me if you want the job,' he said.

I decided I would have to give the offer some thought for a while. It seemed an easy way of earning a few quid but it could get a little involved. I told Sidney I would give him my answer in a week or so. In the meantime, the five of us went out quite a bit together. We would eat most evenings in Casa Pepi where Sidney seemed to be very well known. I began to notice that some very strange people had started to turn up in the places we were using. These strange comings and goings were explained when the *Sunday People* ran a story about the 'man who has a shrine to Hitler'. Sidney offered me a lot of money to do something about the guy who had written the article. I thought that was a good moment to bail out.

It was about this time that I first met the Kray twins socially. They had the snooker hall in Eric Street and the Double R Club in Bow. I had already met their older brother Charlie, who used to take the twins to Bill Kline's gym when I was training down there. They were both very good amateur boxers and Charlie was showing them to a big promoter from Canada, who was very impressed with them. I found them to be very likeable people and they had a good name by everyone who spoke of them. But it wasn't until I got seven years shortly after this that I got to know them a lot better. That's when Ronnie got three years for wounding and Reggie 18 months for demanding money, which some believed was a questionable charge as the Old Bill had been taking a bit of notice of them. It was their way of testing the water.

In those days it would be usual for all of the guys to go to Freddie Mills' night-spot in Charing Cross Road. Although it was supposed to be a Chinese restaurant, it was more of a meeting place for practically anyone – ex-fighters, entertainers and gangsters. There would always be plenty of drink flowing, a small cabaret and a happy and relaxed atmosphere. I seem to recall Freddie had a partner who was Chinese and whose name was Eric. Freddie's wife, Chrissie, whose father, Ted Broadrib, had managed Freddie's illustrious boxing career, would sometimes be present. She had been married previously to a South African heavyweight named Don McCorkindale. More often than not the conversation generally revolved around boxing.

Sadly all was not well with Freddie. He died a violent death. For many years, people have conjectured about whether Freddie committed suicide, or whether he was murdered. I would bet my life that Freddie killed himself. He was getting himself involved with a lot of people who were very different from the types he had grown up with and his character seemed to change just before he died. I also don't believe there was anyone who was capable of sitting Freddie in the back of a car, pointing a gun in his face and pulling the trigger. As for the later theory that the Kray twins had anything to do with Freddie's death is totally ridiculous. Anyone who knew the twins would know that they both admired people like Freddie and if they had known that

THE BRUTAL TRUTH

he was in financial difficulty, they would have helped him out. The twins always had a great admiration for any guy who had made his living in the ring as they knew themselves what a hard business it was.

A case in point is the way they treated the ex-welterweight champion of the world, Ted 'Kid' Lewis, arguably the best fighter this country has ever produced. Kid Lewis had had an illustrious career in America, where he beat one of the all-time great fighters, Jack Britton, to gain the world title. He was to have 20 epic battles with Britton over the years, which caught the imagination of every fight fan on both sides of the Atlantic, none more so than Sophie Tucker, the last of the Red-Hot Mommas. She had a soft spot for the Kid. I remember being at Vallance Road one morning when Reggie told me that the Kid was coming to the house that day. They were going to fit him up with a suit and other smart gear as they were taking him to see Sophie Tucker at the Talk of the Town. They also arranged for a big bouquet to be sent backstage with a card saying 'To Sophie From Ted'. When Sophie came on stage they all had tears in their eyes as Sophie talked to Ted from the stage, reminiscing about the days in the '20s when Sophie Tucker was one of the biggest stars in America and Ted was the world champion.

I had by this time become a trusted member of the Kray fraternity. Whenever I went over to the twins' house in Vallance Road, we would invariably go up to Bethnal Green Road for a cup of tea in Pellicci's Café. This became known as a meeting place for anyone who wanted to do business with the Kray twins. I would think that there were more deals done in there than in any office in the country but there were never any leaks from Pellicci's.

The meetings each morning were conducted in a quiet and respectful manner, whether the discussions were about someone who had stepped out of line and needed a visit from the 'firm' to have a few words about their future conduct or whether it was to organise some benefit for friends who may have fallen on hard times. Or maybe some guy's wife and kids were finding it hard to make ends meet because he was serving a little time as a guest of Her Majesty. But whatever problem was discussed there would always be a solution found in Pellicci's.

As well as safe-cracking, I was also having a few unlicensed boxing matches. Butty Sugrue had set up a ring in the Carlton Club and was making more money with a few ex-pros and street fighters than the average boxing promoter. He was an incredible guy who came over from Ireland with a team of strongmen. They used to go around the pubs challenging all-comers to various feats of strength that normally featured a barrel of beer. Butty could lift a man with his teeth – while the guy was sitting on a chair. For some pretty substantial bets he would bury himself in a coffin for twenty-four hours. There was obviously some trick to it but everyone was very impressed. He had a sidekick called Bert Azorati who was the ex-world wrestling champion. Bert was one of the toughest men I ever met and when things got a little rough, which they usually did when the Irish boys thought they had been duped over some of the results in the boxing ring, Bert would be there to sort it out. Bert seemed to positively enjoy people picking chairs up to use as weapons against him. He wouldn't duck or ward off the blow, he'd just 'nut' the chair and stand with a big grin while his antagonist would make a quick exit.

I got involved with Butty and his team as a boxer in his 'gee' fights from which we were all getting a few quid. A 'gee' fight is one that has been rehearsed before the customers arrive and only we know the result, so all of the betting done was pretty much in our favour.

I also became friendly with Jack Rosa, a professional thief who had gained notoriety through his battles with the authorities in prison. After many years of the same type of treatment that I had received, Jack had attacked a screw pretty badly and had been sent to the Old Bailey for trial. With only about three weeks of his existing sentence to go, he was sentenced to a further five years. We had a lot in common and used to swap stories about the brutality we had both experienced – Jack, like myself, had also been flogged with the cat-o'-nine-tails. When I first met him, he looked as if he had been through some tough times, but the first thing you noticed about Jack was his quiet demeanour. He seemed a gentle guy but very determined. Although Jack was from south London, we did our socialising mainly in the West End or the East End.

One place I was spending a fair amount of time in was a spieler in Clarendon Road, Notting Hill· Gate. These old-type spielers had an atmosphere all of their own. Whilst supposedly legitimate, they had the feel of illegal gambling joints. There was none of the respectful air and subtle chink of chips that you found in a casino. It was ready cash only in a spieler and no one took their coats off. A few bums, often ex-thieves, would stand around ready to run errands, hoping to cop a few quid if a friend won. The clubs would attract the aristocracy and others from affluent backgrounds who would rub shoulders with the flamboyant fast-living criminal fraternity. It would be quite usual to see Lord and Lady Docker gambling with Peter Scott, rated Britain's most successful cat-burglar. When £300,000 worth of jewellery was stolen from Sophia Loren whilst she was filming at Elstree, Peter was suspected of the crime. Although there was never any proof, his status grew as a result of the allegation.

One would always know that a big game was in progress when Peter's 'Roller' was parked outside the spieler. I often saw 'Taffy' Raymond and 'Taters' Chapman leaving the club after losing quite heavily, return within the hour and sit down with the governor of the place, haggle over a piece of jewellery they had just acquired and then go straight back into the game.

Occasionally poker games would go on for days, with some guys just taking a short nap before going back to the table. There was never any trouble and there was always good-humoured banter between the punters who arrived at regular intervals. Some of the greatest characters from all walks of life would use the various spielers that were dotted all over London.

Sometimes one place would become more popular than the others and Clarendon Road was one of the favourites at this time. 'Shaky Sheila', a lady who ran a number of 'clip joints' in Soho, was a frequent visitor to the speiler. A clip joint was a near-beer place with a number of sexy girls encouraging mainly tourist punters to buy the exotic-looking drinks at exorbitant prices and promising to meet them when they finished 'work'. But the girls never turned up at the meeting place and if the punter returned to complain, he would be fobbed off by a menacing bouncer. Sheila was from Liverpool and was a great favourite in the spieler. She would earn fortunes in the clip joints but would lose nearly every penny at the dice table.

Clarendon Road was where I renewed my acquaintance with my old colleague Joey Mayo from St Vincent's approved school. Joe had grown into a handsome guy, over six feet tall with curly fair hair, who always had an attractive girl with him. One night Joe told me about two girls who were using a flat directly opposite the spieler to 'entertain' their clients. One of these was a well-known MP whose special fetish was that he liked to be treated as a skivvy. Joe arranged for myself and a couple of mates from the old Nash gang to go up on to the verandah where we could get a good view through the french windows into the flat. We couldn't believe our eyes when we saw who the client was. He was well known by sight to us all. When the girls started to verbally abuse him and threaten him with a beating, we could hardly contain ourselves as he cringed and pleaded with his 'tormentors'. The spectacle continued but when the girls took his trousers down and started to beat his bottom, we could not stop ourselves from bursting out laughing. When he heard this he came to the french windows and stood there fuming whilst we pointed to his diminishing manhood. We then went back to the spieler and left the girls to convince him that they didn't know who we were. They must have done a good job as I often saw his car parked outside the flat after this incident. I sometimes wondered how he must have felt when a question was asked in the House about the growing industry in pornography and the dangers involved to the fabric of society. Well, the industry has certainly prospered since those days and I know many people, supposedly pillars of society, who have indulged and also many who have become wealthy as a result.

I had become quite friendly with Johnny Nash about this time. John was to become one of the most notorious faces in the London underworld. His good friends in those days were obviously his brothers. There were five of them. They all came to prominence because of their individual personalities, but in times of adversity they were a very close-knit group not to be tampered with. They are still a very respected family and successful business men.

But forty years ago, John's little firm was with Ronnie Diamond and one Ronnie Marwood, who was to be subsequently hanged for the murder of a policeman. This affected the Nash family, because they were convinced that Ron wasn't guilty of that murder. They even contemplated breaking him from Pentonville Prison. In fact they would have succeeded had they not been tricked into believing that Ronnie Marwood was going to be reprieved.

But I'll leave that story for John to tell as I do believe he will write all about that in his memoirs, which will have to be called *Peacemaker*.

Many years ago, when we were all young, fit men about town, I remember walking into the Bagatelle Club with Reggie and Ronnie Kray, having been driven there by Albert Donoghue, who had become something of a man-servant to the twins. When we arrived, there was Johnnie and Ronnie Nash, together with Freddie Foreman and someone was holding a *Sunday People* newspaper up. There was the photo of John Nash and a striking headline, 'THE PEACEMAKER'. I still think today that the press had summed up a man perfectly. John is a very intelligent man who has never taken a liberty. I'm glad to say he is still my friend.

I spent a very nice weekend with John and his lovely wife, Linda, in Manchester, where we had lunch in one of my favourite restaurants, the El Rincon. I shall be looking forward to the day when John's autobiography is published. Who knows, maybe John's book will also reminisce about our younger days, and I know for a fact that he will focus on the episode with the MP in the brass's flat.

Who are we to moralise? We were just a bunch of crooks who spent hours in the gambling dens.

Anyway, back to the story, I had other things to think about. I had pulled off a couple of raids that had netted me a fair lump of money and I knew the police were making their presence felt around the circles I was moving in. I had to be careful and try to keep a low profile, but it is very hard to be involved in major crime and stay incognito at the same time.

Because I had quite a lot of success as a professional criminal, I began to frequent the more up-market nightclubs and had become a member of a few of the daytime clubs that were normally patronised by a mix of the gentry, actors, bookmakers, sportsmen and quite a few people who earned a living in nefarious ways. They all had one thing in common: they were raconteurs. They loved alcohol and not many of them ever talked about what they did for a living. I was never surprised when I found out that someone I had met casually at the bar turned out to be a barrister or a bank robber. I met many of the old underworld characters in the most unlikely of daytime drinking clubs where I was to glean a lot of the more interesting stories of the racecourse gangs. These were practically territorial wars, led by the likes of the Sabini gang, Billy Kimber's Hoxton mob and the White family from King's Cross.

But by the time I met any of the remnants of these old gangs, there were only memories left to talk of.

# 10.

## ESCAPE AND THE COCKNEY MILLIONAIRE

I was eventually arrested for a series of robberies that totalled many thousands of pounds. The police raided a flat in Bayswater to arrest me and two of my pals, but I managed to escape through a back window. However, I was caught in a gambling club in Notting Hill Gate later that night while arranging to get a false identity and was remanded in custody to Brixton Prison. After a series of identity parades, I was committed for trial at the Old Bailey. I knew I had a few months to wait for the trial and I was expecting to get a big sentence. Since I had by this time become pretty well known in London's underworld, I thought I would have a fair chance of getting a bit of help to escape.

Then what seemed to be a bit of luck came my way.

A couple of chaps I knew slightly were arrested for robbing a bank in Mitcham and I knew they would be interested in any plan that would afford a means of escape. But as soon as I approached them, I was delighted to find they had already started to put their plans into operation. One of the guys, Teddy Rees, told me how they had been arrested and I thought they must already have had all the bad luck that they could have in a lifetime – which I hoped meant we should have some good luck in making good our escape.

Ted and his three pals had decided to rob a bank in Mitcham over a bank holiday weekend so that they would have until Tuesday morning to work without being disturbed. At first, everything went according to plan. They gained access to the bank and fixed the alarms without any problems and whilst two of them were setting up the vault for blowing, the other two opened the big safe in the bank proper. The safe yielded £48,000, but the vault had jammed and they needed more 'jelly' to get into it. So it was decided that two of the gang would take the £48,000 home and pick up some more explosives, while the other two would await their return. Ted was one of the two who stayed in the bank. They expected to wait at the most about three hours; after 12 hours elapsed, they started to get a bit jittery. They were imagining all kinds of disasters, especially when they decided to phone one of the other guy's homes and found that he hadn't been back. Eventually, they had to leave the bank. On the way out, while climbing over the wall, Ted gashed his finger on a piece of glass at the top, which cut out a lump of his glove at the same time. When they eventually arrived home they found that their companions had been stopped by an ordinary police check and were taken into the nick. The Old Bill couldn't believe the amount of money in their possession. They obviously wouldn't enlighten the law as to how they had acquired it and so were charged with possession on Tuesday and taken to the magistrates.

Later that day, when the word went out from the bank, the Old Bill knew where the money had come from. When they went to the bank and found bloodstains around the walls, they knew someone else was involved. But the unluckiest thing of all, from Ted's point of view, was that an eagle-eyed copper found the piece of Ted's glove and there inside the glove was preserved a nice piece of skin from Ted's finger. After the fingerprint people had done their work, Ted was hauled in to explain how the piece of skin missing from his finger had ended up on a bank wall in Mitcham.

So here we all were, walking around the exercise yard, plotting our escape. The good thing was that Ted's other mate was still at large. We were all on the same landing and, as luck would have it, I was in the cell opposite Ted's, which looked out on to a compound at the rear of the prison. It was decided that we would cut the bars in Ted's cell and if we could have the job completed by one of the coming Sunday mornings, Ted's friend would come over the wall of the compound. The signal for the accomplice was when we dropped a cigarette packet; he would then throw a rope up to the cell.

Our first problem was getting the hacksaws into the prison, as people like us were pretty closely observed. Then we had another bit of luck. A guy called George Dawson came to Brixton on remand for allegedly ripping-off the government over a consignment of orange juice. Dubbed the 'Cockney Millionaire', he had made a fortune out of scrap metal after World War Two. He had a yacht in the South of France and would entertain government officials and the aristocracy at his home or in the Mediterranean. Therefore, when he was arrested and sent to Brixton, he was treated with respect. When we went to and from our court appearances we would be taken in the 'meat wagon', a large van with tiny cubicles down each side with a very narrow piece of wood to sit on. We would each be locked into a cubicle and when we got to the prison, we would be thoroughly searched. But George used to travel to and from court in a private car and would go straight back to his cell with just a perfunctory rub down. We set to work on him until, after a little cajoling, he agreed to bring the blades in for us.

The blades which Ted's friend brought to the court were only six inches long and were made of high-tension steel. He wrapped them in a rubber covering and put them in a greased condom and told George the best place to hide them. George was by this time becoming very reluctant to carry out the mission and as he was about 20 stone in weight, he had a bit of manipulating to do before he got the blades into place. Then, to everyone's horror, the screws who came to our cell to load us all up in the meat wagon, said, 'You as well Dawson, your car's not here today.'

George nearly died. We could hear him pleading with the screws, saying, 'There's no way I can get into a little space like that.' But the screws were adamant and eventually managed to squeeze him into a cubicle. We were kept on the verge of hysterics all the way back to Brixton. Every time we went over a bump in the road, we would hear George moaning piteously. But we did eventually get the blades back into the wing, even though George couldn't sit down for a week or two.

Now we had to set about a plan to cut the bars with the least amount of risk. It was decided that I would take my spy-hole cover off so that I could see as far as two or three cells on either side of Ted's cell. We then set about loosening the rail which ran the length of the landing. Anyone walking along the landing would make the rail shake and should we have any intrusion, I would drop my chamber pot lid on the floor a couple of times to warn Ted.

This was going along without any hitches until the con in the cell beneath me began shouting up complaints about my constantly dropping the lid of the pot. This started a bit of controversy, so after he'd left his cell the next morning to slop out, I went and hit his light fitting with my shoe hoping he would be moved to another cell. But no, they sent for the electrician and got him a new light fitting. Plan B was that I should knock him out and have him taken to hospital. This was soon accomplished.

Now we found another problem. We had started to fill the saw-cut with nougat brought in on our visits and this had started to attract hundreds of flies. Everyone on the landing was complaining about this unusual plague and Ted's cell seemed to be full of them. It was amazing that the screws didn't get wind of what was happening. But at last it was the Saturday before the morning of the escape and Ted was certain that only the paint was holding the bars together.

We were going to have to move quickly on Sunday morning, so we kept pressing Ted to make sure that the bars only needed a couple of rubs before they came apart. Ted decided to give them a little touch-up prior to us going out to exercise with the result that, when he shut his door, one of the bars fell down and hung loose. We were all very quiet in the yard and carefully watched every screw just to see if anybody had noticed anything amiss. The suspense was agonising but we got back to the cells without incident. Everything seemed normal. We were quickly trying to wedge in some matchsticks or anything we could find to hold the bar in place, thinking that everything was ready to go when I heard the rail rattling slightly. I got up to look out of the spy-hole and there were about six screws creeping towards Ted's cell. I leapt over to the pot and banged it on the floor but my door was flung open at the same time as Ted's and we were taken down to the punishment cells. We were a little worried about Ted's mate coming the next morning but though he had actually got into the compound with the equipment, when the cigarette packet hadn't come over the wall as a signal to throw the rope, he aborted and left unseen. We found out later that no-one had grassed us up; some screw had just noticed that the bars had been tampered with and alerted the others.

# 11.

## Is There a Mr Big?

After a trial at the Old Bailey, I was sentenced to seven years and my friends both got five. On the same day one of my old pals, Jack Rosa, was given four years for another robbery. The screws at Wandsworth were far from happy to see the pair of us as they knew that Jack and I would not be standing for any of their bullying tactics. We were both put on the same landing in A-Wing and it was funny the next morning when the landing screw came to look in on the new faces to hear him moaning that it wasn't fair, 'I've got the pair of them, I'm seeing the chief about this.' He must have convinced the chief as Jack was taken to another wing that afternoon.

In Wandsworth at that time, there were many prisoners who were later to become quite notorious underworld figures. It is a common misbelief that behind every big crime committed there is a shadowy 'Mr Big' doing the planning and that the actual perpetrators of the crime are paid a set fee. Nothing could be further from the truth. In actual fact most big crimes that have occurred in this country over the last 30 years have been planned and executed by people I have known, either as friends or acquaintances. Most are ordinary criminals who have progressed up the ladder from petty thieves to being involved in the planning and execution of some of the world's biggest robberies. For instance, the Great Train Robbery was planned and executed by quite a few of the blokes who I'd met at various times in my life.

I first met Douglas Goody while we were both on remand for ordinary crimes in our teens. He was a smash-and-grab specialist who was sentenced to be birched for doing no more than the ram-raiders do today. Jimmy

Hussey, like most criminals, came from a working-class background and as he got older he looked around and found that the more privileged in society were having a ball. He got involved with a 'jump-up' firm, doing exactly the same type of thing as I was doing myself at that time, taking loads from lorries. We used to see each other quite often in Manchester in the '50s where, after a tickle, we'd end up at the same bars and parties. A good time was had by all, until Jimmy got five years for taking a lorryload of cigarettes.

I met Ronnie Biggs and Bruce Reynolds in Wandsworth Prison in the '50s. We were all working in the brush shop. The no-talking rule was in existence in those days, so you only got to know each other through brief snatches of conversation on the landings, on the way to and from work or in the exercise yard. There would invariably be some poor chap on report every day, sentenced to three days' bread and water, seven days' solitary confinement and seven days' loss of remission for breaking the rule. So if you needed to convey any information to each other, it would be done by writing a 'stiff' on prison toilet paper.

Ronnie Biggs, at that time, was just a run-of-the-mill professional thief. He pitted his wits against the law and when he was caught he expected to get a prison sentence and just as naturally he would try to escape. He was always a 'special watch' prisoner. Ronnie was tall and gangling with a permanent smile on his face. He had a friend called Terry who was very similar to Biggsy and the pair of them were always plotting their escape. They would frequently be given a 'dry bath', i.e. a strip search, but they usually managed to be one step ahead of the screws.

Ronnie Biggs also struck up a friendship with Bruce Reynolds which developed through their liking for jazz. In those days, the only reading matter you were allowed to have sent in was either two magazines, which were approved by the authorities, usually *Picture Post* and *Illustrated*, your local paper – which would be heavily censored – and a trade magazine. The jails must have been full of musicians because the most popular paper in prison was the *Melody Maker*. Bruce Reynolds used to get it sent to him every week and he would lend it to Biggsy who once got a dose of bread and water for being in possession of another prisoner's magazine. Even at that early age Bruce Reynolds was a serious thinker. He was in his twenties and he was doing four years for robbing a bookmaker. I've never seen a guy go to the lengths that he did to get time off his sentence. In fact, he nearly lost his life over it.

It happened after Ronnie Kray arrived at Wandsworth. Ronnie had been doing a three-year sentence for wounding a guy. He'd been sent to Grove Park Mental Hospital where the inmates were allowed to wear their own clothes. Reggie went to visit him there, wearing identical clothes to his twin brother and just swapped places with him. When the 'nurses' came to tell

Ronnie to go back to his cell, Reggie said, 'No, I'm Reggie. My brother's gone to arrange some tea for me.'

Of course, they realised they'd been duped, but they had to let Reggie go on his way and put a warrant out for Ronnie's arrest. After Ronnie was eventually caught, he was sent to Wandsworth and ended up in the brush shop where we were all working. Bruce Reynolds came to me in the exercise yard and said, 'Do you think Ronnie would mind if I had a gun brought into the prison and put near where he is working?'

Ronnie couldn't have cared less because he knew he was going to do nearly all of the three-year sentence for his escape from Grove Park. Bruce arranged for a gun to be brought in by some friends and then went to the governor to say that he'd heard there was to be a breakout and a gun had been hidden in the brush shop. Once the gun had been found, Bruce was told that he would be given a few months' remission off his sentence.

But this wasn't enough for Bruce who soon had another idea. He got someone to write a note threatening him for spoiling the escape plan and saying that he would be 'done'. He showed the note to the chief officer, who immediately took him to the governor. They both assured him that it was impossible for anyone to know it was him as they were the only two people who had this information.

Not daunted, Bruce tried again. His next plan was for Frank Mitchell, 'The Mad Axeman', who had come back to Wandsworth after his second escape to attack him in the bath-house. Frank was told there would be a few quid sent to his sister if everything was done according to plan and Bruce was happy to receive a superficial wound. Unfortunately no one planned for Frank's enormous strength. He nearly killed Bruce who was found weltering in his own blood in a bath cubicle. When I later asked Frank what went wrong, he said, 'I only meant to give him a little nick, but it went right through him.' Bruce Reynolds got a bit more time knocked off, but he also nearly got himself 'knocked off'.

Ronnie and Reggie were already well known in the London underworld as two pretty formidable characters although they had not yet gained the national notoriety of later years. The story of the way they duped the staff at Grove Park earned them a different sort of respect from the cons in Wandsworth. Ronnie was very quiet and did not mix much with the other prisoners but by now I had gained something of a reputation, so the twins were both very friendly and showed me respect. About a month after Ronnie was discharged, Reggie Kray arrived, doing 18 months for demanding money. He and I hit it off right away and became as friendly as two people could do. We had a mutual respect for each other. Reggie would never let anyone push him around, although he kept quite a low profile. He probably stood for more pettiness than he would ordinarily, as he was only doing eighteen months and was awaiting an appeal, so he couldn't risk having too many fall-outs.

I was working in the main mail-bag shop at the time. George Dawson was sitting next to me and was still a bundle of nerves following his little escapade with the hacksaw blades. Reggie came in and sat in the same shop. As we were all on the back row, as far away from the screws as possible, we could have a chat without too much aggravation. One of the cons decided to relieve the boredom of the shop by sneaking up to the pile of finished mailbags and setting fire to them. As the flames started to get bigger the only one who couldn't see them was the screw in the observation box. That is until George Dawson helpfully shouted, 'Fire, sir!' George didn't realise that he risked getting set upon by half the cons in the workshop, he was just reacting naturally. So Reggie and I had a few words with the chaps and it was all forgotten.

Just after this incident, Reggie and I were on a visit together. Ronnie came up to see Reggie and Charlie came up to see me. As Ronnie got up to leave, he noticed a guy on our side of the visiting room who had upset him before he went out. Ronnie started to give him a coating and just as the bloke went to open his mouth to verbal Ronnie back, Reggie flattened him and had to do a bit of 'bread and water'.

Shortly after this, Reggie was discharged following a successful appeal. On the day he was released, he gave me all the possessions that he'd accumulated in prison and promised to keep in touch. He said, 'By the time you get out we should be doing well in business and you won't want for anything.' Most people in prison make such promises to their friends, promises to keep in touch, to do some little thing for the family, but promptly forget them when they get out. Not so the twins – they spent a lot of time thinking of the people they had left inside, remembering little things like sending a book or ensuring that some kid had a Christmas present sent to him 'from his dad who was away at work'. Most cons respected the twins for this side of their characters. I had this feeling for Reggie especially, as he was the one who always kept in touch to see if I needed anything. In fact, the twins had their own particular friends and it was noticeable that certain members of the 'firm' would be closer to one or other of them, though in all it was one big happy family.

Wandsworth was always known to be a very violent prison, but there would sometimes be considerable humour about the place. Quite a lot of light relief which existed in many of the prisons in those days focused around the homosexual prisoners who had been sentenced to fairly long terms. Some were quite tragic figures, but in general, most were amusing and had a good sense of humour. Nearly all had female names and they would stand out immediately due to their plucked eyebrows, the rouge made from the dye of book covers and their pronounced mincing walks. Some came from good families, while others were basically runaways who had been persecuted. But whatever their particular background, they would all be treated as weirdos by the courts – which is the last thing that they were. In fact, most were very intelligent and well able to look after themselves in any verbal contest. It was very noticeable that most of the screws made sure that they never became involved in arguments with the gays as they were normally made to look pretty foolish.

I remember two of them well from my time in Wandsworth. Pat and Paula were both very different, Pat being tall and self-confident, whilst Paula was very petite and nervous when he first arrived in the nick. However, Pat soon took Paula under his wing and in no time at all Paula was mincing around with all of the assurance of an old-timer.

It was quite common knowledge that some other prisoners would become very friendly with the gays and the odd screw would also show favours to them. In the evenings, when certain screws were on duty, one would hear the sound of a spring lock slotting into place as they crept around the landings, paying visits to the 'girls'. We would question the individual who we knew had received a visitor the previous evening. If it was someone like Pat he would be very open and say, 'Oh him, he comes to see me once a week. I have to talk dirty to him and give him "one off the wrist", but it makes my life a lot easier in here.'

But it wasn't all so humorous. There was once a very violent knife fight in D-Wing involving a gay called Bobby who had been seeing two different blokes at the same time. Both of these guys had reputations as hard men and it eventually erupted into a bloody battle as one of them, who was besotted with Bobby, decided to take the life of his rival. But the potential victim managed to wrestle the knife away from his assailant and in turn inflicted some horrendous wounds on him. Strangely enough this incident wasn't considered any more serious than any of the other acts of violence which occurred regularly in that establishment. In fact, it was treated with humour by most of the inmates with comments like, 'I hear there has been a bit of domestic trouble in the married quarters.'

It wasn't long after this incident that I heard that I was on the transfer list. My allocation had come through and I was sent back to Dartmoor.

# 12.

## BACK TO THE MOOR

Having been in Dartmoor once before, I knew exactly what was waiting for me. First, there was the cold and dank surroundings. Moss-covered cell walls; photographs curled up with the moisture; your bed was always damp. This was in the ordinary wings. The punishment block was unbelievable – even colder and wetter; absolutely silent except for the occasional cries and shouts of the people being beaten. I spent a few years in that punishment block without seeing another prisoner, just hearing their screams of anger or pain. And any prisoner might find himself in the punishment block accused of offences – whether guilty or not – against the good order and discipline of the prison.

The following typical scenario will illustrate how easy it was to get put into the punishment block. I spent 13 years in Dartmoor Prison, a few of those spent in the prison quarry. Our job was to break the rocks with a 14lb hammer until they were small enough to go into the crusher which would reduce them to stones for road-making and breeze blocks. This was a very arduous task – you were not allowed a break except for the lunch period. You were not allowed to speak. There were screws observing you all the time, either from the floor of the quarry or from the gun turrets, one near the entrance to the quarry and one in a type of sentry post above us. When we were marched back into the prison, we passed the 'tally point' where the chief and his sidekick would stand taking the numbers. If there were 65 men working on the quarry, for instance, the screw in charge of discipline would come by and usually say, 'Sixty-five, all correct and two reports.' This would mean that there were two prisoners on report in the morning for some breach of discipline. That was a guaranteed loss of remission, bread-and-water diet and a minimum of a week in the punishment block. On the rare occasions when the screws would come by and say, 'Sixty-five, all correct and no reports,' the chief would narrow his eyes and look very pained. If this was repeated over a period of a few days, the chief would call the discipline screw back and say, 'Do you mean to tell me that you've got 65 convicts working in the quarry and not one of them has broken a prison rule in the last three days? I don't think you can be doing your job properly. I'll have to make a note of that.'

Everyone on the quarry would be aware that someone would have to go on report the next day, so they all made sure that they just kept on hitting those rocks without any let up. Late in the day, when it was obvious that no one was going to do anything wrong, some poor sod would notice the screw standing next to him.

'You know you're not supposed to talk whilst working.'

'I ain't talking, guv.'

'Are you calling me a liar, prisoner? Take that threatening look off your face.'

The con would try talking his way out of trouble, but he would find himself on report with five or six charges, typically that he was lazy, persistently talking and when told about it adopted a threatening attitude and used abusive and foul language. This would usually earn the poor chap fourteen days' loss of remission, three days' No. 1 diet and seven days' No. 2 diet, plus 14 days confined to cell, in addition to receiving plenty of abuse.

Unfortunately, this was just the usual run of the mill stuff that the average prisoner put up with and no one took any real notice of it. However, there were a few cons in the Moor who were prepared to stand up and be counted and not just take the knocks. This helped a lot of the other cons to get on with their time.

I was only in the prison a matter of days before I was put in the punishment block. My file made it clear to the authorities that I was one of the handful of prisoners who wouldn't stand their sadistic ways. I think that the majority of prison staff just wanted to get their job done, draw their wages at the end of the week and go home to their families. But there was always a crowd who took pleasure in inflicting as much misery as they could – with the result that all the screws became hated. A con who had been involved in an incident and been subjected to some degree of violence in the punishment cells, would probably feel that he wanted revenge. Then something harmless would set him off – for instance, a screw might unintentionally walk into him. Even though this screw was not involved in the violence he'd suffered, the con would lash out, seeing only the uniform. No one would think of looking to the cause of what they would term an 'unprovoked attack' on a member of staff. Instead the heavy mob would arrive to administer the expected beating and the cycle would start again.

It would take a prisoner about three months to finish his punishment after an attack on a member of staff. This would include a period on bread and water and then a period of CC. On one occasion I was given three lots of this punishment, plus the beatings, all to run consecutively and several times I was sentenced to rule 36, 'that the prisoner will be kept segregated from the rest of the prisoners for the good order and running of the prison'. In this case I would have no idea when I would be released.

The most upsetting feature about these long periods in the punishment block, was the silence, broken only by the distant sounds of violence or the odd shout of 'Bastards' by some con who managed to remain defiant. Worst of all, was the sobbing of some prisoners who were completely beaten and despairing.

To be fair, the odd member of staff would show some pity or humanity. Sometimes when you collected your bedclothes from outside the cell at night you would find a book hidden inside the roll. And the chaplain might call to see you and perhaps bring a book. But these little gestures of kindness were few and far between.

There were a few cons in those days who I will always remember and admire for their guts, as I spent many years in the punishment block with them. Tommy Flanagan was one in particular. His determination and courage could only be measured by the men who knew the odds that he fought against. Tommy spent many years in Dartmoor's punishment block, but they never looked like breaking him. Instead he broke a few of them.

During my second term there, Dartmoor was going through an exceptionally violent period. One con had been found dead in B-Wing in funny circumstances and it had been hushed up as another suicide. I was actually in the hospital wing in a strongbox called the strip cell when I heard screams of terror from a guy called Nelson in the padded cell next to me. I could hear the thudding of the sticks on his head and body and his voice pleading with them to stop. It wasn't until later that I learned he died after this beating which occurred that day and night. I was later to read in the local press that the coroner had asked how he got so many appalling injuries and the prison doctor said he had thrown himself against the walls of his cell. Considering he was in a padded cell at the time and that it was standard practice to use a straitjacket on prisoners in these circumstances, which they may well have done, I find it hard to believe that even they could have got away with that one.

I've recently been back to Dartmoor to photograph the place where Nelson was buried with a little stone showing his initials and the year. I would bet that the validity of everything I say about the prison authorities could be proved by the exhumation of his grave.

As the years passed, some members of the 'heavy mob' stood out as being unusually sadistic, even by their standards, with a fascination for beating men between the legs and trying to put their batons into some pretty painful places. One bloke liked to boast that he was a boxer of some repute. He was always sparring up to people and, even if most people there would have liked to have taken up the challenge, they knew the consequences, so they just put up with his bullying. But a few of us knew that he was always diving down to the punishment block whenever the 'fun' was going on. It was decided, therefore, that he should be 'done' himself. There were probably half a dozen guys in our wing who could have taken care of him. But it was felt that he had to be given a hiding in front of everyone, by one prisoner, to show him for what he really was – a coward and sadist. I said I wanted to be the one to perform this task, so it was agreed that we'd wait until he was on duty in the evening. I wanted as many men as possible to see what he was really made of. I sat around with Tommy Flanagan, Cyril, Don Adams and Lennie Crooks, waiting for the one-and-a-half-hour session when we were allowed to associate with each other to come to an end. I said to them, 'Don't get involved and leave it to me, it's got to be a man-to-man thing to prove the point.'

Finally the screw shouted, 'Right, pack up, back to your cells.'

I stood up and said, 'It's too early, we've another five minutes yet.'

He replied, 'You heard what I said, get back to your cells right now.'

I then asked him if he thought he could put me in my cell. I could tell by his face that he realised this was a confrontation. He was looking around for help and all he could see were the pitiless faces of cons looking at him. I said quietly, 'Don't worry, it's just you and me. No one else is getting involved. I'm going to show everyone what a coward you are.'

He started saying, 'Look, just go back to your cell and I'll forget what you said. You'll hear no more about it.'

I knew his bottle had gone, so I said, 'If you can really fight on your own, start fighting because that's the only way out for you. It's just you and me.'

With that I hooked him in the belly. He had no chance. All the frustration and pent-up anger rose up in me. I wouldn't let him drop. I just kept smashing him in the doorway of one of the cells until finally I stood back and let him slump to the floor.

By this time, about six or seven screws had arrived with the chief. I just stood looking at them and my pals walked towards them. Tommy Flanagan acted as spokesman. He said to the chief, 'If he gets done in the chokey block, I am going to hold you personally responsible.'

I can only say that Tom's words must have had some effect for, as I walked to the punishment block, it was the first and only time that I never got a beating. In fact, the chief brought Tom down to the strongbox to make sure that the heavy mob hadn't given me the usual treatment. It started to dawn on me then that maybe I was winning my battle with the authorities.

It was after my punishment for this assault on a screw had finished that I met Obedyne face to face. I first heard of him in the mid-fifties: a Nigerian of abnormal strength, he was one of the most fearful characters that they ever had to deal with in the prison system. They used to say he was mad, but I got to know him pretty well and didn't find him so. I think it was a case of the system creating its own monster and then not knowing how to control it. It is my view from my experience that some of the police and the prison staff were racist. It was bad enough if you dared to object to their treatment of you but if you were black as well, then God help you. There were not many black guys in prison in those days, so consequently there were one or two who were sent to jail, whom I encountered, who had a pretty bad time. This was the case with Obedyne.

He had originally been arrested for not having a ticket when he came through Notting Hill Gate Tube Station. There was an incident in which the ticket collector received a punch. Obedyne then ran off. The police were called and someone who knew Obedyne, told them where he lived. The police duly arrived at Obedyne's flat, where they immediately began to manhandle him. He fought back, putting three policemen in hospital. Suddenly a siege had started which went on for hours. The police sent dogs into Obedyne's flat only to find them being flung out again with knife wounds. He was eventually overpowered by their sheer weight of numbers.

He was sentenced to 14 years for the attacks on the policemen and their dogs. By the time he arrived at the prison he was like a wounded lion and just wanted to get his own back on the authorities. I was in Wandsworth Prison when they first brought him there and, as usual, I was in the punishment block. It wasn't long before I realised that they had someone in the block who was giving them plenty to think about. I knew he was black by the racist remarks that were being screamed at him.

That's all I knew at that time. But I soon heard the stories that were going around the jail of this enormous Nigerian with immense strength who refused to give in when they were beating him up.

We had both been in the punishment block at Dartmoor for quite some time, but had never met because of the requirements of segregation and solitary confinement. You would be locked in your cell all day long. There were three or four cages at the back of the cells which were used for exercise purposes. The only time you came out of your cell was to go into the cage for about half-an-hour a day. So it wasn't until I came out of the punishment block that I first met Obedyne.

The circumstances of that first meeting were very strange because the authorities decided to put Obedyne and myself to work together! I will never be able to fathom the reasoning behind the move, but I don't think the result was what they were hoping for. Although Obedyne had come from the punishment block, they still kept him segregated from the rest of the prisoners and put him to work in the wood-shed. There he sat on a wooden bench with a chopping-block in front of him and an axe. He was expected to chop sticks for the screws' fires whilst we were all freezing to death in our cells. I was seen by the governor a few weeks after Obedyne was put to work in the wood-shed and told that I was going to be let out of the punishment cells. The Home Office had decided that I was to work on my own for a while but they already had a man on restricted association at work. The result was that Obedyne and myself were put together to do our tasks.

The next morning a screw came for myself and Obedyne. We went to the chief's office where he signed for a flat wooden box and we were then taken to the wood-shed. The working arrangements had already been sorted out. There were now two wooden benches to sit on, one opposite the other, both with a chopping block in front of them. Obedyne sat on one bench; I sat on the other. Then the screw just slid the box into the middle of the floor between us. We looked down and saw two axes lying neatly in the box.

We both took an axe apiece and started looking at each other. It was deadly silent in the wood-shed. We both stared at the screw who appeared to be on the verge of a heart attack. Obedyne turned his gaze back to me and said, 'I like you. I no like him,' pointing at the screw. I agreed with him. We then started to play little games like chopping quickly at the block of wood to make the sticks fly toward the screw's chair. Within a few days his nerve had gone completely. I was sitting in my cell reading, while the evening association privileges were going on, when the door opened. It was the screw – shaking from head to foot.

He said, 'I want to make a deal with you. If Obedyne ever attacks either you or me, if you help me, I'll give evidence that you saved my life.'

I just looked at him and thought of all the times those people had me helpless in the body belt or straitjacket and not once had there ever been the slightest mercy shown. I just got back to my book and didn't even answer him.

I never saw him again but within a few days the new wood-shed party had been disbanded and they put Obedyne in the laundry and me back into the quarry.

Although my attitude to most of the screws never changed, a sort of truce was gradually established. I remember sitting in the mat shop one day, not doing any work, just looking at the screw who was sitting by the alarm bell. Immediately behind him was a guy called Pierre, who was located a few cells from me. Pierre was enormous in stature and came from Trinidad. One day he approached me and asked, 'Why don't they make you work?'

'Well,' I said, 'it goes back many years, you see. I used to clash with the authorities but now we've kind of called a draw, so they don't bother me and I don't bother them.'

He started to tell me how hard he found it to do the job. His hands were so big that he found it very difficult to keep the coir around the ropes suspended on the frame and his fingers were red raw. I said, 'I know, I've done plenty of that in the past but now I don't do it.'

The next day in the workshop, Pierre just sat there doing no work until one of the discipline screws noticed and started to remonstrate with him. The next thing the screw saw was a hospital ward when he finally regained consciousness after the terrible hiding Pierre had given him. I didn't see Pierre for a few months and when I did meet him again, he was still getting over the beating they had given him. But he had a different job and he seemed to have settled into it. He could just manage a grin when he said, 'At least they never put me back in the mat shop.'

One guy I felt particularly sorry for in Dartmoor was doing life for killing his wife. His name was Robbie and had been sentenced to death in the Channel Islands, then been reprieved and sent to the mainland to do his life sentence. Apparently, there was a rule that a guy couldn't be released on-licence to the Channel Islands unless he had someone to sign and be responsible for him, which Robbie didn't have. He had been sentenced in the '30s and by the time I first saw him in the '50s, he weighed about six stone and had been sewing mailbags for 14 years. He always looked freezing and hungry and when the new boilerhouse was built and we got central heating pipes in the cell blocks, Robbie would rush into the wing after work and wrap himself around an upright pipe in the corner of D-Wing. It became known as Robbie's Corner. I remember the Salvation Army campaigning for his release and after about 25 years they eventually gained his freedom. He hadn't seen any of the war and as there were no newspapers or radios in prison in those days, he didn't know much about life outside. He was a little scared of going out and seeing the speed of cars and such things. I heard later that he died about two months after his release.

Perhaps some of the most interesting people in Dartmoor in those days were the quiet guys. One in particular was Rubber Bones Webb. You wouldn't have given him a second glance but all the same he pulled off one of the greatest prison escapes of all time. The fact that he was on special watch as a potential escapee made his feat even more outstanding.

When Rubber Bones decided to escape through an air vent that ran under his cell, he studied every detail of the screws' actions: when they did their bolts and bars check which, in the case of a special watch prisoner, was very frequent. He noticed that regardless of who did the checking, there was one part of the cell that they never stood on. It was just off centre on a straight line to the bars on the window; they only checked the outside wall and window as the potential escapee would still be in the cell block if he dug in any other place. They knew it was practically impossible to go through the walls, because unlike most prisons, Dartmoor's walls had been built by French prisoners of war using solid rock hewn from the quarry. However, Rubber Bones had noticed, whilst in the exercise yard, that there was a grill about eighteen inches by nine inches with a large lock on it, situated just about three feet below his cell. There had to be an air shaft of some description.

Rubber Bones quickly went into action. He first needed to enlist the help of a couple of trusted men because, as he was on special watch, he never came out of his cell on association. Association worked to a set of established rules. If a prisoner was on second-stage, that is after doing 18 months of his sentence, he was allowed two one-hour periods out of his cell per week. If he was on third stage, after doing two and a half years of his sentence, he was allowed three evening periods per week.

Rubber Bones recruited a man from each association period to sit near his cell while he dug down to the airshaft. The floor was covered with a bitumen-like material that most cons polished with the wax that was used on the threads we sewed the mail bags with. Each period, Rubber Bones would take the cover, which he had made with the help of a chap in the carpentry shop from the hole he was digging and each evening he would replace the cover and then polish it to match the rest of his floor. He got rid of the stuff he was digging up (mainly sand), by dribbling it through his trousers onto the exercise yard, which was a rough stony area directly outside D-Wing. A couple of his friends would get rid of the stuff in the same way. Dartmoor, having the type of weather it does, every prisoner was issued with a heavy waterproof coat which made it easy to conceal a fair bit of the sand. It was a painstaking and nerve-wracking operation but the delight when he eventually hit the airshaft could be seen in his demeanour as he went to and from work.

But the really hard part was still to come. He knew the airshaft was too narrow to get through with clothes on, so he would have to rely on the guys giving up their meagre margarine ration to rub on to his body when he was ready to go. However, the real stumbling block was the problem of how to get the lock off the grid on the outside, once he'd gone head first down the shaft, as there would be no coming back at that point. Eventually, one of his friends acquired a steel bar, like a jemmy, from the tool bag of one of the civilian maintenance staff.

At last, Rubber Bones was ready to go.

He waited for the first check after lights out – he would then have a half light in his cell, as did all special watch prisoners. He set up a lifelike dummy in his bed, stripped completely naked and smeared himself with the complete margarine ration of about ten cons for the week. Then, pushing his small bundle of clothes in front, he proceeded head first down the hole. It took him about one and a half hours to get to and bust the lock on the grid. Once outside D-Wing, he made his way to the builder's yard inside the prison, snapped the lock with his jemmy and helped himself to a ladder. Within minutes he was over the wall.

He knew that given a fair bit of luck, he would have about four hours before they missed him, so instead of going over the moors – which had been the downfall of many potential escapees, such as Billy Day who died in the bogs when he escaped with Dennis Stafford – he decided to go by road via Oakhampton. When the boys in the Moor knew that he'd arrived in London, there were a lot of smiling faces walking around the exercise yard, even though everyone knew that there would be extra bread and water dished out over the next few months for any trivial offences.

There was one guy in Dartmoor who never smiled at anything. He was always very deep and I wasn't surprised to read, years after he had finished a life sentence, that he had been re-arrested and charged with molesting little girls at a hotel where he worked. His name was James Camb and he was serving a life sentence at Dartmoor for one the most celebrated murder cases after the Second World War. It was known as the Porthole Murder Mystery. James Camb was a steward on one of the big ocean liners. On this liner was a very attractive actress returning to Britain from South Africa. When the journey was halfway completed it was discovered that the actress had disappeared and when the ship docked the police went aboard and questioned certain members of the crew. Eventually Camb was arrested. After a sensational trial at the Old Bailey, he was found guilty and sentenced to death. He was later reprieved and served a life sentence instead. Many blokes in Dartmoor tried to discover from Camb whether he'd killed her and pushed her through the porthole but his eyes just glazed over and he refused to talk about it.

I remember one incident in the Moor that gave all the guys in my wing a little bit of light relief. We had an old screw on our landing who got on well with everyone, never bothered putting people on report and just did his job. Most people were glad to see him come on to the landing at unlocking time. One night I was listening in my cell to a radio programme that featured a 'mystery voice challenge'. When the mystery voice came on I immediately recognised it as belonging to an old pal of mine who had been in the nick with me years before. Since getting out of prison in the '50s, he had become a successful writer. His first book, *Bang To Rights*, was very amusing, about all of the characters he had met in jail. Years later when I met him in his old haunts in Soho, I couldn't believe it was the same Frank Norman. His voice was now much plummier, except on the odd occasion after we'd had a few drinks in the Colony Club. So when I came out of my cell in the morning, knowing that a lot of chaps tried to guess the mystery voice, I said, 'Did any of you recognise the voice?'

No one did and they all thought it would go to the maximum prize of £100. I approached the old screw and said, 'Get your wife to listen in and send a card to enter and when they ask the name, say it's Frank Norman the author.'

The competition seemed to go on for weeks. Each night all the cons on our landing would sit up and wait for them to phone the three contestants and eventually the prize reached the magic £100. Every night the old screw would come in and say, 'The missus is still waiting for the call.'

Finally, the night came when the presenter said, 'We are calling a contestant in Princetown.' We all listened attentively. Sure enough it was the screw's wife. When asked what she did she said, 'I'm the wife of a prison warder in Dartmoor.' Then when she said who she thought the mystery voice was, the presenter got excited and said, 'Yes, you're right!'

A big cheer went up around the cell block. Then the presenter asked, 'How did you guess the name?'

'Frank Norman's friend is doing time on my husband's landing,' she said.

'Will you be sharing the £100 with the prisoner?' he asked.

'Oh no! I'm not allowed to do that but my husband will probably give him and his mates a bit of tobacco – but don't tell anyone,' she replied.

Her husband nearly got the sack over that.

# 13.

## MURDER IN THE CHAPEL

Violence had become a part of our daily life and not just the violence between screw and prisoner. More often it was between prisoners themselves. Most cons in Dartmoor carried a weapon and nearly every day someone was attacked. The situation came to a head in the chapel in the beginning of the '60s. It was a Sunday afternoon and we were all going to a picture show entitled *The Blue Lamp*, a drama about a policeman being murdered. A few days earlier a friend of mine, Cyril Birkett, had been charged with attacking another prisoner and two other cons had given evidence against him. To inform against another inmate was one of the worst offences in the eyes of your fellow cons and it was normal to put a 'mark' on the offender. This sort of justice seemed entirely natural to us – we had our own rules that we lived by.

When it was seen that one of the grasses was lining up to go to the pictures, it was decided that he would be attacked when the lights went out. It wasn't hard to arrange. All you had to do was to be the 18th person after him when going into the chapel and you would be able to sit behind the victim. Dennis Thirkettle, another friend of Cyril's on our landing, placed himself in the relevant position, with me next to him.

The film started, the lights went out and everyone settled down to watch. The film had not been rolling long, when I heard a cry of pain from the man just in front of us. He stood up and I could see his silhouette against the screen as he pulled a knife from his back. He turned and lunged at Dennis. The knife went straight into Dennis's heart. I immediately wrapped my jacket around my arm. As the lights went on again I threw it up in front of the guy with the knife and knocked him to the floor. Prisoners were scrambling over the pews to get out of the way and I was fighting with a couple of screws who'd seen me knock down the con who stabbed Dennis. Everyone seemed to have decided to settle their differences, myself included. The result? Mayhem.

The screws decided to make a quick retreat, so they ran out leaving the doors open. This was a sign for everyone to get out, quickly. There was one man lying dead and about twenty others injured. Within minutes, prisoners were hurrying back to their cells, hoping they hadn't been noticed in the chapel. During the confusion, four of us decided to raid the kitchen as we knew it would be a long time before we got another meal. We helped ourselves to as much grub as we could carry and returned to our cells.

It was about six in the evening when the screws came for us. They had the police with them. They took six of us to the punishment block and over the next month, the police tried to piece together a case. Eventually the trial came up at Exeter Assizes and everyone was found not guilty. After a period of time in the punishment block, the Home Office decided to split us all up. I was sent to Walton Prison in Liverpool, where I was to meet up with a lot of old friends, including Jack McVitie. Tommy Flanagan went to Winson Green, Birmingham and Donnie Adams went to Strangeways, Manchester.

On arriving at Liverpool, I was taken immediately to the punishment block, in H-Wing. The next morning, the governor and his merry men came to the cell and informed me that, as I still had a couple more years to go of my sentence, it had been decided by the Home Office that I would be kept in solitary confinement for the duration. This was stated as being in the interests of maintaining good order and discipline within the prison. However, the governor relented after a short period and allowed me in the prison proper. I was left to get on with my time without any problems whatsoever and I could come and go as I wanted to. My old friend from my early days at Dartmoor, Mixie Walsh, used to visit me from Blackpool where he lived.

Walton Prison at this time had just come through a major shake-up as a result of the actions of a remarkable lady, Bessie Braddock MP. Her enquiries and determination led to the exposure of the brutality that had been going on at the prison. Many prison warders had been charged, some were given a short prison sentence and many others were disciplined. The dust had only just settled when I got there.

There were a few screws who had avoided punishment and they were among the ringleaders of the heavy mob. Jack the Hat, who had been transferred to Liverpool from another prison because of his bad behaviour, took an instant dislike to one of them. Jack would taunt him about his reputation as a bully and challenge him to come to Jack's cell and 'fight like a man'. The screw was unable to oblige as he was still under a cloud after the Braddock enquiry. Jack became very popular with the other cons for keeping him in his place.

Like Jack, I had a bit of a reputation myself, though the reaction of other cons was not always what it seemed. One day a fellow inmate came up to me and said, 'Are you the guy that had the cat-o'-nine-tails?' I nodded and he started to ask me what it was like and would I describe it to him. As I obliged I noticed his eyes becoming glazed.

When I told Jack about him, he laughed and said, 'Didn't you know that he was a school master and used to get all the sixth-formers to beat him with the cane. He's having the time of his life talking to you about being flogged.'

Although I was still inside, I was aware of what was going on in the lives of the Krays. When Reggie and I were in Wandsworth, while we were working or walking in the exercise yard, we'd talk about our plans for the future. I didn't want to go back to crime when I got out and Reggie said he and Ronnie would help me set up my own business. The only business we were interested in was nightclubs. Nightclub bosses seemed to have a glamour about them with a bit of shadiness that appealed to people like us.

After Ronnie had been discharged, he and Charlie used to come up to visit Reggie and myself. A little while after Reggie had been released, Frank Mitchell and myself were told that the Home Office had stopped any future visits from the Kray family. I'd just received a visit from Reggie at Dartmoor when, shortly afterwards, a guy who was quite a well-known prisoner put himself on protection. He must have realised that Reggie had told me how this guy had tried to fit him up many years before. In fact, Reggie had told me but he wasn't vindictive about it. He even made excuses for the guy by saying, 'He was only young in those days and he didn't know any better.' I never found Reggie a vindictive person. It was a well-known fact in the East End that if you'd upset the twins, you could always go and have a word with Reggie and he'd calm Ronnie down.

Although life outside prison seemed very far away, Reggie kept me informed of all the news in the letters he used to write me. I've always kept his letters and reading through them now, I realise that Reggie looked on life as one big merry-go-round. He had a very good sense of humour. In one letter he mentions someone who 'broke Tony's jaw the other day. The guy who did it was the guy who left you a tin of syrup when he went out.' This was a coded message from Reggie who was referring to himself. In this way he let me know that the Krays were taking over Tony Snyder's rackets.

During the time I was in Dartmoor, the twins had started to get friendly with people from America. Frank Sinatra's son, Frank Jr., had been kidnapped and soon afterwards he did a tour of Great Britain. As a result of the earlier incident, it was arranged that his minders would accompany him.

A couple of guys came over with him, one of whom, Eddie Pucci, I later met in Stockholm. The twins were also contacted to make sure Frank Jr. had no problems. So by the time I was released from prison, the twins were well on their way in every respect. They were making plenty of money, had plenty of friends and not too many enemies. Most of the celebrities on both sides of the Atlantic liked to be in their company.

My own view is that the twins never set out to become gang bosses as a lot of people think. It was something that just happened as a natural consequence of the fact that they were both very likeable personalities and also known to be very tough. They attracted people to them and they were heroes to a lot of guys.

Charlie at this time was dabbling in the world of pop group management and had a nice recording studio and dance club in partnership with the American dancers, the Clark Brothers. On the morning of my release from Liverpool, Mixie Walsh and Steve and Jimmy Clark picked me up. The twins had asked the two brothers to collect me and had sent a few quid as a coming home present. That was a wonderful day, one that I thought many times I would not see. I didn't get back to London until the next day as Mixie and a few of his friends had laid on a big party in a club in Preston owned by Joe Lancaster, a chap I was to become very friendly with a year or so later. I promised to return and visit them after I got settled in London.

# 14.

## WEST END CLUB OWNER
## AND THE 'FIRM'

After celebrating my homecoming with my friends in Blackpool, I caught the train down to London. I was met by 'Duke' Osbourne whom I'd met during my early days in prison and who has been a friend of mine now for many years. He had a great personality, was tall and slim and always had a smile on his face. He was into every racket that he could find, both in prison and out. He was always the prison 'baron' as well as being the prison bookmaker. I believe he ended up getting into drug smuggling and was wanted for this when he was found dead under strange circumstances, probably drug-related.

Duke was also a very good friend of Reggie and Ronnie Kray. So as soon as I stepped off the train, we went immediately to 178 Vallance Road where the twins lived with their mother, Violet. It was one of a small block of terraced houses in Bethnal Green and had become the meeting place for all of the firm. Everyone was well mannered and respectful when they visited Vallance Road, mainly because the twins' mother was always in the house. She was a really nice person. She always had tea and sandwiches on the go and would bring them into the little front room where the twins held their meetings.

The twins arranged for us to have another celebration at the Cambridge Rooms that night, so I could meet members of the firm whom I didn't already know. The twins, by this time, had many and varied business interests and Reggie had also married Frances, a girl he used to tell me about

THE BRUTAL TRUTH

in his letters. When we arrived at the Cambridge Rooms it was packed with guys, who in one way or another, had an interest with the twins. Whether it was in the best interest of the twins or not, is another matter.

One of the guys there that evening was called Les Payne. Les seemed to have a fair amount of influence over Reg and Ron. He was always trying to involve them in his wild money-making schemes and, I believe, was mainly interested in using them for his own good. Eventually he realised that they were getting wise to him and he was the one who finally helped the police nail them. He wrote a book about the twins and his activities called *The Brotherhood*.

Also there that night was Teddy Smith, whom I first met in Wandsworth and had introduced to the twins a few years earlier. I bumped into him later at the Colony Club, where he introduced me to one of the greatest characters I ever met, Francis Bacon. Although Ted was close to the twins, I think he would have liked to get away now and then to be with his artistic friends and every so often, he would say to me, 'Do you fancy a drink in Soho?'

Most of the original members of the firm were there – Micky Forsyth, Johnny Davis, Terry O'Brien, Dicky Morgan and Curly King. I also met Stubby Kaye, the American actor who had appeared in *Guys and Dolls*, and Terry Spinks, ex-Olympic gold medallist, both of whom liked to socialise with the twins.

Everyone seemed to be friendly and enjoying themselves, and even the bookmakers and publicans who used to help financially seemed happy. I knew many of the people in the company but as I'd been away a few years, there were a lot of new faces on the firm. However, everyone was, as always, very polite and it was a good evening.

The cabaret act that night was a very good singer called Lennie Peters, who remained a good friend of mine until his death. This was before Lennie had met Diane Lee to become Peters and Lee. Lennie was always a good friend to the people who tried to help him and he kept in touch with Reggie and Ronnie. We used to meet now and again and chat about the old days over a couple of drinks. He was one of the very few people who never changed over the years and he had the same old sense of humour. We often mentioned his early days in the East End when he had a partner, Brian 'Butch' Royal, who was another great singer. They used to sing at the Greengate in Bethnal Green Road and all the firm would pop in to catch the show. Those were marvellous days. You would never know who would turn up to have a drink or a chat with the boys, listen to the music – even get on stage to play along with Lennie and Butch. One particular night, a girl called Winifred Atwell, who was a big star in those days and a brilliant pianist, came down to perform on stage with Lennie and we all ended up going back to her flat in Mayfair after the show. She was rather intrigued by all these smart young men with their nice cars and ready cash. Quite innocently she remarked, 'You're all obviously from good families.'

Shortly after coming home in 1963 I became the proprietor of the Emerald Beach Club in Soho. It was a basement premises that had become very popular and I heard from a friend I'd met in Dartmoor that the owner was having trouble with some local heavies. My friend was sure that the owner would offer me the business for a nominal rent, which indeed is what happened. Then Maurice King, who was the proprietor of the Starlite Club, was offered the Brown Derby Club for a very reasonable price. He'd heard of my success with the Emerald Beach and came to me with an offer of a partnership in the Brown Derby, thereby ensuring himself protection in the Starlite for no cost. I ran both clubs with some excellent staff and loved the lifestyle. Comparing it to my previous way of life, I think this was my idea of going straight!

Maurice had a very thriving business in the pop world. He managed quite a few of the stars of the day including Shirley Bassey's affairs and those of Jackie Trent. Quite a few of the successful bands of the '60s, such as the Walker Brothers and the Rockin' Berries, were on his books. Maurice rarely came over to the Brown Derby. His headquarters were at the Starlite Club in Stratford Place, Oxford Street. But if ever he got any problems with hardcase customers he would give me a ring as it would only take me a few minutes to pop over. It was an ideal partnership. If Maurice had any customers who wanted to go into Soho and look at the shady side of life, he would call me and ask me to keep an eye on them. Consequently, I would end up with a pretty mixed clientele of villains, sporting personalities and pop singers, plus all of the people such types seemed to attract.

One of the nicest of these was Terry Murphy. Terry would always look in if he was in the West End and would be accompanied by a couple of ex-fighters and business associates. I was always pleased to see Terry and his friends as they were the tops as far as drinking customers went. Terry had been one of the best middleweight fighters in the country in the '50s. His fight with Lew Lazar for the southern area middleweight title was the first fight to be televised on the independent network. I had some great nights out with Terry and his friends, one of whom was Terry Spinks.

One evening we were in the Mayfair Hotel having a nice drink. It was getting late. One member of our party was having difficulty finding the toilet. He was getting desperate when he noticed a tropical stream which was part of the decor, complete with palm trees and real crocodiles. He decided to have a quick wee into the stream which was nearly the biggest mistake of his life, as the crocs were not too pleased with our friend relieving himself on top of them. I don't think the management were too happy either.

I think the boys I became closer to were the Rockin' Berries. Clive Lee,

THE BRUTAL TRUTH

119

Terry Bond, Chuck Bottfield and Jeff Turton from the original band were, perhaps, my particular friends in those days and they came to visit me when I was in prison. I have seen them all at different times over the years, Chuck being the only one of the original Berries left when I last saw them. I saw quite a lot of Clive after he took over from Russ Abbott to front the Black Abbotts.

Some time ago I was in Jersey on business and took six Chinese friends along. We had all been out to dinner and decided to go to a nightclub to end the evening. The hotel porter told us there was a nice club called Ryders just fifty yards from the hotel, so myself and three of my friends went along there. It was getting late and there was no one on the door. We walked in and followed the sound of the music until we found ourselves in the club bar. I was looking for someone to introduce ourselves to when I heard a voice say, 'I don't believe it, is that you, Eric?' It was Terry Bond the ex-drummer of the Rockin' Berries and he was the governor of the place. It was a very pleasant surprise. We swapped a few stories that night and all went back for dinner the following evening. We had a really nice time.

One of the hardest days I ever had with that lot was when we promoted a show at Sofia Gardens in Cardiff. P.J. Proby was topping the bill with the Berries and a few other bands. The front guy was a most outrageous character. He was a lovely guy called Tony Marsh and was, in his day, Britain's number one DJ. Maurice phoned me the night before the show and said, 'Eric, for God's sake don't let Proby and Tony get near the booze before the show.'

'Don't worry, Maurice, I'll stick to them like glue,' I promised.

I thought I'd done a good job, but when we got to Cardiff, Proby nearly fell out of the car and Tony had a big grin on his face. As I'd been driving those two had slipped a bottle out of a holdall in the back seat and finished it off. All was well in the end, although I nearly had a fit when Proby almost fell off the stage. However, his voice carried him through. It's sad when a guy with such talent falls from grace.

Tony Marsh had a bit of a traumatic life in the business because he was always clashing with the powers that be and got into more than one scrape. The most noticeable one came when he was introducing the Rolling Stones on stage at Slough. He dashed off stage and was changing in the wings when he realised a lot of the audience could see him with no trousers on. He was in fact charged with indecent exposure and fined £25. The incident finished his career.

I remember throwing a party for the Dreamers, the boys who backed Freddy Garrity. They had just done a concert at Hammersmith, with the Beatles and were then off to America. We had the party as a good luck send-off. On stage at the Starlite were four top rock and roll bands. Every few minutes another face walked into the club. Eric Burdon of the Animals came in with a guy no one had heard of in those days and Eric asked if the kid could do a spot. With a request from someone like Eric Burdon, the kid was soon on stage. He was incredible. His name was Steve Marriot. Tom Jones turned up with the drummer from his band the Squires. Elkie Brooks was also there, I remember. She was about 15 years old then and she still remains one of my favourite singers. It was an incredible night. Ray Davis and the Kinks, Jackie Trent, P.J. Proby and many other musicians turned up, a tribute to the popularity of the Dreamers. We also got some gate-crashers who started to pester people and made a nuisance of themselves. Speaking into the mike, one of the boys in the band told them to leave in no uncertain terms. To show that if you give a dog a bad name it sticks: one of the well-known music papers of the day ran a story about the evening. In the article it enquires, 'Who was the delightful chap who told the gate-crashers to fuck off? Was it Tony Marsh.' Poor old Tony. He got the blame for starting everything in those days.

I used to see Reggie Kray every day and in the evenings we would go out together into the West End, usually ending up in the Stork Club. One place we used to pop into quite frequently was the Flamingo in Wardour Street which quite a few of the superstars of the day used to frequent. Long John Baldry was the name in those days and he used to play there quite often, as did Georgie Fame and the Blue Flames. But it was the kids who used to hang around there – hoping to make it some day – who were the ones who stood out. And they certainly did that. I love the music of some of those kids, who are not kids any more, such as Elton John and Rod Stewart. The boss of the Flamingo was a guy called Rick Gunnell and he loved to introduce Reggie as his pal to the various 'faces' who visited the club.

One day I was sitting in a club enjoying a quiet drink. There were a few people we recognised as a party from another firm. Oliver Reed, who was with some friends, upset the party that was sitting a few yards from us and one of the guys smashed a glass into his face. We hustled the guys – who wanted to smash the place up – out of the club and went to look at him. There was a lot of blood about and one or two bad cuts, but he didn't make too much fuss about it. This episode didn't seem to do his career any harm. In fact the scars could have enhanced his reputation!

It was around this time that Reggie and myself went to Stockholm with another friend, called Johnny Squibby. Johnny was a very amusing guy, full of fun and practical jokes. We were sitting in the plane at Heathrow just before take-off. Reggie had already admitted his dislike of flying and had downed a few large brandies before boarding when John started his non-stop banter. 'I'm sorry we've got this type of plane as it's got the worst record of all for crashing,' he informed us.

Then, after we had taken off it was, 'Can you hear that funny noise coming from the engine?'

Reggie nearly exploded, 'The only noise I can hear is coming out of your mouth, so just button up!'

We had to change at Copenhagen and Squibby was larking about in the duty-free when Reggie said desperately, 'I can't stand much more of this. Is there a boat we can get on?'

We eventually landed in Stockholm and went straight to the Grand Hotel where Frank Sinatra had the whole of the floor above us booked for his entourage. In Sinatra's company were a couple of minders who had come to England with Frank Jr. and it was one of these, Eddie Pucci, who'd phoned Reggie inviting him to Stockholm to meet Frank and a few other people. They would be there for the boxing between Floyd Patterson and Eddie Machin and, as there were a few British fighters on the same bill, it would be an ideal meeting place.

It wasn't long after we booked in that Eddie Pucci phoned our suite to let us know what was happening. As there were a lot of press people about we would have a proper meeting later. We were to meet at the weigh-in and later have dinner at the Flamingo Hotel after the fights. As we had planned a week's stay in Stockholm, we decided to go and give the town the once over on the first night. We had a superb night, met some nice people and found the girls very friendly. Reggie was always shy in front of women but they found him very attractive.

The next morning we went to the weigh-in at a night club in Kingsgarten, called the Ambassador. As we walked in, the place was packed and on the stage were all of the American crowd plus a couple of English fight managers, Denny Mancini and Johnny Campbell. Both had fighters on the bill. We went straight to the stage where we were greeted by everyone. In the American contingent was Nat Fleischer, editor of *The Ring* magazine. I'd met him when he came with Rocky Marciano and Al Weil to England and they visited the prison I was in at the time. Some of those involved in the American boxing world of the '50s and '60s had links with organised crime due partly to the practice of rigging fights. So Nat was thrilled to find himself chatting away about the British penal system with a top criminal on the stage of a nightclub in the Swedish capital.

When it came to fight-time, scheduled for the afternoon, the word went out that Sinatra wasn't well and wouldn't be attending, so would friends from London like to use the seats. Everyone in the place was watching the seat with Sinatra's name on it. When we arrived Reggie sat in Sinatra's chair and he was nearly mobbed by dozens of girls who then sat at his feet throughout the fights. Between fights, all the local celebrities came over to shake hands. I'm not sure whether they thought we were in Sinatra's company or were the 'men from London' as everyone referred to us. Ingmar Johansen, who was the ex-heavyweight champion of the world, joined us and was very charming. But I could tell by his conversation that he didn't know who we were.

Later that evening, we went to dinner at the Flamingo where we were joined by Johnny Campbell, his fighter Ray Sheil and a bookmaker friend, Burt Ashman. I was to meet Ashman again years later when I was involved in a big betting coup. This was supposed to be Frank Sinatra's dinner but he was the only person who didn't attend. Later that night we were taken to Burns nightclub to meet Sinatra and his friends. One bloke in particular whom I enjoyed meeting was the film actor Van Heflin. Van was very good company. Sinatra was very impressive, too – he was the perfect host. Everything was noticed and no one's glass was left empty at any time. It was a memorable night. In fact, we had another five days after that. It was one of the most enjoyable weeks I ever had. But our visit, as it had to, came to an end and we returned to London.

Both the twins and Charlie were frequent visitors to the Emerald Beach and the Brown Derby. It was on one of these visits to the Brown Derby that they met Maurice King. While I was having a drink with Reggie and Ronnie the phone rang and it was Maurice, who seemed rather agitated about some customers who were giving a bit of trouble. I told Maurice I'd get over straight away and then said to Reggie, 'I've got to pop over to the Starlite for a few minutes.'

Reggie said, 'We'll come over with you.'

I could see they fancied a change of venue and they'd never been to the Starlite before so I said, 'I might have to "talk" to a couple of people over there and then we can have a nice drink.'

Once we arrived at the Starlite there was no problem as the people who had been causing the aggravation had already left in rather a hurry as I understand it. We settled down for a pleasant evening.

At this time, the twins were doing business with Dino Cellini, who had brought George Raft from America to front the Colony Casino Club. Dino had an interest in quite a few other clubs in London and the twins were 'on wages' to see there was no trouble. Whilst we were chatting to Maurice in the Starlite club, it was mentioned that there was plenty of room for gaming tables in the club. Within a few weeks, a casino was set up and everyone was happy. Dino's staff were running the show, Maurice was getting his rent plus the extra clientele and the twins were having their few quid. But one night there was a slight hiccup.

I used to pop into the Starlite most evenings and on this particular evening I looked in as usual, on my way to the Astor Club in Berkeley Square for a late dinner. Whilst in the Starlite I had a drink at the bar and mentioned that I was on my way to the Astor and said good night. I'd no sooner sat down in the Astor when Sulki, the manager, came over to me and said, 'You're wanted on the phone urgently.'

I went to the office right away and it was one of the barmaids from the Starlite sounding distressed and muttering, 'Eric, we've been stuck up by four gunmen and robbed. They've taken everything. They've made everyone take their clothes off, taken all the money from the casino and gone with the punters' clothes, wallets, handbags and jewellery.' She said one of the customers had phoned the police.

I said, 'Phone Maurice and tell him to get down there straight away and when the law have finished with you, come to the Astor.' I then phoned the twins who were not very amused. 'Who would do this to us? They've got to be found. We can't have the word going round that people have robbed us! See what you can find out,' they said.

I did find out. But not until many years later, when I was sitting with a couple of chaps planning a bank job and they started to laugh and mentioned the Starlite robbery. They recalled the circumstances. They had just pulled up ready to go in to hold the place up, when I arrived and walked into the club. They decided to wait until after I'd left as they knew that I wouldn't be too long. But I had stopped to talk to the barmaid and I was a bit longer than I normally would have been. So there were four chaps sitting outside the club, with shotguns, waiting for me to leave before they would go in! To this day I think I'm the only person who knows the identity of the guys who robbed the Starlite.

In the meantime, I had been introduced to Peter Rachman, who the twins did some business with. Rachman was a Polish Jew who had suffered in the Warsaw ghetto and in a concentration camp. He had learned to be a survivor at a very early age. He landed in this country just after the war and, when he was in his twenties, he acquired a sizeable fortune from developing slum properties. His methods of getting sitting tenants out of their flats left much to be desired. When I knew him, he lived in a mansion in Hampstead's 'millionaires' row' and was just starting to get fat. He still had a very charming manner and women found him fascinating. His girlfriend at the time was Mandy Rice-Davis. He surrounded himself with heavy guys, mainly ex-boxers and wrestlers and could often be seen at the Cumberland or Regent Palace Hotels where there was a carvery offering as much as you could eat for £2.10. It was a sight to see Rachman and about five or six giant ex-fighters tucking into everything in sight. They'd go through a leg of lamb, a joint of beef (or pork for the non-Jews), heaps of potatoes and vegetables and then tuck into mounds of cheesecakes and trifles. Rachman died in Edgeware General Hospital about twenty years ago from dissipation. I believe they had to cut all of the gold from his wrists and fingers because he had become so fat. One of Rachman's managers, Lenny Royal, gave me a lovely flat in Kensington rent free. I had a name for myself after being flogged in Wandsworth and was known for my battles with authority. That kind of reputation meant something to men like Rachman; by giving me a flat, he neutralised someone who might be a threat to him and had the added bonus of being able to point me out as a 'friend', showing that he knew some heavy people.

At the end of '63, I got the Beach Club in Gerard Place and the twins would come at least once a week and bring all of the firm. I still used to spend most of my days with the twins but I saw a lot more of Reggie than I did of Ronnie. They liked to have their own friends and get away from each other for short periods, just for a bit of breathing space. Whenever we met in the evenings it was now invariably in the Grave Maurice or the Widows. The twins would always be together.

There was a very unfortunate incident one night when we were all to meet at the La Monde in King's Road, Chelsea. The club was run by one of the twins' oldest friends, George Osborne. The meeting had been arranged for that evening at Ossie's and everyone had been invited. In the end there were about twenty of us awaiting George's arrival. But no George. So Ronnie enquired politely, 'George is late coming down to greet us?'

A girl serving behind the bar, who happened to be George's step-daughter, said in a matter-of-fact voice, 'George won't be coming tonight. He and my mum have decided to stay in.'

The girl's attitude didn't help put Ronnie in a better mood. Suddenly he said, 'Get that arsehole on the phone.'

After Reggie and Ronnie had a bit of a row and Charlie had tried to calm things down, the girl got Ossie on the phone. By this time, Ronnie was beside himself with rage. He grabbed the phone and started to scream at Ossie: 'You ungrateful bastard. We've given you everything you've got and now you're over here with your poncey Chelsea friends you want to blank your old mates. So keep your ear on the phone and you can listen to what's going to happen to your lovely little club.'

With that, he turned to the few regulars who were in there and said, 'Just sit where you are, don't move and you won't get hurt.'

Taking a soda syphon, he smashed all the mirrors and optics behind the bar. Then he systematically smashed up the rest of the club without anyone saying a word. When he had finished he picked up the phone and said, 'We're going off to drink with real people.' And we all got in our cars and went off to another club.

The next morning Reggie phoned me and said, 'Will you come over to Vallance Road right away?'

When I got there, Reggie, Ronnie and Charlie were sitting in the front room of the house looking very serious. Ronnie was down in the dumps and he asked if I thought what he'd done was right. I told him – being diplomatic – that in a way he was right. This seemed to brighten him up a little. But then I said, 'You can't really blame George, he's now married to the lady and she obviously has a lot of influence over him. He definitely wouldn't snub you. He thinks too much of you.'

With this, Ronnie, tears coming to his eyes, said, 'Reg, get Ossie on the phone, I want to speak to him.' He then apologised to Ossie and said, 'Spare no expense, get the club fixed up and send the bill to me.'

Ronnie was a very complex person. Reggie and Charlie were the only two people who could handle him when he was in one of his moods. But he had another side which was charming and humorous. He was also very generous. Ronnie would see an old lady in the street looking as if she had a hard life and would take all the money from his pocket and stuff it in her hands.

Money was just something to give away to others – I don't think material things interested him at all. He was happy to live at home with his mum and he only got the flat in Cedra Court so he could entertain his own friends. His generosity got him into an embarrassing situation once when I was at Vallance Road. The rest of the family were at the shops and when the milkman called round, Ronnie, who'd given all his money away again, was unable to pay him. He walked into the room where I was sitting and, looking deeply uncomfortable, said, 'Will you pay the milkman? I've got no money.' That sort of situation would embarrass Ronnie but I've seen him in a nightclub be handed a bill for a couple of hundred pounds and, without turning a hair, just say that he'd pay next time he was in.

I've enjoyed some good days with him and also some bad. I was with him and Reggie at Cedra Court when Edith Piaf died. Ronnie took it as if it was his own sister who had died. He wanted to go straight to Paris to pay his respects to her.

# 15.

## HOW ORGANISED IS THE NORTHERN UNDERWORLD?

**B**y this time I had acquired a certain amount of knowledge of what was happening in most of the cities in the north of England. Any time the twins wanted information concerning the people who ran the nightclub scenes, they would give me a ring. Consequently, when Billy Daniels, the famous American singer, phoned from the States to say that he was booked to sing at the Dolce Vita in Newcastle and enquired whether they would be able to see the show, Reggie phoned me to ask if I knew someone in Newcastle. I did. I phoned the person I knew and was introduced to the Levy Brothers – David, Marcus and Norman – who ran the Dolce Vita.

David Levy said, 'Leave everything to me. Just let me know how many are coming from London and tell me what time the train arrives. I'll do the rest.'

Which he certainly did. There were seven of us and as we stepped out of the station two Rolls waited to take us to the hotel where Billy Daniels was staying. Later the cars came to take us to the club. First the boys showed us around and said there were a few people coming tonight who would like to meet the twins. Reggie and Ronnie were by this time getting quite a reputation all over the country. As the evening progressed, we met the guys who ran things in Newcastle in those days. Everyone was very polite to each other, as usual, and we had a wonderful evening. Billy Daniels joined our table after the show and also another guy called Angus Sibbert who ran the one-armed bandit business in that city.

It wasn't long afterwards that Angus Sibbert was gunned down. Two men were later to be given life sentences for his murder. One was a Londoner whom I knew very well in those days. I met him in Dartmoor where he'd made a dramatic escape with another prisoner, who had died in the attempt to get away from the Moor. After our visit to Newcastle, I bumped into him in London and he said, 'I hear you've been in Newcastle.' I told him we'd only visited socially and he said that he was thinking of settling up there as he was making a good living. He asked me whether I wanted a bit of the action. I'm glad I refused his kind offer.

Some time later I was in Manchester to visit an old friend of mine and to spend a bit of time getting to know the nightlife and meeting new friends. As I walked into the Manchester Piccadilly Club, the boss of the casino, Joe Marlow, said to me, 'There's a call from Reggie Kray. He said would you ring him at the Shoreditch number.'

I phoned Reggie that evening and he asked me if I thought the casinos would pay £2,000 to have Joe Louis, the ex-heavyweight champion boxer of the world, to appear for a week or £3,000 for two weeks.

I said, 'Leave it with me and I'll call you back in about an hour or so.'

I went back immediately to Joe Marlow and put the proposition to him, but added a monkey to the fee for my own expenses. I knew from experience what it would cost. Joe said the best thing to do would be to go to see Alan Kaye and Gus Demmy at the Salford Casino, which we duly did and came away with a two weeks' deal which suited everyone. I relayed this news back to Reggie with the message that it wouldn't do to have too many 'faces' going to Manchester, as the Old Bill were very much on view in the club scene up there.

'No, there'll only be Charlie and a boxing promoter and one of his aides to escort JL to Manchester,' Reggie reassured me.

It was decided that I would organise everything in Manchester and we set about the publicity and other arrangements. On the Sunday we had all the press and photographers on parade as the train pulled into Piccadilly Station. As flashbulbs exploded around me I stood staring, hardly able to believe my eyes. There, in front of us all, was every top villain in London alighting from the train, smiling happily for the cameras with Reggie and Ronnie in the forefront.

I hastily gathered them all up and took them immediately to the Midland Hotel to book in. There was a great danger that Joe Louis's appearances would come to an immediate end if the Old Bill knew who was behind bringing him to Manchester. Unfortunately the chaps were determined to go out and give the town the once over and as all of the local villains used the same two clubs, it was guaranteed that the Old Bill would be using them too. It was no use thinking we could visit those clubs without the Old Bill

The whipping block at St Vincent's.

Above: Lennie Cain (ex-fighter), myself and Dave Barry.

Left: Painting by Larry Rushton of the punishment block at Dartmoor.

Nelson's gravestone.

The view of Dartmoor looking across the French
P.O.W. graveyard.

Brian Beck – a
lovable rogue.

Left to right: Connie
Whitehead, 'Frosty'
(one of the Kray gang)
and myself.

Left to right: Charlie Dice, Terry Spinks and
myself at the London ex-Boxers Association.

Left to right:
Billy Cox,
Peter Kelly
(bank robber),
'Frosty' and
myself.

Patsy Manning, Johnny Prescott, myself and
friends in West Bromwich.

Top: Joe Khan, Mickey O'Sullivan (grandfather of
Ronnie O'Sullivan, World Snooker Champion) and
myself at the London ex-Boxers Association.

Above: Roy Belling (racehorse trainer), myself
and Eddie Gray (Mr Leeds United).

Johnny Stones
and Jimmy the
Weed on their
reunion.

Ricky Hatton (Inter-continental Light Welterweight
Champion), myself and Max.

My Scottish friends, in Edinburgh.

Myself and Max in the Hare and Hounds.

tumbling who the strangers were. So we devised the plan of opening the Piccadilly Club, which was usually closed on a Sunday and having a private party. Joe did miracles that night. He only had a few hours to organise everything, to get hold of his regular staff, musicians, doormen, bar staff and kitchen staff. A few of the regulars and a couple of good mates added to the scene and made everything seem like a normal evening in the club.

All was going well until one of the waiters who Ronnie took a shine to, Bertie Burton, who was later to tell the Stalker Inquiry that he was Ronnie's driver, said, 'They've brought us all in to work on our day off to keep you boys happy when there are two very swinging clubs open just around the corner.'

From then on the charade was over. All the blokes wanted to go to one of these clubs and there was no stopping them. We started with the La Petite where there were quite a few entertainers on their night off enjoying life with plenty of pretty girls and one or two local villains who were obviously put out by the arrival of some obviously very heavy opposition. After a few drinks at the La Petite, we went to the Portland Lodge, owned by Bernard Williams, a nice guy who I still see now and again. By this time the word was out as to whose firm was in town – there were plenty of visitors to the club, some with heavy boots drinking modest halves of bitter, others just rubber necking.

One guy upset Reggie with a remark he made and Reggie duly knocked him out. After this, it was decided that everyone should go back to the Midland Hotel to retire and get together the next morning prior to the twins going back to London. The twins had managed to meet a few club owners and had also sent messages to a couple more to come to the Midland in the morning. There was mention of these particular people giving a few quid to help people who had some problems in London.

The next morning saw us all together. It was a very cosy scene. There was Reggie and Ronnie amiably chatting to a couple of local club owners with several of the 'firm' sitting about. As well as a few entertainers and friends, I remember Stubby Kaye sitting next to me and a couple of ex-fighters I knew. Suddenly the hotel lounge filled with the Old Bill. Ronnie immediately asked me if I thought I could get out of the hotel without going past the police.

'Yes, I think so,' I said.

He then gave me a packet of money and said, 'Can you bring this down to Vallance Road in a couple of days?'

'Leave it to me,' I said.

I went straight to one of the hotel staff and said, 'You must recognise me from my show on the TV. I've got a lot of my fans outside and I want to miss them. Is there a way out the back?'

'Yes, sir,' he said, 'follow me.'

He took me to the rear of the hotel and I walked off. I went around the block in time to see all of the firm getting in taxis on their way to the station with a very heavy escort of the Old Bill. They had been asked to get the next train to London. It was just another experience to the twins; they had a laugh and went on their way.

I spent a lot of time visiting old friends in different parts of the country. Invariably Chris Lambrianou would accompany me. He was a big guy, about six foot and weighing about 17 stone. He was fun to be with and had similar aims in life. I don't think he set out to be a gangster, he just wanted to make a bit of money and enjoy life without too many hiccups. He could look after himself, but he wasn't interested in getting into any bother. I think if he could have got through the rest of his life without falling out with anyone he would have been happy.

I would often go to Liverpool to look up Billy Grimwood, who was an old mate from prison. He was making a few bob from the legalite tables, the only form of roulette that was legal in those days. Chris's brother, Tony, would join us on the odd occasion. I think he had illusions of becoming a gangster even in those days.

By 1965, I had got rid of the Brown Derby Club but still had a share in a casino in Mayfair. I had plenty of time on my hands and was making a few quid without having to show my face. So I decided to give my friends a visit, stuck a few grand in my pocket and arrived in Blackpool, intending to stay for a week or so. But the visit lasted a lot longer than I had planned. I met a girl who was appearing at the theatre in St Annes and we got pretty involved. Things seemed to be going right for once. I was enjoying life.

# 16.

## THE RICHARDSONS

I might have known things were going too smoothly. It was while I was part of the Krays' circle that I was nearly killed by the Richardsons, a rival firm, although the seeds of our disagreement had been sown before I became friendly with the twins.

In Tony Lambrianou's book he talks about my fight with the Richardson gang. He also mentions how he asked me to call on him when I made a comeback. Let me examine the truth of that statement.

Firstly, Lambrianou at no time got in touch with me with the intention of any comeback. In all the time I knew him he never had the bottle to make one in any row with a man, whether it be a villain or a wimp. All he has ever done is to live a life of make-believe and follow people whom he rated as tough, like a lap dog. My friend, Patsy Manning and I have many a laugh whenever we see him pontificating about what a tough guy he was. We knew him for exactly what he was and still is.

The only person who ever got in touch with me, other than the people who were involved in the row at the Astor Club, was my good friend, Mixie Walsh. He let me know that he had a dozen or more people around him who were more than willing to come down from Blackpool to stand on with me for whatever had to be done. I always knew, though, that I had those kind of pals – not the type who paid lip service. Mixie and I are both 70 years old now and we have always been able to hold our heads up all our lives. I'm just pleased to know that I've got a few friends whom I consider to be real men.

As far as my association with the Krays is concerned, I was their friend for many years, but never on the payroll. I earned my own money and I was

THE BRUTAL TRUTH

always capable of fighting my own battles. It has never been my game to run to anyone for help if I came unstuck. Now let me explore the beginning of my rows with the Richardsons.

The Richardson brothers, Eddie and Charlie, had gained a reputation as heavy people through taking a lot of liberties with people on the fringes of the underworld. They were the proprietors of a scrapyard in south London, Peckford Metals and were in a position to buy stuff from the lower end of the criminal fraternity. The only trouble was that they wouldn't pay the going rate and if anyone complained that he had been duped, the Richardsons would see that he was beaten up for his pains. As time went on and they got wealthier – they actually owned a mine in South Africa which added to their riches – they started to torture people for a variety of reasons, but all aimed at making themselves wealthier and more powerful and feared by the average criminal. They surrounded themselves with psychopaths and started a reign of terror that lasted a few years, until they were arrested and charged in the infamous Torture Trial case during the late '60s. Charlie was sentenced to 25 years in prison and Eddie got 15.

My first run in with the Richardsons took place in south London. My friend Jack Rosa asked me to come for a drink with him to the Mason's Arms in East Lane. We had been drinking in a West End club all afternoon and Jack was a little the worse for wear. I decided to stick with soft drinks in case Jack needed looking after in my 'minder' role. I tried, unsuccessfully, to talk Jack out of going to south London as I knew he had the hump with a few people from there, in particular a guy called Jimmy Brindle. Some members of the Brindle family were pretty notorious. Jimmy was married to the sister of Frank Fraser who was also a notorious guy. In fact, Fraser had a similar life to my own, up until his involvement with the Richardsons. He was sentenced to 15 years after an affray at a club in south London where one man was gunned down and many others were injured. Fraser was later sentenced to another five years over an uprising in Parkhurst Prison. He had earned a certain amount of respect from the majority of cons for his battles against prison brutality and, like me, was transferred around the country many times. Jimmy Brindle wasn't in Frank's class. It was only the fact that he was married to Frank's sister that made him think he could tangle with the likes of Jack Rosa.

As soon as we arrived at the Mason's Arms, I felt that the atmosphere was a bit heavy, to put it mildly. But Jack was determined to have a go at Jimmy Brindle. I could also see that there were several guys with their heads together, obviously contemplating what to do in the event of the situation going further than just words. I had just managed to get Jack to leave it till another day when he was more sober and we were about to go through the door, when out of the corner of my eye, I saw Brindle making for Jack. I pushed Jack out on to the pavement and flattened Brindle on the doorstep. Another guy tried to take a swing at me so I immediately dropped him. As I tried to get Jack into our car, I saw Brindle getting up from the floor. I then gave him a good belting and left him in a heap on the pavement.

It was when I saw that another of the gang, who had just climbed out of a wagon, had something in his hand, that I realised the situation was about to get a bit heavy. I jumped into our car and drove away.

'Let's go back and give them some more,' Jack muttered.

I would have been quite happy to go back to west London and have a few drinks, but Jack insisted on going to the Reform Club, which was just around the corner from the pub we had just left.

We had only been in the club about twenty minutes when there was a hush and a regular who was standing at the bar said, 'Hold up! Here come the Richardsons and they're tooled up.' I looked up and saw about half a dozen men bearing down on Jack and myself. The only one I recognised was the guy I had left on the pavement shortly before. They immediately started to hit out at us with iron bars. We fought back and although Jack and I had a couple of wounds, we gave as good as we got. The Richardsons eventually fled, leaving Jack and myself grinning at each other. I had the lobe of my left ear hanging off and a couple of gashes on my head. Jack looked as if he had been through a mincing machine.

We went back to my flat in Kensington and cleaned up. We then tooled up and drove to the scrapyard in south London where Jack said the Richardsons had their headquarters. It was deserted. Then a guy stopped in a taxi and as the cab pulled away, Jack said, 'He'll know where they are.' I don't think the guy wanted to co-operate, he only seemed interested in depositing the booze he had consumed into the gutter. We left and went back home.

Then we started to do some homework with the intention of making a comeback. Before we could take any action, the police swooped on us for a series of robberies for which I received seven years. It was whilst I was doing the seven years that Reggie Kray arrived at Wandsworth. On the exercise yard, Reggie said to me, 'I hear you put Brindle into hospital.' I nodded and he said, 'His brother-in-law has just arrived in the nick for his accumulated visits. So be on your guard.'

I saw Frank Fraser a couple of days later in the bath house but it was just a glaring situation and nothing came of it. I was allocated to Dartmoor and shortly afterwards Fraser arrived. He had a few of his pals with him but I was never very concerned. I knew that in the nick things are pretty even. I also knew that there was not one of them I would have any trouble with if it came to a man to man situation. In fact, I had one or two guys who approached me in the Moor and said, 'If it goes off, we're with you.'

But I got involved with one of my battles with authority shortly after arriving in Dartmoor and found myself in the prison hospital. Fraser, who was working on the bin party, arrived at the hospital and said to me, through the cell door, 'Eric, people like you and me shouldn't be falling out. We've got one common enemy so let's call it a day and be friends.' This was certainly all right as far as I was concerned.

A short while later, following the murder in the chapel, I was transferred to Liverpool. It was after my release, when I had settled into club life, that I again bumped into Fraser. I was having a drink in the Log Cabin Club in Wardour Street when he came in with Eddie Richardson, Jimmy Brindle, Jimmy Andrews – who was later gunned down in the street and died – and about six other guys.

Fraser came over to me, held out his hand and said, 'Will you do me a favour and shake Jimmy Brindle's hand and let's all have a drink together?'

I was quite happy to agree, although I was rather surprised at how friendly everyone was – even Brindle. I was still on my guard as I'd learned over the years exactly how much you could trust the word of a gangster. Nearly every word they speak is designed to enhance their own power and if it suited their purpose to befriend you, they would tell you anything. I've heard all the claptrap over the years: 'We must stick together', 'I'd die for my friends', 'You can trust me'. All phrases that roll easily off the tongue and are meaningless. But I shook Brindle's hand and we then went our different ways.

The next time I saw Fraser and Eddie Richardson was when I got into a bit of trouble with the law whilst trying to release a guy who had been arrested outside my local pub. The law turned their attention to me and I was arrested instead. The Kray twins sent Teddy Smith to the police station with a few quid to have a talk with a top detective. I was subsequently bailed to appear at Clerkenwell Magistrates' Court the next morning on a reduced charge. After being bailed, I went to my club in the West End and I met Fraser and Eddie Richardson who had heard that I had been in trouble. They immediately gave me a few quid to help with the straightening process – to prove that bygones really were bygones. So up to then I had no problems with anyone.

A few months later I was doing business with two friends of mine, involving the laundering of some money from a small African republic. We had arranged to meet the ex-finance minister of this country at the Astor club, Berkeley Square. My two friends were Harold Cashman, known as Boot, and Johnny Barnham, who was a member of a well-known boxing family. As we entered the Astor, we saw Eddie Richardson, Fraser and most of their firm entertaining a group of Scotsmen, some of the top-rated gangsters of the day, including Jimmy Boyle, who was wanted for murder and had been brought down to London to keep out of the way for a while.

There were about twenty in the group, sitting around a large table in front of the stage. We all nodded to one another in recognition and were waiting to be shown to our table when one of the jocks, who was a bit drunk, said to Johnny, 'How did you get that flat nose? Did you fall off your bike when you was a kid?'

With that, Johnny hooked the guy and he went down in a heap on the floor. All the people at the Richardsons' table jumped to their feet and Boot knocked the nearest guy to the ground.

Then all hell broke loose.

Most of the Richardson firm grabbed bottles and started to smash them on our heads. I saw someone stab Boot. I saw Johnny run out of the fire door at the rear of the club and bent to lift Boot from the floor. I felt a knife being stuck in my head but it wasn't a serious wound and I knocked down the guy responsible. Then I heard someone shout, 'The Old Bill's arrived!'

Everyone seemed to disperse in a flash. I looked at Boot lying on the floor. He was in a bad way and I was determined to go after the Richardsons and give at least one of them the same treatment. So, without thinking of the consequences, I followed the mob up to the club entrance. A few of them were standing around outside while one solitary policeman in uniform made his way into the club. I saw a car pull up with Eddie Richardson driving it and I said to Fraser, 'Do you or any of your mates fancy getting into a car with me? Let's see how good you really are.'

The sweet-talking Fraser said, 'Come on, let's go somewhere else before we get nicked.'

I was willing to go with any two of them for a fight, man to man and when Fraser told me to get in the car, I thought he was accepting the challenge. As soon as I got in, about five of them dived in after me, pulling out weapons. They were all stabbing at me with knives while I tried to get out of the car. It seemed that within minutes, we were pulling up in a side street off Tottenham Court Road. As the car stopped, I put one of them down and had broken out of their clutches. I almost escaped, but the guy on the floor held on to the bottom of my trousers and this gave them the chance to regroup. I could hear a few more cars pulling up and the next thing I knew I was being dragged into a basement – a workshop for one-armed bandits. I had a shotgun stuck against my head and dimly heard voices urging someone to pull the trigger. Someone else was whacking me with an axe. I heard one of them say, 'Cut his hands off. He won't be able to fight again.'

I saw the axe coming down once and put my hand up to shield my head. The blow pinned my hand to my skull. It was then I realised that I had serious injuries as I couldn't speak or move parts of my body. I must have lapsed into unconsciousness. I have only vague memories of being in a car but I recall someone saying, 'I know where to dump him.'

The next thing I remember was waking up in hospital. I still couldn't pronounce my words but I could hear people, as if at a distance, telling me I was lucky to be alive. Apparently I had been dumped on a piece of waste land and a drunken wino had stumbled across me, thinking I was a sack of rubbish. When I groaned it had nearly scared the life out of him. However, he called for help and I was taken to hospital in the Holloway Road. I had over thirty serious injuries, three fractures to my skull and over three hundred stitches in various parts of my body. The only visitors I can remember, were Ronnie Knight and my girlfriend, Brenda. The first my family knew about it, was when they read of a 'gangland attack in Mayfair'. They were a little frightened and couldn't understand the kind of life I was obviously leading.

I was ill for some considerable time. But when I came out of hospital, I saw the Kray twins at Vallance Road. They asked me what I felt like doing about it. I appreciated their offer of support, but I had already realised that any retaliation would have triggered a major gang war, possibly resulting in loss of lives. Therefore, I had decided to deal with it in my own way, doing the same to the Richardsons as they had done to me. Jimmy Humphries and Jack the Hat came to see me with offers of help in case I needed it. I wanted revenge but I was still suffering physically and mentally from the attack on me and knew I didn't have a chance on my own.

One night Jack and I were following a couple of guys who had been at the Astor club with the Richardsons, when we were involved in a car accident and I ended up going through the windscreen. Visiting me in hospital, Jack said, 'I don't think you're having much luck this year. Perhaps next year will be a better one for you.'

It certainly was a better one than he had.

I stayed at Jimmy Humphries' farm for a while to recuperate. Whilst there my friends Boot and Johnny came to visit me and we planned an ambush in south London. We sat outside a block of flats expecting four of the opposition to arrive. The weather was atrocious and we ended up underneath a lorry in order to keep dry. We were there until the crack of dawn but the 'firm' never arrived and we found out later that they had gone to a party at another house.

When I thought I could trap a couple of the firm I would carry a gun. I think if I had been able to corner them, I would have shot them. I've often reflected on this period of my life and been glad the way things worked out. Nothing seemed to go right for me while I was planning my revenge; it seemed as if the Richardsons had a charmed life. And I was risking a long prison sentence for carrying a gun, which was completely alien to me anyway.

In fact Johnny, Boot and myself were turned over by the Old Bill who were searching for guns, as it was common knowledge that we were running around London together looking for the Richardsons. Johnny had a very lucky escape. He heard the Old Bill outside his house and stuck his gun into a shopping bag. John's wife walked to the door as if she was going shopping and was surprised to find the Old Bill outside and just about to knock.

She shouted back, 'There's some old friends at the door. I'm going to the shops.'

The Old Bill charged right past her as she calmly went off down the road.

A little while after this, I heard that the Richardson firm had gone to Southport. They were nicked on their return for torturing some people and some of the firm got done for the Mr Smith's Club shooting and affray. A few people were shot and one died and there were some pretty badly wounded. They were sentenced to terms of imprisonment ranging from 15 to 25 years.

A lot of the minions who made up the firm were now left to their own devices. One day I was lucky to bump into one of these in a club in Bayswater. He had been boasting that his firm had done Eric Mason, when I locked the door and introduced myself. I then told him that he would have to prove to all the people present how he had destroyed me, using his own words. I then gave him a humiliating time, a clout and unlocked the door to watch him scurry away.

I had another run-in with a guy who liked to boast about being a member of that firm. I was walking in Gerrard Street, Chinatown, when I recognised a man standing in the doorway of a Chinese restaurant. I immediately set about him and he squealed like a pig being slaughtered. But although satisfying, actions like this were not earning me a living, so I had to get back to the graft.

The only other time I've set eyes on any other member of that firm was when I was attending a boxing event in Manchester. My friend, John Shearer, came over and told me he had just bumped into John McVicar at the bar. John Shearer had said that he was with me and John McVicar had said he would join us. Upon hearing my name another guy with McVicar had said, 'Come on, it's time to go.'

A short while later, I was talking with a friend, Jimmy the Weed, when he told me that the other guy with McVicar was Eddie Richardson and apparently they were all going to a party at the Film Exchange. So I thought I would go along, as I hadn't seen John McVicar for about twenty years and Eddie Richardson for even longer. We never met as they didn't go to the party.

The roots of the underworld as we know it today were born at the turn of the century with the likes of Arthur Harding, who was a legend long before I was born. People would speak of him in awe. When I was 25 years of age, I met a man called Dodger Mullins. He was then in his fifties. He was to tell me many stories of Arthur Harding. Dodger was in Dartmoor Prison at this time doing five years for shooting at Arthur's house, hoping that a stray bullet would find the target in a man who was still feared, even though he was about 65 years old.

Arthur Harding started life in Bethnal Green in 1886. He was a child of the slums. His mother was either the second or third wife of his father and as he began to explore the East End streets, he would often meet boys around the same age as himself, with the same surname as his. These, he learned, were his step-brothers. He also had natural brothers and sisters.

He was always up to mischief. He once got caught by the law aged about eight. He had already learned that you never told a copper where you lived in case your family had something at home that was stolen. So he told the police that he had no family and nowhere to live. The police took him along to Dr Barnardo's home, where he was to stay for the next four years before he was allowed to go home. His mother, who had been crippled in an accident with a horse and cart, earned a pittance by making matchboxes for Bryant and May. They would supply the cardboard and sandpaper and she had to buy the glue from her meagre earnings.

Arthur got various jobs, the most lucrative being cleaning the dung from the street. He would dodge between the horse-drawn buses, delivery carts and brewery drays with his bucket and shovel and then on Sunday he would go with all the other poor people to Sunday school to get his 'tickets' for breakfast at the mission. This was another con, as the school was at the back of the mission: after eating, you would go straight into school.

He grew up very streetwise and tough. By the time he was released after a short period in Borstal for thieving, his first actions were to go to the local pubs and frighten the life out of all the publicans, with the intention of stopping them serving his mother with drink. She had become a bit of an alcoholic owing to the misconceived idea that it would alleviate the pain she suffered after her accident.

It wasn't long before Arthur found that people were a bit scared of him, so he decided to exert a little more pressure, with a view to earning a few quid. He soon found out that more publicans were happy to give him a few quid because his reputation was becoming legendary. Most of his friends were professional boxers, but they never chanced their arm with Arthur. He was a prize-fighter but there was nothing fancy about his way of fighting. He never used a knife – he would say 'that's for foreigners and toe-rags'. All his life he had an aversion to knife wielders. His most derisory expression about people he disliked was, 'He'd stab you in the back.' That went for 'grasses', 'stroke pullers' and what he called 'scumdicknicks'.

There were many ways that Arthur earned a living and one of the more lucrative ways was what he called the 'Wardrobe Racket' – today called charity shops. Arthur and his firm, two of whom were called Kray, Jimmy Kray and his brother Charlie Kray – who was the father of Reggie and Ronnie Kray – would go to the outskirts of London with their horse and cart and later with an old disused Army motor vehicle and collect clothes from the toffs. The women would then tidy them up and they would be sold in Arthur's second-hand clothes shops. Nearly forty years ago I would go round to Vallance Road in Bethnal Green where the Krays lived, sit in the kitchen where old Charlie would tell me stories about the old days. You could bet your life that Arthur Harding's name would come up. It seemed to me that one day I was destined to write about Arthur Harding, as I followed him for many years of my life. I followed him to Portland and then to Dartmoor.

His reputation was enhanced by the events that the press called the 'Vendetta Affair'. It started by Arthur being asked to sort out a guy called 'Greeny' who was the leader of the Hoxton Mob. He had been giving the stall holders in Petticoat Lane some aggro and Arthur duly obliged. Apparently, though, the Old Bill had given Greeny a bit of extra treatment, causing him to spend many months in hospital. As Arthur found out later, the Old Bill had the needle to Greeny more than the stall holders, owing to the fact that Greeny had given the Bill a terrible beating a while before. Greeny had also given grief to Benny Hall in Sunshine's spieler, so all of the Jewish mob were very happy with Arthur, who had always grown up with the Yiddishers and they had a good rapport. Arthur then had a bad fall out with the Titanics, who were a stronger and more intelligent gang of villains. It began when one of their firm started giving grief to the Brick Lane stall holders. They had the Old Bill straightened, so they set Arthur's firm up and they all got nicked. But it wasn't illegal to carry guns in those days and so the only evidence was intent. They were all acquitted.

But things began to develop in the East End when it all blew up in the Blue Coat Boy public house in Bishopsgate. This was when Arthur heard that an old friend of his, George King, who had spent time with Arthur in Borstal, had befriended a man called Isaac Boggard and Boggard's accomplice, Philip Shorck. Isaac Boggard was known as 'Darkie the Coon'. He was Jewish and a very villainous character. He had amassed quite a number of convictions for violent disorders, with police and other local hard men. He carried a gun openly in his belt and they let it be known that they were gunning for Harding. Arthur Harding also had a very hard firm around him who's favourite tool was a six-shooter. And so a meeting was made and they met in the Blue Coat Boy. Boggard immediately offered Harding a drink. Harding as quickly threw it into Boggard's face, glass as well, then all hell let loose. Harding's firm had seven guns between them and they inflicted quite a lot of damage. It was reported after eight members of the Harding gang were found guilty of various charges: 'EAST END VENDETTA GANG BROKEN UP AT LAST'.

The state of lawlessness and terrorism existing in the East End revealed by the Vendetta case was the subject of strong remarks made by Mr Justice Avory at the Old Bailey on Saturday, 23 December 1911. On passing sentence on the eight prisoners in this case, he said that this riot was one of the worst which could be dealt with, owing to the fact that Boggard and King had gone to Old Street for police protection and Arthur Harding and a few of his men had tried to storm the police station with guns. Avory went on to say that some of them went armed to the precincts of a court of law to dispense justice of their own kind and he wished to say that the conditions of things disclosed by evidence – that a portion of London should be infested by a number of criminals and ruffians armed with loaded revolvers, ought not to be tolerated any longer and if the existing law was not strong enough to put a stop to it, some remedial legislation was necessary. The sentences followed: Arthur Harding, 21 months' hard labour to be followed by three years' penal servitude; Charles Callaghan, two years' hard labour; William Spencer, 18 months' hard labour to be followed by three years' penal servitude; William Andrews, 12 months' hard labour; Steven Cooper, three years' penal servitude; William Newman, 15 months' hard labour; Thomas Taylor, two years' hard labour; Robert Wheeler, 15 months' hard labour. They were charged with rioting, assault, shooting with intent and causing grievous injury.

Arthur Harding spent his time in Portland getting fit and strong and reading law. After his release, he was in trouble again, but his law studies stood him in good stead and he was acquitted a couple of times defending himself.

However, he spent most of the First World War years in prison, mainly in Dartmoor or Parkhurst. He spent in all another ten years in these prisons and whilst I was in Dartmoor his name was still remembered as belonging to a very tough man. It seems to be some coincidence that I found I was retracing the steps of characters like Arthur Harding and I suppose of many others. I have met quite a few people who have noticed the similarity in the paths we have trodden. Many who went to Portland became quite notorious later in life. I think it was the fact that to get through the spartan, harsh and brutal life that was Portland you had to come through it with a certain steely determination that you could face any adversary. Portland had the reputation of being the harshest.

But my introduction to the penal system came about 35 years after Harding, so it would not be hard for me to imagine that it would take a very tough man indeed to come through a few years of that regime. I knew what it was like to be subjected to brutality and I had suffered greatly at the hands of those in authority whilst being in St Vincent's approved school. But those years had taught me that you are on your own and it's up to you to respond to brutality.

At the time that I was recovering from my near fatal clash with the Richardsons, Ronnie was responsible for one of the most sinister moments of my life. One night I was driving home, having picked up Brenda, the girl from the Pigalle show who I was living with, when I heard on the car radio that a man had been shot in the Mile End Road. Brenda immediately said to me, 'That's where you take me for a drink sometimes. I wonder if that's anything to do with your friends?'

I didn't say anything, as I had been drinking in the Grave Maurice with the twins earlier in the evening. When I had left to pick up Brenda, everything had appeared to be quite normal.

When we got to the flat and were preparing to go to bed I switched on the radio to catch the late news. The broadcast mentioned the Blind Beggar pub and I immediately knew that it must have had something to do with the twins as nothing happened in that area without them being aware of it.

It was no surprise to me, therefore, when the phone rang shortly afterwards. It was Reggie. He said to me, 'Do you remember the flat over the shops in Walthamstow?'

'Yes,' I replied.

It was a well-known fact that the flat had been used before to keep people out of the way. Reggie then said, 'I want you to do me a favour. Will you go over to the flat and keep Ronnie company for a while? He'll explain everything to you.'

I turned to Brenda and said, 'I'm going out for an hour or so.'

'It's to do with that shooting isn't it?' she replied. I just smiled and left.

When I arrived at the flat, I drove to the rear entrance. I could see just one light on in the kitchen and the dark silhouette of Ronnie Kray. I climbed the stairs to the flat and knocked on the door. Ronnie came out. He seemed in a buoyant mood and said to me, 'Come in. I've got some good news for you.'

As I entered he took his jacket off and loosened his tie. He poured a drink and said, 'You should have been with me tonight. I shot that fucking Cornell's head right off.'

I couldn't believe how calm he was about it. He never told me exactly why he shot Cornell but I feel that in some way Ronnie was annoyed that Cornell, who was a friend of the Richardsons and Frankie Fraser, was adopting an attitude of bravado because they had done me – a friend of the Krays. It may have been that Ronnie was showing me how things should have been dealt with. I stayed for a while, chatting and having a few more drinks, before I made my way home.

Ronnie and Reggie were pulled in for questioning over that business but were both released for lack of evidence. A short while after this incident, I was sitting in a pub, just around the corner from their house, when they were telling a guy from south London, 'We are going to hold you responsible if that bird comes around to the house and throws any more bricks through the windows.' They were referring to the fact that George Cornell's widow had been to the house in Vallance Road and had thrown bricks through the front windows shouting, 'Murderers!' and a lot of other obscenities.

'It's embarrassing having this kind of thing going on while our mum's at home,' they said.

It was after this that Brenda said to me, 'I have a feeling that something terrible is going to happen and I'd like to get away for a couple of weeks.'

I could see that the type of life I was living – which seemed quite normal to me – was having rather an adverse affect on her. I started to notice how nervous she was getting, not for any specific reason, but because of the atmosphere surrounding the people she was mixing with. Her friends in show business knew that the guy she was living with, though a nightclub owner, was connected in some way with some pretty heavy people. In those days the Krays were establishing themselves and I was quite willing to help as they had been good to me. I don't think any of us saw ourselves as bad people – it was just a way of life.

For instance, one evening Reggie and I were in a club in north London when some people made some remarks and looked menacing. Reggie said to me, 'I think we've got a slight problem. I'm going to do this guy – you cop for the other one.' It was all over in a few moments but the word spread like wildfire. It was situations like this that added to the mystique of the Krays.

It was obvious to Brenda that things like this were going on. She'd overhear one-sided conversations on the telephone and she'd see the men go into a huddle away from the girls when we were discussing, for example, what to do in the event of a comeback after a member of a rival firm got hurt. It all seemed more sinister than it was. She'd see the comings and goings of men who may have looked heavy to her, although they were often just inviting the Krays to some social or sporting event. Quite a lot of these people would adopt the dress and air of the gangsters they'd seen on the screen but they were just acting a part, proving to their friends that they were friends of the mob.

Brenda never really got used to this way of life. When I first met her she was an extremely attractive woman, full of life and very bubbly and she worked very hard. One day she would be off to Southampton to do a show for STV, the next it would be a modelling assignment. She was doing a pantomime with Norman Wisdom at Golders Green and then she started to work at the Embassy club in the show with Davy Kaye. On the odd times that we would be together she'd complain that instead of relaxing we were always out meeting my friends, that the phone would go and we'd be off to another meeting. She said, 'It's making me scared.'

I could see that she needed a rest so I suggested we go on holiday.

'I don't want a holiday but I would like to go to see my family in Leeds,' she said.

This seemed a good idea to me so we packed a few things and drove to Leeds. We went straight to Roundhay where Brenda's mum lived. I dropped her off there and went to book into the Queens Hotel. We didn't want her mum to think badly of her boyfriend and things were still pretty strait-laced in those days.

The visit worked wonders for Brenda. Within a couple of days, she was her old bubbly self again. I would pick the family up and take them to lunch and meet all their friends. I was introduced as a businessman from London and I could see that Brenda's family were very proud of her.

At that time Leeds, like most cities, had one or two good nightclubs and because of the lax gambling laws, most clubs would have a few gaming tables. The revenue from the tables would enable the clubs to afford the best cabaret entertainers. I decided to take Brenda and her family to the Cabaret Club in North Street on the night before we went back to London. To make sure that we had a nice time, I thought I would introduce myself the day before. The general manager there turned out to be Eugene Lacy and the last time I'd seen him was in Dartmoor, where he was doing 12 years. We were both surprised to be meeting under such different circumstances.

Eugene introduced me to his right-hand man, Frank Kurylo and told the staff that I was a friend of the governor and to see that my company had a memorable evening. I can honestly say that I still remember that night as one of my best. Brenda was overjoyed as she was introduced from the stage as a local girl who had done well in London.

Frank went on to become Danny la Rue's personal minder and sometimes I would bump into him in Leeds, when I visited the Bridge Inn, where the landlord, Ray Jessop, is a friend of mine.

After the Richardson gang had gone to prison, following their convictions for torturing their victims, I decided I needed to forget about them and look to the future. I was getting a fair living, but the only trouble was that I was doing too much travelling. One week I would be in London, then Nottingham or a period in Manchester and Liverpool. It was like a fast train going nowhere. I was enjoying the journey but I couldn't get off.

I realised that I had become dissatisfied with life in general. I had good days but that is all it was – a day here and a day there. I had thousands of pounds go through my hands, yet I didn't own any property, had no insurance or investments. I felt that one day I was going to end up old and friendless, with nowhere to go except prison. I could see myself becoming one of the many men I'd observed over the years stumbling around the exercise yard 'bumming' for a bit of tobacco. I was finding it hard to carry on living a life that had no purpose.

It was shortly after my war with the Richardson mob that I met Brian Beck. I was still working to regain my fitness and I had to start getting some money. It was quite fortuitous that I met Brian at that time, as I was at a pretty low ebb and he was just the kind of chap to cheer me up. He was a typical lovable rogue – nothing ever seemed to get him down.

He had just finished a three-year prison sentence for putting loaded dice into a casino in south Wales. This was the first time anyone had been prosecuted for any misdeeds in a casino, as gaming houses had only recently become legal. Brian had not been put off by his little spell in Cardiff Prison and he thought we could get rich quick if we worked as a team. It was a new game to me, but it didn't take me long to learn the ropes. We did very well. We travelled all over the country together and we started to get a few quid together.

We have stayed friends for well over thirty years, but after I had gone to prison as a bank robber, I lost touch with Brian. One day though, I was watching a TV programme with Lenny Bennett called *Punch Lines* and there was Brian, with his adopted stage name, as large as life in one of the celebrity boxes. It didn't surprise me, as I knew that Brian had quite a bit of talent and he had worked on it while he was inside.

I was pleasantly surprised recently, when he turned up at my bar and got up on stage to entertain the customers with a few songs and some humorous stories of how we both got a living many years ago.

It was about this time that I met George Downing in a club in Manchester and my life took a different direction.

# 17.

## BETTING COUPS, CARD SHARPS AND CASINOS

George was one of the most flamboyant characters I ever met. When I first knew him, he owned three casinos in Liverpool and had a string of racehorses. He had a beautiful house near Southport, a Rolls Royce, a lovely wife and family. A few years ago I met him in Manchester and he was very ill. He had fallen on hard times but he still had his happy-go-lucky attitude. He was a good friend and it was a privilege to know him.

He asked me to come to work with him almost as soon as we'd met. The first thing we did was pull off a coup with one of his horses, a dead cert he'd been holding back for the right race. George used to manage a few entertainers and he had a showband appearing at a club in the north-east. So we took a few thousand pounds to Newcastle and met the road manager, a nice guy called Dave, who I still see now and again at the races. George left the money with Dave, together with instructions to organise the boys from the band to go to a different town each on the day of the race and find as many betting shops as they could. When we were ready, we would instruct them on how to go about putting the money on the horse.

A couple of days later George and I went back to his house near Southport, having already dropped money off in the Midlands and London and been to see the trainer of the horse. We were now ready. We arrived back at George's house at about 7 a.m. on the day of the race and the phone soon started ringing. The boys were told to put the money on the horse in bets of no more than £50 each. I then drove to Birkenhead, went to a taxi firm and asked if any of the drivers backed horses. They all pointed to one guy.

I said, 'I want you to drive me to as many betting shops as you can. I'll pay your fare and give you £10 for yourself and you can have a tenner on a cert winner.'

I was lucky – my man knew every betting shop in Birkenhead. As I came back to the car and wrote the address on each slip, the driver could hardly contain himself.

'What's the horse, guv?' he asked eagerly.

I said, 'Don't worry, you'll be in on it a couple of minutes before the off.'

When we got to the last betting shop, I took the driver in with me and just before the off, told him the name of the horse. He looked it up in the paper and said, 'This hasn't got a chance. It's never been placed in about ten runs.'

'Don't worry, write your bet out. It's going to win today,' I said confidently.

Reluctantly he put his tenner on our horse. His face was a picture when the horse took up the running in the last furlong and kept on to win by a distance.

I did 23 betting shops in Birkenhead and in total we covered over 1,030. It took three days before we got all the money in from around the country. George and I then drove to London where we booked into the Hilton Hotel and met the trainer and jockey to give them their cut.

Then I went to bed as I hadn't had a sleep for about five days. But not George. He went straight off to Crockfords to play a couple of shoes at chemin-de-fer.

After this episode, my lifestyle changed. Every day it would be racing or casinos and lots of travelling. Being a gambler was as glamorous as my previous way of life, but there was none of the violence I had come to accept as normal. I was happy making lots of money and meeting many interesting people.

Because I had organised the Joe Louis event in Manchester some friends of mine asked if I thought they could make a few quid by taking Billy Conn on a tour of personal appearances in the north of England. Billy Conn was the ex-light-heavyweight champion of the world who had come nearer than anyone to beating Joe Louis when Louis was the world champion. I thought it would be a good draw if he appeared in George Downing's casinos in Liverpool. So we did a deal and I took Billy Conn to Liverpool and arranged to meet the press at the Press Club. But just before we went to the Press Club, I took Billy to Tommy McArdle's Victoria club as a special favour to Tommy, who was one of the great characters of Liverpool club life and loved his boxing. We had a great couple of weeks whilst Billy Conn was in Lancashire. We took him to Haydock Park races where we opened a couple of bottles of champagne with Sir Matt Busby. We stayed at George's house for a couple of weeks and Billy said it was the best couple of weeks he'd had in many years. We certainly enjoyed his company.

At this time we became very friendly with another guy who had a couple of casinos in the East Midlands. Dudley Grace is still one of my best friends and he and George were similar in many ways and great to be with. All three of us went to Miami with a gambling junket (a cut-price holiday arranged for casino members to visit another club abroad) and met Dino Cellini, who was the casino boss. Dudley introduced George to Dino and from then on George was in the casino morning, noon and night, giving all of the croupiers heart attacks with his fearless gambling. When Dino was in London, George and I had dinner with him in the Colony Club. George, who had been losing pretty heavily, borrowed a few thousand pounds on Dino's signature. Quite a few weeks went by before Dino said to me, 'Have you seen George lately?'

I knew what he meant, so I mentioned to George that he should take a trip to London and settle with Dino.

George said, 'Don't worry about it, I'll give him a ring in a day or two.'

But about a week or so later George phoned me to ask, 'Eric, will you go and sort that problem out at the Colony? I've had a visitor to my house and he said some very sinister things about paying debts.'

I went to see Dino and sorted things out. Dino was quite unruffled by the situation. He said, 'Unfortunately, Eric, these things have to be sorted out like this. Everyone must understand that they can't ignore a debt. Tell George to come and have some dinner and we'll all be friends.' That was the end of the matter.

I was now spending a lot of time with Dudley Grace. We'd meet at one of his casinos in Nottingham or Derby and arrange to go racing the next day. One particularly memorable week started at the Cheltenham Festival which, in my opinion, is the greatest meeting in the country. Dudley and I had taken along about £3,000 each, which 25 years ago was a fair lump of dough. After the first day of the three-day meeting, we hadn't backed a single winner, but Dudley said to me, 'Don't worry, there's a good poker game at the 21 Club this evening.' So we went to our hotel to get changed and have a bite to eat. Then after a bit of socialising in the hotel bar, we went over to the 21 Club where there was a very big game in progress.

Knowing Dudley's prowess with the cards, I had sat back to await the inevitable outcome, when I realised that things weren't going according to plan and Dudley finally got pulled into a big pot. We were left without a shilling between us and we still had the hotel bill to pay. We tramped back to the hotel, had a few drinks then bumped into a pal of ours, Billy Foulkes from Sheffield. We didn't have to tell him the story, Billy had been through it all himself on many occasions, so he loaned us a couple of hundred quid.

We went back to the track, where we bumped into a Catholic priest at the bar and he started to tell me about this horse owned by a friend of his in Ireland. Dudley was smiling and getting the drinks set up and I wandered out to look at the price of the priest's friend's horse; it was 10–1. I stuck £100 on it and went back to the bar to tell Dudley what I'd done. He nearly had a fit and said, 'I was going to have the lot on the favourite, it can't be beaten.'

With a certain amount of trepidation we went out to watch the race. It wasn't many minutes later that we were shouting the priest's friend's horse up the hill on the way to the winning post. We kept the priest with us for the next 24 hours and we backed about another four winners. On the third day, the priest was still drunk when he flew back to Ireland and Dudley and myself went on our way.

Next stop was Long Eaton dog track where we knew that we would be given a bit of useful information – and there was always a big poker game after the dogs had finished. We got a few quid at Long Eaton then had a day's rest.

Then Dudley told me of a coup that was being set up in Leicester which was about to be put into motion. It was a rather clever but simple plot. There was a guy who was an expert at picking locks and he'd already got into the Ambassadors Club in Leicester while it was closed. He then opened the cupboard where the casino kept the 'kem' playing cards (these were plastic cards made to stop anyone marking them and they could only be marked by an expert using a special dye). He substituted his own marked cards for the dozen packs the casino had and all he had to do then was to sit in with an accomplice and it wouldn't be long before all the money came their way. Within a few days we had cleaned up and won thousands of pounds.

Dudley and myself had quite a lot of strange experiences in the gambling world. One of the most memorable periods of my life started with what I at first thought was a coincidence – I was later to find out it was no such thing.

Dudley and I were having a night out at the Talk of the Town, in London, when a guy lumbered past our table knocking over a bottle of champagne. I immediately jumped up to remonstrate with him, whereupon he became very apologetic and ordered a bottle of the club's best champers for us. He was very charming and apologetic, so much so that I felt sorry for his embarrassment and invited him to join us in a drink, which he did. When he paid for the bottle we couldn't help noticing that he had a roll of money so big he could hardly pull it out of his pocket.

All we knew at this point was that his name was Joe Robino and he was from the States. He was one of the biggest men I've ever met, weighing about 25 stone. With his big smiling face, he seemed quite harmless. We naturally drifted into conversation about what he did for a living and very shortly we were being invited to Joe's room at the Hilton for a drink and a game of cards.

In London there is a very popular game called rummy (outside London they call it London rummy). Anyway, Big Joe said it was rather like a game he had played with his mum back home when he was a kid. We fell for it hook, line and sinker and over the next couple of hours, he cleaned Dudley and me right out. We were absolutely dumbstruck and had to have a drink and some sandwiches to recover while Joe went for a shower.

He left all of the money he'd won on the shelf of an open wardrobe. When he came out of the shower I saw him glance towards the cash, then he sat down and said, 'Take your money back, you had no chance of winning with me.' He told us what his plan had been from the very first time he'd joined us in the Talk of the Town. He wanted to meet someone who knew all the ropes about the private games in London, or anywhere else for that matter. Just for introducing him and looking after him we would be on 40 per cent of all his winnings. Dudley didn't fancy it and he had his business to think of, but I decided to give it a go.

The first club I took Joe to was the 45 Club in Cromwell Road. It was quite normal for me to go there as I used the place regularly and I also had a business interest in the place. It was ideal as Joe told me he didn't care if there were hustlers or professionals there, he could handle them. Most of the gambling clubs in Earl's Court and Kensington were full of grafters looking for easy pickings, but by now I sat on the same side of the table as Joe, so I thought I would be able to spot something. I also took all the side bets, so I had a very big interest in what he was winning.

I watched Joe very carefully when he played and I couldn't believe my eyes. I saw him pick up his hand and, to use a gambler's expression, he would have a handful of dolly mixtures. Then after two or three dips at the pack, his hand would be 'pat' and he'd call up. It was uncanny. I watched him operate hundreds of times in various clubs throughout Britain and I never ever saw what he did. I made thousands of pounds with Joe.

I was in the Colony Club one night having dinner with George Raft and Dino Cellini when I asked them if they knew Joe.

Dino said, 'Eric, whatever you do, don't play with him or he'll skin you alive. He's the best and his photo is in every casino in the States. That's why he's over here.'

I didn't say any more but when I saw Joe I told him what I'd heard and he just laughed.

He said, 'Don't worry about them, you'll get a better living with me and certainly more laughs.' He was right about that.

The last time I saw Joe was as I was going into the Mount Club in Mayfair. There was an Australian guy telling Joe that the place was closed – we couldn't understand it as it was always open. Joe and I went for a drink and I saw the Aussie later that night and he said to me, 'I'm sorry I couldn't say anything about what happened earlier on, as I didn't know who the big guy was, but Scotch Jack Buggy was shot in there earlier on and they were still getting rid of the body.'

I took the story with a pinch of salt at first, then I read a while later that Scotch Jack's body had been found, rolled in a carpet, by two off-duty policemen fishing in the sea.

I was also acting as minder to some of the Arabs coming over to London with money to burn. They all loved to gamble and never seemed to go to bed. A friend of mine made his living by organising parties and trips to casinos and nightclubs for clients who were mainly Arabs. He would ring me and say, 'There's this prince' – they were all princes or sheiks – 'who wants to go to a few clubs and spielers and he also wants to go to the Derby. Would you look after him?' I'd agree and then meet my friend later at the Stork Club where I'd be paid. I could earn £500 on a good day. I met some great guys from the Middle East, including the son of the Jordanian ambassador who was to be a good friend for quite some time. He was also a very good card player.

It was around this time that I started to hear rumours that Jack the Hat had been murdered and that he had died a pretty horrific death. It was also said that he had been lured to his death by some people who were supposed to be his friends, as well as mine. Gradually the story began to take shape and it seemed that the Lambrianou brothers had made sure Jack had enough drink inside him to be incapable of defending himself. That, to me, is a cold, calculating, heartless way to treat someone who was supposed to have once been your friend.

I couldn't help thinking of the time I was nearly hacked to death in the basement off Tottenham Court Road – Jack must have felt much as I did when Reggie Kray stabbed him to death. There was a difference though – my row was a gang fight brought about by a clash of personalities; Jack was completely unaware of the fate that was waiting for him when he was drinking at the bar of the Regency Club with people slapping him on the back and telling him what a great guy he was. And then when he was nearly incapable, saying, 'Let's go to the Kray Twins' party.'

I often think of all the times that I had with Jack. I couldn't have had a better mate and I can relate a score of incidents that prove Jack was a different person to the out-of-control gangster I've read about lately. I've spoken, quite recently, to people who knew Jack as well as I did and most say he was the type of guy I've described. Admittedly, there are others who say, 'Eric, you didn't know him a couple of years before he died – he'd changed.'

Jack must have changed a fair bit but I can't imagine him deserving the kind of death that befell him. One of the saddest moments of my life came when I met Anne, Jack's ex-wife, at a party. She asked me if I knew exactly what had happened to Jack. I told her what I had heard and she said, 'Jack never deserved that kind of death. He was a good man, he never meant any harm to anyone.' I was completely choked up.

I like to remember Jack as the chap who stuck with me through some pretty grim times, someone you could always rely on. I'm sure I'm not the only person who remembers Jack with a lot of affection – he was a brave, tough, fun-loving guy.

I was also beginning to hear rumours about the disappearance of my good friend, Frank Mitchell, who had apparently been gunned down after he had been sprung from Dartmoor by Teddy Smith and Albert Donoghue (who was one of Ronnie Kray's gofers).

I wasn't convinced that those two had anything to do with the killing of Frank. Firstly, they'd have been frightened out of their skins at the thought of being asked to do Frank in and, secondly, because he was such a likeable guy, nobody would have wanted to do it anyway.

Although the rumour was very strong, no one seemed to know who had actually killed Frank, but the stories still persisted in the underworld.

Apart from the sadness about losing two friends, I was otherwise coping with life. I spent quite a lot of time commuting between London, Nottingham and Liverpool. I'd sometimes pop in to see old mates when I was visiting London and sometimes there would be a bit of lucrative work. It was at one of these particular jaunts that I renewed my acquaintance with John McVicar.

# 18.

## JOHN MCVICAR
## AND THE AUSSIE SHOPLIFTERS

I first met John McVicar when I was the owner of the Emerald Beach Club in Soho. John was in his early twenties and he started to frequent the West End in the company of his sister, Janice and a few of her girlfriends. He was always very quiet and polite and seemed out of place with most of the clientele of the club, as they were mainly guys who had acquired a few quid and wanted everyone to see that they had been successful – notwithstanding quite a lot of them would be skint within a few weeks. John always seemed to have a few notes to spend but didn't talk much about what he did. His sister was a bubbly type of girl, well liked by everyone and it was always nice to see them in the club.

I then took over the Brown Derby Club which was frequented by much the same clientele. I saw John a few times and then heard that he was in trouble and had received a fairly long sentence for armed robbery. As the years pass, you hear or read things in the newspapers about people that you've met and so it was with John. I read that he and some other cons had overpowered the screws on their way from one prison to another and eventually had their sentences extended to over 20 years.

A few years later I had given up the club business and had gone back to crime myself. It's a funny life; you come out of prison hoping to go straight, build up a business, work 16 hours a day and as soon as you get on your feet you have the law harassing you for every trivial thing they can think of, until you are forced out of business and back into crime. They'd come to the club at all times, checking that all the customers were members or bona fide signed-in guests of a particular member, checking a genuine meal was supplied for the supper licence extension. It was impossible to stick to the letter of the law and be successful, as people wouldn't come to the club if they were being hassled all of the time. I couldn't hold a licence with my criminal record, so I had to find someone else to be the licence holder. Of course, when the club was charged with some infringement, it was the licensee who was fined and as a result, licensees were hard to come by. In the end I was forced out of the business and ended up doing the same as most of my ex-customers – executing a robbery and going to the various clubs to spend the proceeds.

It was a few days after a particular robbery when I read the papers and saw that there had been a daring escape from Durham Prison. One of the people who had escaped was John McVicar, together with Walter Probyn, my old friend from the Wandsworth days. Alas, poor old Walter had broken his leg in their dramatic bid for freedom.

Like most people, I followed the story for the next 48 hours, while the press made John public enemy No. 1 and said he was surrounded and couldn't get away from the north of England. I then went on my usual rounds, ending up in a club called Oscars in Albermarle Street, Mayfair. As soon as I walked in, a friend came over and said, 'I've been phoning around for you. There's someone here to see you.'

I thought I was dreaming – there stood John McVicar at the end of the bar. Every policeman in Britain must have been thinking what a feather in his cap it would be if he could nick John and there he was calmly drinking a soft drink in one of the most popular clubs in London.

I was working with a little team from north London at the time and one of them was from a well-known boxing family. No one would think of his house so I took John there straight away. John, myself and a couple of pals, sat around half the night chatting and generally working out John's immediate plans. He was safe where he was for a couple of days, but then he needed to get together with his missus and little boy. We organised a few quid, clothes and a car and with his missus got them a flat in south London.

I saw John a few times after that. There were a few hairy incidents at the time and we nearly walked into an ambush once. John was to meet me and another guy in Stoke Newington. He arrived at the meet early and decided to go into a betting shop nearby. Quite by chance, there was a policeman inside who had been involved with John on a case before he went inside. Luckily John recognised the policeman at the same time as the policeman recognised him. As we arrived we saw the Old Bill charging up mobhanded. If John had not spotted the policeman and he had followed John, we'd have walked into a trap.

John, meanwhile, sprinted off and being a pretty fit guy he soon disappeared from view. Discreetly leaving the scene ourselves, we saw John drive off in the car we'd found for him so we knew he was safe for the time being.

Some of the people that I worked with in those days were like me and enjoyed travelling. We would spend quite a lot of time on the Continent, mainly in France, Italy and Switzerland. It was amazing how quickly we would find who the local villains were. I think it is because all villains like the night life, no matter what country they are from and once you are noticed spending plenty of money in the clubs the locals soon cotton on. So it wasn't long before we were meeting people in Shalako's in Brussels, the Red House in Zurich, or the Lucky Strip in Paris and swapping tales with each other. One guy we met in Paris was an old retired villain named Jacques. He had a hotel in Paris and another home in Vichy. Jacques was to become a very useful connection for me, especially when I was travelling around the Continent with the shoplifting gang.

In the early '60s, just before I was released from prison, I used to manage to get hold of the odd newspaper, even though I would probably be in the punishment block. One day I read an article entitled 'The Australian Shoplifting Gang'. What made it interesting to me was that a guy who had been mentioned in the article and had been arrested with the Aussie gang was an old friend of mine and was rated as a very smart operator among the fraternity. So I thought: what is he doing mixed up with a load of petty thieves? Then it seemed that nearly every day there was an article in the press about the influx of Aussie criminals coming into this country and, far from being petty criminals, they were getting away with millions of pounds.

It wasn't long after my release from jail that I met a lot of these guys as they moved in the same circles as myself and some of them used the Brown Derby while I was the proprietor. They were not just the ordinary shoplifters. They would walk into a jeweller's shop, very smartly dressed; invariably with a woman wearing an expensive mink coat and carrying a bouquet of flowers, all props to distract the assistants; they would cleverly open the showcases or the window displays and come away with thousands of pounds worth of diamonds.

They were not only into shoplifting, but were some of the smartest con-artists I have ever met and done business with. It was the type of thing that now appealed to me, along with gambling, as no one ever got hurt and there were some pretty rich pickings and relatively light punishment if you were caught, plus the opportunity to travel regularly.

With all of the publicity that the Australians were getting it was a lot better if they had a few people with them who didn't speak with their accent, to 'front up', whilst visiting certain well-known Bond Street jewellers. I was to spend a couple of years with our Commonwealth cousins and I made a lot more money with those people than I did as a bank robber.

The first Australian I was to do any business with was a guy with a similar background to my own. He had done 15 years in Australia and was a known tough guy. He had realised there were people making a fair living who were only risking a few months in prison if they got caught. His name was Keith and he, like a lot of the Aussies, found that there was a much bigger pond to 'fish in' by getting a flight to the mother country and having an extended holiday.

I soon came to know everyone in the team. Nearly every one of them had a nickname, most, self-explanatory. They were Jack the Liar, Crying Steve, Morrey the Head and Roy the Boy amongst others. There were about twenty of the original team including some very smart girls, such as Carmen, who I was to visit later in Holloway Prison when she was on remand, awaiting trial for stealing nearly £250,000 worth of jewels from the Hilton Hotel. I also remember Grace, an elegant lady, who got out of a northern town with her bra stuffed with diamonds.

I was to have many escapades with my Australian friends. One of the cleverest of the team was a guy called Barry. He was a great character, always laughing and absolutely fearless. I remember at the height of all the publicity about the Australian gang, the police told the press that they were to give a lecture and demonstration at a particular jewellers on how best to combat this rising new crime wave. Barry couldn't wait for the day and he duly turned up at the jeweller's where the police were demonstrating the best methods of preventing the criminals from stealing jewels. You can imagine the laughter from the team when the evening papers splashed the headline: 'JEWEL THIEF STEALS EMERALDS WHILST POLICE DEMONSTRATE ANTI-THEFT METHODS'.

I went all over the Continent with Barry, Roy, Keith, Danny and Grace. We had some great times. One of the best things that happened to us at this time was when we booked into a nice hotel just off the Rue Lafayette in Paris. We got into conversation with the proprietor, Jacques, and found he was an old retired villain. Within a very short time he was buying all of our gear, so we didn't have to keep taking the risks by bringing the fruits of our labour back through the customs at Heathrow.

In Paris alone, we had about ten good tickles from jewellers' shops. In fact we were responsible for one of the biggest heists ever and did so using variations on a standard method for tricking the staff. It all seemed so easy at the time. It was nothing for us to fly out of Paris to Switzerland in the morning, and to be back the same day with the contents of some jeweller's window. We found that Amsterdam was a veritable Aladdin's cave. We could go to practically any street in Amsterdam and find enough work to keep us in absolute luxury. We stayed in good hotels in all the cities we worked in. One day we'd be in the American Hotel in Amsterdam, the next it would be the FrankfurterHof in Frankfurt or the SwitzerHof in Zurich, then possibly the Grand in Stockholm, or the Palace in Milan. Then, when we'd get back to London, there would be another member of the team with a different scheme to go for.

Danny, one of the Godfathers to the Australian contingent, always had somebody arriving from Oz with some new scam or other. One of the best of these was a guy who arrived accompanied by a little chap who was a dead ringer for Ron Hutchinson – the top Australian jockey who was riding in England at that time. As I was to find out, it was no coincidence that he was his lookalike. All they had to do was find the big punters, which was pretty easy to do if you kept your eyes and ears open at the race tracks. They would engage the punter in conversation, arrange a series of meetings and, by a strong coincidence, the Ron Hutchinson lookalike would arrive at the restaurant or bar or wherever the meeting was being held. They would then get into deep conversation with Danny and pass over what was supposed to be inside information, for which the 'Hutch' would be seen to receive a large packet of money, presumably for past information provided. The punter would be very impressed, especially when he was manoeuvred into going to the car park to see the Hutch off to his car, which always had some jockey's gear lying casually on the back seat.

It was then that the hard work had to be done by finding a winner to give to the punter. Danny was a pretty good tipster anyway and by the time the punter was ready, he would trust the boys completely. The whole art of the con game is to make the punter impatient to get on with the business, so if anything went wrong, you could always say, 'You should have had more patience and then things would have gone right.' However, after a time they found that by getting a few punters, they could give two or three red-hot tips in the same race to the individuals, thereby guaranteeing a 'pay-off' to at least one very satisfied punter. This game eventually came apart when, a few years later, another jockey, George Moore, came from Australia and the same lookalike method was used. However, when a few disgruntled punters started to threaten the real George Moore at the race tracks and started to send nasty letters to his home, Moore being a completely innocent party to the scam, went to the police. I believe the publicity forced the fraudster to go back to Australia.

Everybody seemed to benefit from the influx of the Australians, especially the club owners and restaurant proprietors in Bayswater and Queensway as it was normal for all of the team to meet in the various clubs that were dotted around the area. There was a favourite place in Bayswater Road called the Caravelle Club. It was a regular haunt for the criminal fraternity and also for many actors and sportsmen. One actor who seemed to use the club quite regularly was Ian Hendry, who was a very popular chap with the Australians. He had recently made a film called *The Hill*, where he played the part of a brutal prison guard. One of the Aussies took umbrage to Ian after seeing the film and started taking him to task for being so brutal to the prisoners. Everyone soon realised that the guy who'd seen the film had got the part that Ian had played mixed up with reality and that things could get out of hand. Then Ian barked at the guy, 'Stand to attention and put that drink down when you speak to me.' The Australian, without thinking, did as he was told and everyone in the club burst out laughing. The tension was gone and Ian became one of the most popular guys in the club.

A great friend of Ian Hendry's, who used to visit the club regularly, was Ronald Frazer, another well-known actor, who used to relate great stories about Robert Mitchum. We would spend hours in that club drinking and telling stories. Whenever any of the girlfriends of the Oz crowd came over from Sydney or Melbourne, they would get very excited and come to the various clubs and drink at the bar with actors like Ian Hendry, Ronnie Frazer and Sean Connery. Sean was a really charming fellow and I remember one Australian girl just couldn't believe she was standing next to the great man when he said, 'I've got to play in a golf tournament in Bognor tomorrow, so I'll have to get to bed early.'

I said to Sean, 'I'll give you a lift to your hotel.'

When I got back to the club, the Australian girl was in a state of shock and could hardly speak. It took her months to get over the fact that he was just an ordinary guy who had gone off to bed early – on his own – so as to be on time for golf the next morning.

There's a lovely story that arose from the association between the acting fraternity and the Aussies. A well-known actor was about to get engaged and casually mentioned that he was looking for a nice ring for his prospective bride. The word was given out that there was a customer for a good ring. Roy the Boy just happened to be in Harrods a couple of days later and asked one of the assistants to show him some rings. With a little bit of sleight of hand, he acquired a nice stone worth £5,000. He immediately brought it over to the club and sold it for £2,000. That ring would be worth well over £50,000 now, so some lucky actor made a good investment in his early days.

I believe most of the Aussie team eventually ended up back in Australia after a tour through the United States, where they apparently got some pretty rich pickings.

After the Aussies went back home I hung around in London for a while and then went back to work with George Downing. We would travel about quite a lot: Manchester, Liverpool and Southport, always using various casinos to pick up a few bob. It was amazing to see the number of grafters who were all using the same clubs. You could walk into a club in Southport and see Geordie, who every card sharp and grafter knew, then a couple of days later you could walk into another club in Birmingham and there would be the same Geordie. Or maybe you'd see Scotch Alec, who happened to be Greek. It didn't matter who you saw but that you saw then working at all. I don't know where the nickname came from but Scotch Alec was a remarkable chap who nearly always worked on his own. His only gimmick was a handkerchief he used to mop his brow with. He loved a drink and I've spent many hours with Alec after he'd just cleaned up on some gaming table.

The British casinos in the '60s were like manna from heaven. I think every grafter in the world came here for easy pickings. I've seen them all and seen some amusing incidents in various clubs and casinos all over the country.

I was in a casino in Manchester with George Downing and Joe Marlow when they had the croupier straightened as he was dealing seconds. To make it easier to slip the second card out, instead of the top one, he used french chalk on the cards and when he shuffled, he would do the cut shuffle by running the cards crossways into each other. All of a sudden, he forgot himself and rippled the cards in the normal way and a big cloud of dust went into the air.

There was a stunned silence and a punter who had been losing pretty heavily, got up from the table and left the club. He was back in about twenty minutes with two parcels. He threw one on the table with a thud in front of the croupier and started to open the other. Both contained a small axe.

The fellow said calmly, 'Am I going to have my money back or are we going to duel for it?' There was no argument, the bloke got his money back and everyone went for a drink.

Malcolm Rance was a great character from Manchester who I first met years before in Dartmoor. He was a very tough guy but he'd retired from the heavy game and had learned a bit of sleight of hand. He wasn't as good as some of the chaps I had seen but he still made a fair living. I was in a club in Wales with him one night when he was working the blackjack table with extra cards. He used to sit at the blackjack table with his legs bent up and would lodge the spare cards at the back of his bent leg. Now one of the croupiers tumbled that he was using extra cards and told security. I saw the security man go to phone the police so I tipped off Malcolm. He didn't turn a hair. He called the security bloke over and said, 'Could you organise me some drinks and have one yourself.'

With that he handed the security bloke a tenner to give to the girl at the bar.

Unbeknown to me or anyone else, Malcolm had put the spare cards into the security guy's pocket. When the police came and accused Malcolm he was very indignant and said bitterly, 'This is the way they treat people just because they win.' He demanded that the police search him, which they did. Of course they didn't find anything. Everyone ended up apologising and off we went. I would have loved to have seen the security guy's face when he found the cards.

One of the most embarrassing incidents in my life happened to me in Nottingham around this time. The British middleweight title fight between Wally Swift and Johnny Pritchard was being held at the ice-rink. I had an interest in a business in Nottingham so a few friends had phoned me to ask me to arrange the tickets, hotel, dinner and nightclubs. I was pleased to do this as I hadn't seen some of them for a year. In the end I booked about ten people into the Old Victoria Hotel.

Everyone arrived about midday and we all got together for lunch and a few drinks. I arranged to call at the hotel later and take everyone to the fight. After the fight we went to the Pigalle Club where some ladies joined the company. Then one of the boys said, 'Eric, I hear they have a big chemin-de-fer game in this town?' I told them that it was at the Society Club but it would be hard to get a place at the table. They were still keen, so I said I'd see what could be done.

I took three of the guys to the Society and signed them in. The boss of the club was Polish, a very nice and affable chap, who made us all welcome. I asked him if he could fix a spot in the game for one of my friends. As soon as somebody left the table, he beckoned me saying that there was an empty place. However, when I told my pal that there was an empty place, he said to one of the other guys in the party, who I didn't know, 'Bill, you take the seat while I have a drink.'

I didn't think there was anything suspicious about this until I noticed how often I was hearing 'Neuf à la banc'. Bill was starting to amass a pretty sizeable fortune. By now everyone was surrounding the table, drawn by the phenomenon of a guy doing something like a twelve-timer. I watched him closely but couldn't detect anything untoward, except that every time he got his cards, he made a rather flamboyant gesture towards the canopied lightshade.

Eventually the game broke up with nearly everyone skint apart from Bill who had all of the money. We moved back to the Old Victoria Hotel. It was only when Bill wanted to give me a large bundle of notes, that I was certain the game had been bent. But they denied it when I raised the matter so I had to accept what they said. I left shortly afterwards and went back to my flat.

I was to get a rude awakening in the morning with someone banging loudly on my door. When I looked through the spy-hole I saw Jon the Pole, practically foaming at the mouth. He had a large pack of cards in his hand and when I opened the door, he tossed them all up in the air shouting, 'Neuf! Neuf! Neuf! Where are your friends? I count 20 spare neufs in my box!'

After I had calmed him down, he told me that when he checked the box that all the used cards had been thrown into, he had found 20 spare nines. Eventually I was able to convince him that I had also been duped. It wasn't until a few months later that I obtained the truth. I was at Cheltenham races and bumped into my friend. He admitted to me that Bill had plotted it all before they came to Nottingham. I was also right in my supposition about him ringing the cards as his hands went past the light shade. I don't know who coined the phrase 'honour among thieves' – I've never seen much of it.

When I heard that the Kray Twins had just been arrested, I was saddened but not surprised. I had grown up in the criminal fraternity and had gone along with all of their clichés about themselves – 'We'll stick together', 'I'd die for you', 'We're men of principle'. In reality, 'men of principle' meant 'men of money'. It didn't seem to matter how many principles a man had so long as he had money. A bloke who was spending money with the firm was a lot more important than a guy who would stick with you if you were outnumbered in a battle. I found that all of the people I had been associating with had the gang mentality. They had surrounded themselves with hangers-on who had become mixers and held a certain sway because they had plenty of ready cash and were able to settle a few personal scores. It suited them to mix it for people like Jack the Hat because he openly slagged them off as wimps and hangers-on. When I heard the rumours about what had happened to Jack, I thought, 'So much for sticking together.'

When the Krays and other members of the firm were arrested my first thought was, 'I'm glad I'm away from it all.' I had in fact just pulled a job that had netted myself and a friend a fair bit of money and we were busy enjoying ourselves. But I gave a lot of thought to the twins' mother, Violet, as everyone who met her was impressed by her devotion to her sons. She never saw any bad in them and I knew that she would be thinking that they were being fitted up by the law. She was a wonderful woman.

I followed the story in the press and through the grapevine and it began to emerge that only staunch people were sticking by the twins. I felt a kind of sadness because I had had some good times with them. I realised that because of the kind of hangers-on they had attracted they had gone down a different path to the one they had planned in the early days.

# 19.

## FIRST-DIVISION CRIMINAL

S hortly after my little forays around the British casinos and as a result of a chance meeting in the South of France, I started to associate with some of my old 'bandit' friends. I was staying at a hotel in Nice with a couple of friends and we happened to visit the Mediterranean Casino. As soon as we walked in, we saw a couple of guys I'd known for a few years who were pretty heavily into bank robbery. They assured me that this was purely a pleasure trip after a successful raid in London, so we had a sociable couple of days in Nice and then moved down to San Remo on the Italian Riviera where we spent a lot of time in the casino. But it was costing too much to live in that style, so it wasn't long before we were back in London and I was renewing acquaintances with my old mates. We quickly pulled off a couple of raids that netted some fair money but we were always on the lookout for the 'big one' – the ambition of every first-division criminal.

As the years had passed by and bank-raiders had got more daring, so the security of the banks became more challenging; it also became something of a challenge to beat this increased security. At first, when people started to carry out daylight raids on banks, it was usually as a blagger; that is, snatching the money from the security guards, taking wages or spare cash to a feeder bank. Although security in that area got tighter, you could still easily leap over the counter and take money from the nightsafe and the tills.

Raids were frequent. Those in the know could identify the different operators by their *modus operandi*. We all seemed to use the same clubs and pubs and we became rather like an exclusive social club. It would be nothing

THE BRUTAL TRUTH

for a particular team to ask someone from another to join, if they were short-handed on a particular robbery.

I think I must have met every bank robber who was active at that time, either by 'working' with them or socialising. They were all good company and, with a few exceptions, were all trustworthy.

There were about six teams working the banks in those days and there were about four bank robberies a month, so most 'bandits' (as they were known) would be working about once every six weeks and each would be netting about £5,000 each month. You could buy a fair house for about £15,000 in those days, so you can see how lucrative the game was.

There would come a time, though, when the odd big one would come up and it was good times for all. There were never any 'Mr Bigs' or masterminds, but most bandits were fairly intelligent. They were mostly fearless and respected each other for their individual prowess, whether it was as a driver, for agility or even downright cheekiness.

There were 'characters' on every bank robbery team. I think the guys who stood out a little above the rest were the drivers. There was always a good driver on every team and I've met and been in a car with every one of them. Danny Till, later given a 14-year sentence as one of the Wembley bank robbery team, was, without a doubt, one of the best. But he was about Formula Three class in comparison to Mickey Greene, who was in the top bracket Formula One class.

Mickey Greene was given an 18-year sentence for a string of robberies that made legends of the men who were all sentenced in that infamous trial. This is where the word 'supergrass' was first coined. It was 'Bertie' Derek Small who decided to save his own skin by throwing everyone whom he had ever worked with to the wolves. His closest friends were Mickey Salmon and Mickey Greene and they must have been sick when they read the statements. I believe, though, that they all got on with their time and came out a little wiser than when they went in.

Unfortunately, Mickey Greene has been a marked man since he was released. As a consequence, every time there is a money scam perpetrated, he is alleged to have been involved somehow – it's a matter of 'give a dog a bad name'. The press make him out to be a cross between a superman, arch criminal and a Midas. In fact, he's quite an affable person and I can see that when he is apprehended, if ever, the press will make sure that he won't be given a fair crack of the whip.

The banks started to put bandit-glass up in front of the tellers, so you had to keep yourself fit to enable you to get over the top. Eventually the glass was fitted right up to the ceiling and it became hard to find a bank in London without this type of barrier. So we started to look further afield and eventually we discovered that Cardiff had never had a bank robbery – until then. As I also knew of a safe house in that city, a friend and I went there to have a look at a few banks in the city centre. The first one that interested us was a major bank. On first inspection it looked an ideal job – plenty of money to be had and a very good escape route in the event of anything going wrong. We soon realised, however, that it would take too big a team to do it successfully, but we looked around and found at least half a dozen banks that would be fairly easy to do.

Finally we settled for Barclays, Albert Road, as the getaway route was a lot better than any of the others. Also, the security van which delivered and took money from the bank always arrived on time. We had no difficulty in setting the whole thing up.

After a few weeks of observation, we decided to raid the bank on Monday at 10 a.m. We arranged to travel to Cardiff early on the Sunday to give us time to make sure that everything was in place for the following morning. There was a Transit van with all of our tools; there were two cars as changeover vehicles; and the last check over the getaway route to be organised was made to make sure there were no road blocks since we'd last been over the route. The safe house was a mile away from the city and was the house of an old retired villain who could be trusted. The Transit van had been stolen a week before and the number plates had been changed to correspond to a similar van that we had taken the tax-disc from. Hence there were two identical vans that hadn't been reported missing. We did the same to two Ford Cortinas on the Saturday before the robbery. The one that we took from outside Chelsea football ground, we later discovered, belonged to a police inspector.

When we arrived on the Sunday, I went to my old friend's house to check that he'd rented a couple of lock-up garages. He was rather thrilled at the prospect of being involved in a bank robbery, albeit only in a non-active role. As he pointed out, he was getting a bit old for jumping over bank counters, but he'd settle for the excitement and a few quid, which he could certainly do with.

One of the team had already travelled to Cardiff from Paddington Station with some ordinary-looking baggage, containing two sawn-off shotguns, balaclava helmets, gloves, valises for carrying the money, plus one or two extras that go to make up a bank-robber's working kit. The shells in the shotguns had been doctored to make them non-lethal by taking out the pellets and substituting ordinary household rice. However, they would sound just the same when fired. We were a team of experienced people who had all boxed at various levels – a couple of pro-fighters and the others could look after themselves – in any circumstances, so we didn't need shotguns as weapons. The idea was to create as much confusion as possible whilst we helped ourselves to the rewards.

THE BRUTAL TRUTH

We knew that on Monday at 10 a.m. there would be 14 or 15 night-safe pouches on the ledge behind the counter. There would be four tills open with about £3,000 in each. There would also be a large bag waiting for the security people to take to the main Barclays branch. They would also be delivering a bag of new notes. We knew from experience that it would take us only one minute after entering the bank until we left with the loot. The press later referred to us as the Minute Men.

Everyone knew their job. The bandit-screen was only built to a height of about six feet above the counter, so two men would immediately leap up on to the counter and then drop down inside the working area of the bank. By this time the two security men would have been overpowered by the other two members of the team. The job should have gone according to plan, without a serious hitch; but there was always the chance that the odd incident, either scary or amusing, would occur. This particular robbery had a bit of both.

When the van pulled up outside the bank, the two security men went immediately to the hatch at the rear and, as it opened, took a large package from it. One of them carried the package into the bank while the other, brandishing a baton, followed him in. It was then we struck. My job was to take care of the baton man, who would be standing just inside the door while his mate would go to a communicating door to transfer the money bags. Terry and I went through the door immediately behind them. Terry's job was to smash the glass in the door frame and fire a shot into the ceiling, thus causing maximum confusion. My job had been taken care of in the split-second I'd taken to flatten the guard. The other two were already on their way over the counter.

There were four customers in the bank. I told them all to sit on the floor and nothing would happen to them. Three of them complied without a murmur, but one guy, who was paying in his takings from an ice-cream firm, wanted to argue with the bank staff as to whose money it was. Quite oblivious of the danger he was in, he kept insisting that as he had already put his money on to the bank's counter, it was, therefore, legally in the bank now. The bank teller was begging him to do as he was told and get down. In fact, all the bank staff wanted to do, by this time, was comply with our demands and lie down behind the counter. I took the disputed bag of money from the counter and threw it into the valise with the other we had taken from the security man. Although he'd finally got to the floor with everyone else, the ice-cream man was still giving a running commentary on the legal implications as to liability for the stolen money.

The two chaps behind the counter were hurriedly filling their valise, which was soon bulging with the money from the night-safe pouches and the tills. As they came through the communicating door, they picked up the bags that were waiting for the security men, plus the two which were on our side of the counter. We were all ready to leave. As we came out of the bank a passer-by attempted to obstruct us; he was pushed aside and we leapt into the Transit van for the getaway. That chap was later rewarded for his bravery.

As we pulled away from the bank, we immediately began to pack everything into the two large bags, the money into one and all the equipment into the other. We were soon at the first change-over. I drove one of the Fords to the safe house with the money, while the other dropped the guy with the tools at the station to take the first train out, wherever it was going; eventually to make his way back to London. The cars were parked in another part of the city.

After taking out the 'bung' for my friend, we then cut the money up into equal shares. One of the boys took two shares, his own and one for the guy who had gone with the tools. He made his way back to a van with pigeons in it, as these were his cover. He drove into the countryside, releasing the pigeons as he made his way home. We all met the next day without any hitch. After the usual shopping spree it was out to our favourite club where we analysed the previous day's work. There was the usual feeling of exhilaration and a few laughs of disbelief at the guy who was arguing about the ownership of the money whilst the robbery was in progress. We also had a laugh at the expense of the bank teller, haughtily telling one of our team who had leapt over the bandit-screen, that he shouldn't be this side of the counter – before she realised it was a bank raid. There was also grudging admiration for the guy who had tackled us.

Ironically, it was the takings from the ice-cream firm that allowed the police to finally build up a strong case against us. One of the team had some of this money on him when he was arrested and the cashier from the ice-cream firm recognised his scrawl on the notes. A handwriting expert gave evidence to support it.

I was at the time living with a girl who I'd previously met in a club and we had one of those old-fashioned televisions that looked like a piece of furniture with doors on the front. It also had a large space with speakers on either side with a big gap in between. I put a few thousand pounds into the gap, screwed the back cover on and left it. It was about two weeks after the robbery in Cardiff at about seven in the morning, when there was a knock on the door. Thinking it was a builder, who had come to do some work on the house, I told my girlfriend to tell him to come back as it was still too early in the morning. The sound of her footsteps on the stairs was immediately followed by the heavy thump of boots. I'd heard this sound before and was just sitting up as they burst through the door. I found myself staring down the barrels of two guns.

'Move and you're dead,' said the plain-clothed inspector.

It wasn't difficult to see that I wasn't concealing a weapon as I didn't have a stitch on. They let me pull on my strides and shirt. By this time I could hear them tearing the place apart. There must have been about a dozen of them and the only place they didn't look was inside the back of the television. We were all arrested at the same time, courtesy of a little information from the brother-in-law of one of the team.

We were taken to Cardiff, charged and remanded to Cardiff Prison. We were the first Category-A prisoners to go there and after a trial before Mr Justice Bridge, we were sentenced to long terms of imprisonment. I got ten years.

# 20.

## 'THE ARAB'

After being sentenced for bank robbery, I was sent back to Wandsworth Prison for assessment and allocation. I found that in the years since my release from my previous sentence, a lot had changed inside. Following the Mountbatten Report, a system of categories had been introduced and people such as myself were immediately put down as Category-A. This meant that we were considered to be a danger to the public, other prisoners and to anyone who worked within the prison.

Consequently, a Category-A prisoner was locked in his cell for 23 hours a day and only allowed out into the prison yard to exercise, by himself, under the supervision of three or four screws. This would go on for a couple of months until he was either allocated and sent to a top security Category-A prison, or deemed by the allocation board to be considered worthy of another chance and made Category-B. In the latter case, he was still probably locked up for 23 hours a day, but was allowed to exercise with other prisoners.

Being locked up nearly all day, I had plenty of time to reflect upon my life, both over my past and what the future had to hold for me. It was a pretty gloomy picture. This prison stretch was different to the first. I was older and I knew that if things went wrong for me, I would probably never see life outside of the prison walls again. I had mellowed a lot and had got used to a comfortable lifestyle and now I had the prospect of some pretty spartan times ahead.

I knew, of course, that I still had a fair lump of money hidden, but I didn't think that my girlfriend was the type to wait a few years. I had visions of some other man sleeping in my bed, wearing my clothes and spending my money. I knew from experience how seldom a man's partner will wait for him once he is locked up. In fact I was lucky – she waited a few months before she did the moonlight flit. I was expecting it and when the chaplain came to my cell with a letter in his hand I was a little prepared.

He said, 'The governor's concerned about this letter that's been sent to you and he's asked me to come to speak to you, in case there's anything we can do.'

I thought, 'Well, at least she's taken the time to write to me.' As I read the letter telling me that she had met someone else and that she had been worried about the 'stuff' in the television and burned it, I was hurt but quite calm. I thanked the chaplain for his concern and asked him to thank the governor and told him not to worry that I'd do anything silly.

Getting that letter was the real turning point for me. It brought back the futility of the life I had led, the realities of what a small world the underworld is. I met a lot of good people during my life of crime and rebellion, people I have a lot of respect for, but I also met many who had no redeeming features, who were beneath contempt. Today, being free and being part of the real world, I get an enormous feeling of pleasure and contentment with the simple things of life.

I was rather surprised to find that on my return to prison, not one of the prison staff seemed to want to renew the old antagonisms of the past. I was taken in front of many boards, who were sitting to assess me and my past conduct was nearly always referred to. However, this was done in an enquiring manner, typically trying to understand my present attitudes and whether I still had the same hatred for everyone which I had shown in the past. I used to smile and reply that I couldn't forget all of the things that I had been through and dismiss them easily. I told them that I just wanted to be left as I was and if I was allowed to get on with my time there would be no problems.

Finally I was called in front of the governor and told that I was to be sent back to Dartmoor as a Category-B prisoner. My heart sank upon hearing this news, as I could never imagine being allowed to forget all that had gone on in that place in the past. However, I just nodded and went back to my cell where I sat and thought long about the life I'd led, of the wasted years and whether Dartmoor would be the same. I wanted to think of the more humorous things that had happened but there were so very few of them. I did remember the time Jimmy Kensit, the father of Patsy Kensit, the film star, was in doing a long sentence. He was known as one of the 'bottle' mob (a top pickpocket). Like most of the bottle mob, Jimmy was chirpy and good humoured. There was a screw who looked like a big yokel, but was really a sadistic sod and was always putting someone on report for the most trivial offences. His great day would come every Friday when he got his wages. In those days, they would be paid in pound notes, just a few measly quid. He would take it out of his pocket and hold it up and say, 'That's what I get for locking you lot up.'

We had a word with Jimmy and the following Friday when the screw reached for his money, it wasn't there. He nearly died of shock. Everyone knew and they were nearly all falling about with laughter.

He started to plead, 'Come on, lads, where's my wages? You know I'm not a bad bloke.'

A prison officer screamed up at him to get all the prisoners 'banged up' and he shouted back, 'Somebody's pinched my wages, sir.'

The prison officer couldn't help retorting, 'Yes, I think there might be a thief in this place.'

The big yokel was nearly in tears. He was given his money back but the experience certainly cured him. He never pulled that stunt again.

Would the punishment block be the same? I had visions of that hideous dank cell block and the silence broken only by the clang of keys and the sobbing of guys who had had enough. Would they still be using the cages at the back of the cell block to exercise? Once, after I'd been let into the cage for exercise, icy sleet started to pelt down. It was all I could do to keep moving and when the screws came to open the cage to let me back into the strongbox, the lock was frozen on the gate. I had to wait shivering until they got a blow lamp to thaw it out.

I was smiling to myself as the memories came flooding back to me. They did everything they could to make things harder, but sometimes their best efforts only worked against them.

Every prisoner was allowed a book to read – this being part of the prison rules after the 1940s. If a chaplain or, in some cases, a governor went into a guy's cell whilst in the punishment block, he would always enquire if the prisoner had something to read. So the screws had a store of books which they considered would be incomprehensible to the average con. They would sling the biggest and thickest books they could find into the cell.

I let them think they were getting one over on me, but I read them all, including some pretty heavy material and some very interesting books, like Freud's interpretation of dreams. I had the last laugh when I wrote a petition to the Home Office about my treatment inside the prison. I could hear the Chief Officer saying, 'Somebody must have written that for him. He's used words even the governor can't understand.' He didn't know that the only book that I'd had in my cell for the past few months was a dictionary. I had a great time with that dictionary. I found a new hobby; taking nursery rhymes, proverbs, etc and changing the words to mean the same thing. I passed many a boring hour like that.

I wondered if they had done anything about the terrible bathhouse. Its iron baths were stained brown from the peaty water that came directly from the moors, complete with dead insects, pieces of soil and leaves. The walls ran with condensation and pools of dirty water were everywhere. Everyone suffered with athlete's foot as it was so contagious. It was also a meeting place for some pretty sordid and perverted prisoners. The only light relief that would come from that direction was when a particular child molester from Sheffield would come into the bathhouse. All the cons would say, 'Have a look at this beast, this should be a lesson to them all,' and someone would pull the towel from around his waist to show where he'd been emasculated by a crowd of women who had caught him with a child in a block of flats.

Things would probably be a lot different now since the Mountbatten Report. There would be more segregation of a lot of prisoners and rule 43 was the order of the day for all child molesters.

Then I thought of guys like 'Wanker' Green, who was in Dartmoor for many years. I can't remember ever seeing him without at least a black eye. He had apparently molested a gypsy girl and every year there would be a family of gypsies parked near the prison, who would ask the guys on the outside working parties, 'Will you check Wanker Green's cell card and see if his release date is still the same?' I think they had plans for some kind of reception for him when he was released. I thought I might even hear the result of that on the grapevine when I got back to the Moor.

I was back in Dartmoor within a few weeks of seeing the governor and was immediately met by a few old mates who made me welcome and filled me in with all of the news. I also recognised some of the old screws but from what I could gather, the Moor had lost all of its sinister atmosphere. I was interviewed by the deputy governor the day after my arrival and was surprised to find he was one of the chief officers from the years gone by.

He said, 'Sit down and let's have a chat.'

No one had ever spoken to me like that before, so I immediately thought that this must be the 'new approach'. But no, he was quite genuine and said to me, 'We try to start off on the right foot here now. Have a look around for a few days to see if there is a job in the prison you fancy doing, then if there is a vacancy, we'll see if we can fix you up.'

I gave this a little thought and I then put my request in for a cleaning job in the education block as I would be mainly on my own and I would have facilities to obtain certain materials for my hobbies and pastimes. So for about a year I went about my life in the Moor without any confrontations or incidents. Life in general was more comfortable than in the past – it was warmer following the installation of central heating, there was a new gymnasium, I could watch TV and there were quite a lot of activities going on, which I never dreamed I would see in Dartmoor Prison. I started to use the hobbies room in the education block. As a kid I had always been able to use tools to make things from wood and it wasn't long before I got the hang of it again. With the bit of money I used to earn, I'd buy the raw materials to make a few things to send home to my mother. This worked wonders for the old lady, not only because she liked the things I sent her but also, after all these years, I think a few of her prayers were being answered.

It was at this time that a screw who I knew as 'the Arab' started coming into the workshop and stopping to have a chat. I was a bit suspicious at first as I had known him for about twenty years and his reputation was detestable to say the least. I stayed very cold towards him when he tried to start a conversation, but eventually he put his cards on the table. I couldn't believe my ears when he told me that both he and his wife spent all of their spare time visiting hospitals, raising money for disabled people and kids with various disabilities. He asked me if I would make a few things for a local children's hospital. I agreed and set about the task of making a large dolls house and garage for the children's ward at Freedom Fields Hospital in Plymouth.

When my models were close to being completed the governor called me to his office and said that Mr Richards – 'the Arab ' – had mentioned to him the things I had been doing in my spare time. He had requested that when he delivered the models to the hospital I should accompany him. The governor then told me that he had been in touch with the Home Office and they had given the go ahead. It turned out to be a memorable day for me. The event marked a turning point in my life.

There were a few people from the media covering the story of 'THE DARTMOOR CONVICT AND THE CHILDREN'S WARD'. I met a reporter called Ross Salmon, whom I had heard of before, and we became quite friendly. He was surprised to learn that prisoners were in a position to carry out hobbies and make toys. We struck up a regular correspondence and with his help we got together an exhibition of prisoners' hobbies, arts and crafts. The visitors to the exhibition were amazed at the standard of work that was being shown. Some of the local residents began to take an interest in this work and encouraged the cons to do things for the disabled. A local artist was so impressed by the artistic talent of one of the cons that he requested he should be allowed to visit the prison weekly to work with prisoners with artistic ability. This permission was granted and it was not long before it seemed that half of the prison population had acquired canvas and easels from some source or other.

It was about this time that Lord Hunt – leader of the 1953 Everest Expedition – came to the prison as chairman of the Parole Board, to discuss the parole system with certain prisoners. There had been considerable controversy about this system stemming from the fact that it appeared that only certain cons, mainly white-collar crooks, were benefiting from it. Lord Hunt was very frank and he told us that the Parole Board could not take any chances by releasing bank robbers and serious criminals, as the media would be likely to have a field day if any parolee reoffended. So it was very obvious that I would have to do my time without any hope of parole.

Ross Salmon was still writing to me and he obtained permission to interview me for a radio programme. The broadcast was picked up by another radio show, *Pick of the Week* and much to my surprise and delight, following the broadcast I received hundreds of letters from all over the country from all types of people, both encouraging and congratulatory. I answered most of them and also began to correspond more regularly.

Shortly after resigning myself to serving my full stretch, the governor of Leyhill Prison came to Dartmoor to interview me with the view of getting me transferred to his prison. As I still had three years of my sentence to do, even with remission, I didn't think there was much chance of me moving. At the time, Leyhill was considered to be the most progressive and modern prison in Britain and most of the cons there were white collars, celebrities or bent police. There were also about forty lifers who had nearly completed their sentences and were to be released on licence.

To my surprise I was called up about three weeks after the visit by David Atkinson, the governor of Leyhill and told I was to be transferred there the following week. In a strange way I was sad to say goodbye to a lot of people in Dartmoor, especially 'the Arab', who had been so helpful to me. Before leaving to go to Leyhill I was allowed to go to his home to meet his wife and to have tea; very different from those bad times years before. I have since been back to Dartmoor and discovered that 'the Arab' had died. His grave looked well cared for and tidy, so his wife is probably still alive. I hope she is well – she was a very nice lady.

When I arrived at Leyhill and completed the reception formalities – clothing, property and personal possessions – the screw in reception said, 'Go up to where the prisoners live, ask about the general routine and come back later, then I'll organise you somewhere to sleep and live.'

I looked at him in astonishment. He left me on the main drive of the prison, looking back to the entrance and there wasn't even a gate to stop me walking out. I could see cars driving past on the road. I really thought I must be dreaming. But I was soon to learn the value of a system that gives you the responsibility for shaping your own life and not being told what to do every minute of the day. It was not all a bed of roses, there were some strict do's and don'ts. But it was a place where if you wanted to act like a man you would be treated as such.

I soon met a few people who I had known many years before, including Gus Thatcher, who was in his twentieth year of a life sentence for the Mitcham Co-op murder. Gus had been sentenced to death and was reprieved just twelve hours before he was due to hang. He had become a playwright and artist but he still seemed a very beaten man when I met him at Leyhill.

One of the first guys I met after arriving was Wally Probyn. Wally was the guy who had escaped from Durham prison with John McVicar. Many people had found Wally interesting enough to spend a lot of time writing to him and visiting him with a view to helping him. But Wally knew that even though the people who wrote to him and visited him were genuine and had a real desire to see him get a break, he had upset so many people in authority over the years that it would not be easy. I think that he eventually made it.

Another fellow prisoner was Barry Brogan, the National Hunt jockey. He was a quiet bloke who seemed pleasant and unassuming and was getting on doing his time. He had apparently been convicted for obtaining money by deception. Although he may have been one of the country's top jockeys, he was rather naive about the way things worked in prison. I remember him being caught with a load of tobacco which he shouldn't have been in possession of and being sent back to a closed prison to complete his sentence.

I also befriended a real adventurer called John Miller. He was tall, good-looking and athletic and had been a Scots Guardsman. He had also been a mercenary soldier in various parts of the world. I saw a good deal of John when I visited the gym. After a workout, we would go for a coffee with a couple of guys who were finishing life sentences. We would spend some time each day socialising and telling stories. I would have thought some of John's tales to be far-fetched, if I hadn't seen photographs and letters to prove the veracity of his statements. John regularly expressed his intention to return to Africa to release the 'dogs of war' from a prison called McKindye. Apparently he knew the guy commanding the rebel forces and he had been assured that any escape would be financed by him. He wanted to meet up with me when we were released in order to put his plan into motion. John thought that with all of the people that I knew and with his own contacts, the mission would be a doddle. But I kept trying to convince him that I intended going straight and settling down when I was released. That wasn't going to be the last I heard of John.

I soon got settled into the wood-machine shop and met a couple of lifers who were keen to organise a group of guys to join us in making things for children with various degrees of handicap. I gained permission to visit some places that specialised in spina bifida cases and also met a doctor who treated them. He was very helpful in suggesting things we could make, which would be particularly useful to such children.

We became better organised as time went by. With the help of the governor and staff, and with the approval of the Home Office, we started a Resettlement Group. Eventually we had about forty cons, whose sentences ranged from five years to life, going out at weekends as voluntary helpers in various homes, special schools, community centres and private houses, doing a wide variety of jobs. Each of these men went out without supervision, under their own honour and in the couple of years I was involved, either as chairman of the Resettlement Group or as a voluntary worker, there was not one complaint or infringement of the rules.

Good times came for the group with the arrival of T. Dan Smith, a politician from Newcastle who, with a chap named Poulson, had been sentenced to six years' imprisonment. I met Dan the first day he arrived. He was an imposing figure, over six feet tall. We were playing Scrabble in the billet and he joined in. We got chatting and within a few days I began to recognise in Dan a very strong character.

We would sit together talking of our past lives and Dan would tell me of his early years, when he would take part in the forerunners to the early union meetings and how the police would come to break them up. As the police horses would crash into the meetings, Dan would always be singled out as the tallest man there. Years later, when he attained his office in local government, he interviewed a senior police officer in Newcastle. He recognised the officer as being the one who was always the first in with the batons and took some pleasure in reminding him of those days. He was happy to see that the police officer blushed.

Dan's case was one of the big trials in the early '70s – a case of corruption in the awarding of contracts to rebuild Newcastle. A lot of politicians were quaking when the case unfolded, but most of the big names involved escaped prosecution, and Dan and the architect, Poulson, took the flak – and the punishment.

After hearing what we were doing in the Resettlement Group, he expressed a desire to help. It was the best thing that happened to the group for Dan had not only considerable artistic talent, but also many friends outside. I wrote to many of these people with his encouragement and they helped us by providing the raw materials we needed for our projects.

Dan was tireless and kept everyone on their toes. He was a leading light in all the activities within the prison, including the drama group, where one of his big stars was Leslie Grantham, later to become famous as Dirty Den in *EastEnders*. Leslie was then finishing a life sentence. Dan was involved with the debating society, where we used to debate with teams from Bristol and Cardiff Universities as well as the Round Table. I spent an enjoyable, enriching and memorable time with him.

One day, entirely out of the blue, I received a pleasant surprise: I was told that I had been granted parole. I still had a few weeks to go after this news and Dan spent much of his time contacting many of his outside friends to see what help they could give to me after my release. From these introductions, I met Harold Evans, who was then editor of the *Sunday Times*, and also Sir Monty Finniston, then the boss at British Steel. Through him and other friends of Dan, I obtained a very good job.

# 21.

## GOING STRAIGHT

Going to see Sir Monty Finniston at the British Steel headquarters in Victoria Street at the behest of Dan Smith, was an important moment in my life. First I was made very welcome and, as with Harold Evans, I found people didn't want to dismiss me because of my appalling past. They seemed to take notice of what Dan had to say and were full of constructive ideas as to how the continuation of my apparent resettlement was going to progress. The first thing Sir Monty did was to ring some friends from Political and Economic Planning, to see if there was anyone interested in meeting me with a view to providing employment.

Within a few days, I had a letter from PEP asking me to go to a meeting with one of the country's leading food manufacturing groups where I was to have a very good interview with the managing director. I was asked how I would go about tackling problems of social differences in industry. I put forward a view of the way we tackled similar differences in the class system which existed in the penal system at the time. I argued that if you wanted something to work for the good of everyone, using the example that I was familiar with, namely the Resettlement Group, where there were bank robbers, gangsters, murderers, fraudsters, petty-criminals, bent policemen and ex-lawyers all pulling together with one common aim, then it was essential to establish the correct attitudes and focus upon the tasks required, without even thinking of what background your fellow prisoners came from. I seemed to have impressed the boss because I was offered a job immediately. It was a very good job with a salary to match.

I went to my mother's house (my father had died many years earlier) and said, 'I'm in my forties now and I've just started my first proper job.' There

THE BRUTAL TRUTH

177

were tears in the old girl's eyes and I knew she was very happy for me. Well, I set about my job, which I enjoyed, although there was a fair bit of obstruction from some of the middle management. I think that part of the problem was that I couldn't talk about my past and they sensed that I had something to hide. Perhaps if I could have been more open with them, they would have accepted me better. I've learned not to be ashamed of my past and, although I don't volunteer anything, if I'm asked, I tell the truth – the brutal truth. I've found that most people are okay about it and some are intrigued and want to know more.

I managed to get the social club operational with the help of one of the Asian managers and an Irish worker. We had some marvellous social evenings and established a football team which had regular fixtures with other factories in the north of England. The friendly banter of the supporters from the various teams wasn't about the players' origins, but was centred on the north v. south cultural divide. I stayed at that job until I felt I was ready to start my own business. I had a meeting with the managing director and was given a generous handshake.

I was now rather at a loss as to what to do with myself. I didn't really want to stay in London, as I felt I had done very well and seemed to be putting my past life completely behind me and there was always the chance if I stayed in the City, that I would start to bump into old associates and gradually be drawn back into the false glamour of the underworld. I decided to go back to Bristol where I had made a lot of friends whilst engaged in my work with resettlement from Leyhill Prison.

At first it was lovely to meet some of the people whom I had befriended and had inspired me into taking a different direction in my life, but I had to get settled into a home, employment and generally do all the things that a person does when he decides to keep on the 'straight and narrow'. But although I had some pretty good references from my employers in London, I didn't find it easy to get started. I then remembered a name from the old days, Terry O'Brien. I had heard that he had left London years ago and started an entirely new life in Bristol and that he had become very successful in business. I thought I would try to find him and see what would come of him.

It was simple, I just looked in the phone book and within a matter of hours I was meeting TOB for the first time in nearly twenty years. Not only that, I was meeting his family, Miriam and son Michael, all of whom I was very grateful to, as they were to become my closest friends over the next year or so, making it a lot easier to get started in a new environment.

I worked for Terry and Michael in their business as a kind of 'Jack of all trades'. I even did the signwriting over one of their premises, which I was very proud of, as it stood out for anyone who came into the Bristol area via

Temple Meads Station. I not only worked for them but socialised with them and became one of the family. It was inevitable, however, that I would start to bump into people from my past life. Strangely enough, I never once met anyone who didn't appear to be happy to see that life was going well for me.

Michael liked to go to the casino at the weekend for a meal and a little flutter and he always invited me. I got to know the boss of the casino, Joe Firetto, who was a gentleman. He knew of my past life but never mentioned it. I often think of all of the characters I met whilst I was in Bristol. You'd have to go a long way before you could find a nicer lot of people. They were all so obliging and friendly that I miss them and often have a hankering to go and visit them all again.

I had a very pleasant and unexpected surprise one evening when I went out for dinner with a few friends. I was in a very popular restaurant when a guy sitting at the next table with his back to me turned around when he heard me speaking and said, 'Eric, what brings you to this part of the world?'

It was Johnny Quirk. The last time I had seen John was in Dartmoor Prison at the time I had been transferred to Leyhill. I had got to know him very well in Dartmoor through my old friend Dudley, who John used to work for. John had been sentenced to five years for an affray in a club in Bristol and when he was allocated to Dartmoor, Dudley got in touch with me and asked me to watch out for him and see that he was looked after. I would keep an eye on the list of people who had been allocated to Dartmoor each month and one day John's name was on it. I found an empty cell near mine and arranged for him to be located there when he arrived. John was very quiet when he first came in. I introduced myself and could see straight away that he had a problem. I was soon to find out that John was seriously into drugs – heroin and such – and was having quite a problem fighting the addiction. It was a credit to him the way he finally did beat it. He was to become one of the most respected people in the prison; he was very intelligent and with a great sense of humour. It was a pleasant surprise when I met him in the restaurant and we started to fill each other in with all of the news over the past years. Sadly, as we were talking, I began to realise that John was back into drugs and I hated to see what they were doing to him.

I would bump into John now and again over the next couple of years and would see he was deteriorating in health. He would tell me of friends of his that had died as a result of the habit. I felt that there would only be one end for John but I'm happy to write that after many years of not seeing him, I went to a reunion party in London a year or so ago and he was there, looking great. He had eventually beaten the thing and was now lecturing young people on the pitfalls of the drug scene. He was even going back, voluntarily, to prisons to talk to young offenders. I could see John was a very happy man again.

I got a bit of a surprise when I arrived back in Bristol after a weekend away. Michael O'Brien had left a message for me to go to a certain pub in Clifton to meet a guy who had come from London to see me urgently. When I arrived, there was my old friend from Leyhill, John Miller. He looked very well, tanned and smartly dressed. I was pleased to see him, as I had enjoyed his company when we had been in prison together. But I couldn't believe it when he took some papers and photographs from his pocket. The papers were contracts with a film company which he used to impress the company that hired him the light aircraft and other equipment he needed to implement the elaborate plan to kidnap Ronnie Biggs. It was when John showed me some photographs, recently taken of himself, Biggsy and a couple of other people, that I realised that John really meant business. That attempt failed at the last minute but John was not one to give up easily. I had almost forgotten the whole thing, when I saw a news flash on TV that Ronnie Biggs had been kidnapped from Brazil. I eagerly followed the story over the next few days and sure enough there were the pictures of my old pal John with Biggsy being flashed all over the world. John got him as far as Barbados but the Brazilian government insisted on Ronnie's return.

But it was time to look at a more realistic future for myself. With the help of a bank loan, I was able to start my own club. Because of my background, I could not hold a club licence, so I had to take a partner. I teamed up with very nice guy who was a hotelier and went into business.

We had a very successful start and I was quite happy for my partner to hold the lease on the premises. He was younger than me, only in his thirties, and for a year or so we had a very good business relationship. We paid back the bank loan before the first year was up and had each just taken delivery of a new car.

But my partner had matrimonial problems. He'd split with his wife and although he had a new girlfriend living at the hotel with him, he couldn't get his wife out of his mind. She was also restricting his association with his young son and he began to get very morose and cynical. Then one day I got a great shock. My partner had phoned me at the club about midday and he seemed in a pretty good mood, but about an hour later, his girlfriend rang to say he'd gone to his car, with the hoover and a blanket, and gassed himself.

His family inherited the business, leaving me with nothing. I was financially worse off than when I first started. I began to drink and sit around in bars, going over things, when I decided to look up an old friend of mine whilst visiting Manchester for a football match. This friend mentioned Derek who used to play with the old Dreamers band in the '60s. I'd had some nice times with Derek, who was now a publican in Manchester and I thought I'd pop in to see him and his wife. He was surprised to see me after all those years and we went to a club the next evening for some dinner. There we met another old friend, who was originally from London, but was now also a publican in Manchester. I decided to spend a couple of weeks there to sort myself out and in no time at all, I was booked into Jimmy Donnelly's hotel where I ended up staying for a year.

THE BRUTAL TRUTH

# 22.

## MANCHESTER AND THE QUALITY STREET GANG

I met Jimmy Donnelly (also known as Jimmy the Weed) soon after arriving in Manchester. People always ask me, 'Why do they call him Jimmy the Weed? Is it true that if you do business with him he always has a weed at the wages at the end of the deal?' Now I've always had good dealings with Jimmy, so I'll have to go along with his explanation. He once showed me a photograph of himself and a few of the chaps when he was young and he looked pretty weedy then.

But although he is small in stature, he is very game with a lot of bottle. One evening, Jimmy and I, along with our wives and friends, were invited to a big dinner/cabaret-cum-charity show at the Piccadilly Hotel. The actor Mark McManus, who played Taggart, and his wife Marion were two of our guests and we were all having a great time. Anyone who needed to go to the gents or ladies' room had to leave the main hall where the show was going on and pass a lounge outside one of the two bars. Apparently everyone who had to pass this spot came back complaining of two guys who were sitting there hurling insults and making lewd gestures at passers-by. I thought that if any of our company made a move to go out, I would accompany them, but Jimmy had already pre-empted me. He casually strolled outside to where the two pests were sitting. One of them shouted, 'Hey waiter' to Jimmy, who had just spent about £1,000 on a new dinner jacket and all the trimmings. Jimmy said, 'So I look like a waiter, do I? Then I'd better give you some service.' With that he knocked the pair of them out, came strolling back to the table with a grin and asked the waiter to have them removed from the hotel. Jimmy the Weed was certainly no weed when it came to defending his corner.

Jimmy was a member of the Quality Street Gang, a group of men accused by the press of being behind most of Manchester's major crime. The press are very careful not to mention them by name as they are largely businessmen – men of some substance. They are also very tough boys but I never saw any of them take a liberty.

The name 'Quality Street Gang' made the news during the John Stalker/Kevin Taylor affair. Jack Tricket, a prominent Manchester boxing promoter, speaking on *World in Action*, used the term to describe Kevin Taylor's friends. The name was used very much tongue-in-cheek by people who were jealous of the success of the QSG members, but it stuck and made the association of these men seem more sinister than it actually was.

The John Stalker/Kevin Taylor affair was highlighted in a *News of the World* article by Nick Pritchard, classed as 'exclusive' – the big story the others couldn't get. There were photos with the caption 'Stalker (the copper), Taylor (the friend), and Jimmy 'the Weed' Donnelly (the villain)'. It then went on to talk about a party at Kevin Taylor's house which was attended by every partygoer in Manchester, including members of the cast of *Coronation Street* and sporting figures such as footballers and boxers. Kevin's parties were legendary and the fact that John Stalker was taken off an enquiry in Northern Ireland suggested the far-reaching consequences of those debauched gatherings on public consciousness. Certain people suffered as a result, including Kevin Taylor and Lynne Perrie (Ivy Tilsley of the *Street*), with headlines beginning 'GANGLAND, NAKED ANTICS IN A JACUZZI'.

Donnelly, with interests in pubs and boxing promotions, was quizzed by police.

Another friend of mine, Steven Hayes, was mentioned as being photographed with John Stalker. I saw the picture in question and it was Steve Hayes with John Stalker in the background.

The problems that little affair created were astronomical and the police were forced to pay Kevin Taylor millions of pounds to compensate him. I also think other people suffered as a consequence without being compensated in any way. It was lucky for them that I wasn't photographed at that particular party as I could imagine what the headline would have been then!

The beginnings of the QSG go back to the 1960s, when Jimmy the Weed and his friends were dabbling in the scrap metal business. They progressed into construction and were soon making plenty of money and socialising in all of the well-known nightclubs. The doormen of these clubs were often friends of the QSG and worked with them in their day jobs. As a result, when local drunks or would-be tough guys tried to flex their muscles, any QSG members around would weigh in to give the doormen a hand in sorting out any trouble. It became fashionable for club owners to mention that the QSG were regulars at their club, thus ensuring themselves trouble-free evenings. After an incident at the Wilton Club in 1962, when a noted underworld figure of the day was put in hospital, the QSG were seen as pretty fearless fighting men.

Before the formation of the QSG, there were many respected individuals who the criminal fraternity would look up to or borrow money from, to set up some illegal scam or robbery. I met most of these people over the years as there was a good rapport between the London and Manchester underworld figures. One of the most outstanding was Bob McDermott, who was as well known in the capital as he was in Manchester and would always be seen at the ringside with his entourage at the big sporting events. Bob made a very good living from the barrows. Most guys in the fruit and veg game worked for Bob or at least borrowed money for stock from him, with a small interest attached.

Bob was the proprietor of the Cellar, a club situated in the centre of Manchester and famous with gamblers nationwide. It was frequented by everyone who gambled or had reason to seek help from the many underworld figures who always seemed to be in attendance. It was here that I first started to hear of the QSG and the impression given was far from sinister – they were spoken of as tough, fun-loving guys who all seemed to be quite wealthy. One got the feeling that they were respected because although they were tough, they never threw their weight about.

Deno's in the centre of Manchester was one of the most popular clubs in Britain and most cabaret artists have worked here at some time. There were many fortunes won and lost at Deno's gaming tables and many thousands of bottles of champagne consumed during its heyday. A lot of its glamour came from the fact that the QSG made it their headquarters for a long time.

They also frequented the Cabaret Club in Oxford Road. This was owned by Bill Benny, an ex-wrestler who died whilst making love to one of the many beautiful women who used the club. This particular femme fatale became well known in Manchester for accomplishing a deed many had attempted unsuccessfully and without using anything except her technique.

The head doorman at the Cabaret was Billy Ingham, an ex-boxer who was to become a very good friend of mine. Billy told me that he always looked forward to the QSG coming to the club as he could relax while they were there.

From construction, Jimmy the Weed moved on to become a publican, hotelier and nightclub owner. He helped a few people on their way and as a consequence, the police kept a very watchful eye on him. But though he was arrested on numerous occasions, they could never make their charges stick.

The funniest week I had with Jimmy arose out of a tragic situation which forced him to leave the country very quickly. He was wanted for questioning about the shooting of a man called John Stones in a Manchester pub and Jimmy decided to leave the country for his own good. I received a call from his brother one evening asking me to meet Jimmy. He was arranging a passport and other documents in order to slip out of the country. His brother said that at that moment, Jimmy was with a make-up artist from a TV company, inventing a disguise. But would I meet him in a pub in Stockport later, as there were a few things he wanted me to arrange for him before he left the country?

When I arrived at the pub, Jimmy was standing with his brother at the bar. He faced me and asked, 'What's the disguise like?'

'Well,' I said tactfully, 'I knew it was you because you were standing with your brother and I expected to see you anyway. But otherwise I don't think I would have recognised you.'

This seemed to reassure him and we had a couple of drinks while we plotted Jimmy's disappearance. As we walked out to the car park, an old pal of ours was just arriving with his wife. He immediately greeted us all by our names then said to Jimmy, 'What have you got that funny hat on for, Jim?'

I burst out laughing, while Jimmy muttered, 'I've just bunged a guy £200 for this disguise and everyone knows me.' But everything was all right in the end and I think Jimmy could still hear me laughing as we went through passport control a few days later.

Just recently, I've bumped into Jimmy the Weed and I asked him if he had seen anything of Johnny Stones, the man he was alleged to have shot many years before and Jim's reply was, 'No, but I'd like to,' because he was a man who must be respected.

It didn't take long to set up a meeting and it was arranged that John, myself and Terry Barlow, one of the boxing family from Moston, would go to 'Simmies', a place that all of the old faces would frequent. It seemed an appropriate place to meet, as Les Simms, the proprietor, has always been a bit of a peacemaker and a friend to everyone. I didn't tell Jimmy why I wanted to meet him at Simmies; also John wasn't aware of the reason that I suggested we went there for a drink. I was glad, however, that I mentioned it to Terry Barlow, because the minute we walked through the doors there was an atmosphere of apprehension and emotion that I've never witnessed before. They just embraced each other and I'm sure I detected a glistening in the eyes of them both. We all had a lot to talk about and many drinks to clear the throats that had got a little husky with the emotion of the occasion. Even Simmie, who has seen more of his share of guys wiping the floor with each other, had a job clearing his throat.

It ended up being a day to remember and everyone left the bar that evening with utmost respect for each other. I was only sorry that the Weed's two sons hadn't been present, as Tony and Dominic are two of the most respected boys in Manchester and that would have bridged a gap and set a seal on the occasion. I'm sure one day it will be spoken of as a momentous occasion – I'm glad I was there to witness it.

I'd also met a woman in Manchester who was spending all her time with a Lancashire group who did voluntary work with the disabled. I popped in to see her now and again and would help with little things, but I soon realised that what I'd done in prison was easy in comparison to the dedication given by people who help voluntarily every day of their lives. They are really special and I found I was seeing less and less of them as time went by. I did go back to Leyhill to visit a friend and found that T. Dan Smith was still making the odd trip back to encourage the men we left behind. It was then that I realised why he had stood out as being one of the more special people in my life.

By this time, I had become involved in the wholesale business with a few friends. I had a flat in Prestwich and was living with a girl who was the manageress of the Queens Club. Life had taken on a new meaning for me and I had stopped looking back at what might have been and had decided to enjoy myself and make new friends. When my girlfriend told me she was pregnant, I was overjoyed. We moved into a house with her two sons, aged nine and seven.

I was frequenting the Queens Club a lot of the time, where I bumped into old friends from my gambling days as well as the odd policeman. In fact, it was in the Queens Club that a senior police officer approached me about Jimmy. His alleged victim, Stones, had refused to make a statement about his shooting and the police had decided to drop the matter. 'Tell Jimmy he can come home,' the officer said. I duly did, although Jimmy took some persuading that it really was safe.

Kevin Taylor was one of the faces I knew quite well from the '60s and he seemed to be doing well in business. He was dabbling in local politics and always had a friendly word when we came across each other. He was to be caught up in the Stalker affair, when the Assistant Chief Constable was accused of socialising with Kevin, who in turn was accused both of fraud and of being friends of the QSG. The case collapsed in court, but in the meantime, Taylor and Stalker had both suffered.

I met John Stalker in the director's box at Maine Road. I was introduced by Doug Welsby, who had known Stalker since his early days on the beat. Doug, who was a licensee for over thirty years, said Stalker was the straightest copper he'd ever known. When the storm broke and Stalker resigned, it reminded me of one particular occasion in Blackpool in the '60s.

The police were taking considerable notice of everything I was doing, although I was only socialising with some friends. Nevertheless, word had got out that we were into rackets of some description. The headlines in the papers were: 'HIGHPOWERED GANGSTER USING MOTORWAYS TO COMMUTE'. As a consequence, every time we went out we were escorted. The police were making it very difficult for us to go anywhere, as well as making things difficult for any licensee who served us. At that time I was living with a girl who was in showbiz and the police even went backstage to tell her that I was an ex-convict. So I devised a plan.

I had noticed that some senior police officers would be present at the top social functions, such as charity shows, and two of my friends, Steve and Jimmy Clark, the American dancers and entertainers, were giving an end of season party for all their friends in showbiz at the Win Moreth Club in Blackpool. Everyone was going to be there, so I asked them to invite some senior police officers and their wives. I then arranged to have my own photographer at the party in addition to the official one.

Steve had seated the police at my table, which made for a nice cosy picture and naturally, during the course of the evening, I also asked a few of the wives to dance. I ended up with some very friendly photographs and from then on I was allowed to socialise without any interruption.

The Stalker affair meant that the police were taking an extra interest in the QSG at that time. Jimmy was harassed so much that he decided to leave Manchester and live on the coast for a while. I asked him if he would go back to live in Manchester and in reply he said, 'Not yet,' and showed me a Manchester newspaper and pointed to the headline: 'THREE MEN GUNNED DOWN IN CITY GANG WAR'.

'That sort of thing happens every week now,' he said. 'I think I'll just grow old gracefully.'

Although a lot of the Manchester underworld figures I know do show respect, I find from talking to them that they feel crime in their city is taking the same route as in London. There is a consensus of opinion that the drug scene is responsible for crime sinking to new depths – so much so, that the ordinary citizen can see the average robber as being fairly respectable in comparison. There have always been the footpads (today's muggers) and the highwaymen, but the horrific attacks on the old, the rapes and apparently motiveless stabbings are something new. When Jimmy the Weed tells me about the early days of the QSG, it seems almost harmless in comparison.

Quite soon after meeting Jimmy the Weed, I realised that he had friends in most of the major cities throughout Great Britain. I often travelled with Jimmy to various functions – maybe a boxing event, or a charity cabaret or just a business trip. We spent quite a lot of time in Glasgow, where I met a few old friends as well as making new ones.

The Glasgow I knew in the '50s is a far cry from the place it is now. The days of the Gorbals, when all the differences between gangs or individuals were settled with a razor-slashing, are long gone. You still hear of local tough guys cutting each other, but in the main, the major fall-outs are now over money or area supremacy and are dealt with more ruthlessly. The weapons used today are guns.

There has been a big power struggle going on in the Glasgow underworld which has become more intense since the death of Arthur Thompson, the acknowledged leader for a quarter of a century. One very tough young guy, Paul Ferris, has recently been acquitted for the murder of Arthur Thompson Jnr. but the sons of other well-known ex-villains have ambitions to take over the lucrative position of Scotland's crime boss.

I had rather an odd experience whilst visiting Glasgow one evening. My wife and I had been invited out to dinner and we were taken first to a very nice cocktail bar to meet some friends who were to join us for the meal. We were all sitting quietly, enjoying a drink, just waiting for the last two of our company to arrive, when there was a terrifying noise of skidding and crashing and the whole front of the bar came falling in. A lorry was half in and half out of the bar, about eight feet from where we were sitting. On the back of the wagon was a guy with a machine-gun. It looked like something out of an old gangster movie. Then one of our company jumped up and started to remonstrate with the driver and the guy with the gun. The two guys were soon apologising and saying to our friend that they didn't know he used that particular bar. They obviously had some grudge with the owners but they just backed the lorry out and drove off. We finished our drinks and were trying to make light of things to calm down our wives who were a little unnerved by the incident. Our other two friends arrived and were surprised to see us walking out past a car that had been rammed up against a wall next to the shattered bar front. The only thing we ever heard of that incident again, was when someone phoned our friends' house to say that they were sorry for upsetting the evening out.

Over the years, I've met quite a few people from Scotland, mainly from either Glasgow or Edinburgh. The majority of them have been either sportsmen or underworld figures, but there has been the odd ordinary businessman. Whatever their particular profession, I've found them to be reliable, honest with each other and very hospitable. There is always the exception to the rule, but in general, I've had some great moments in Scotland and also some quite humorous times. I remember the night I was invited to a boxing dinner at the Barrowlands in Glasgow. Every dignitary in the city was there along with just about anyone who had a reputation. Now, it was quite well known that the Barrowlands had been the place where many of the top villains had earned their reputations as young men at the Saturday night dances. It had become quite notorious through the many books and articles written about it. I was sitting at one of the long tables with a lot of smart-looking guys all dressed in dinner jackets. There were champagne corks popping and everything looked like a gentlemen's night out until the MC started to deliver his welcoming words. He first greeted all of the dignitaries and personalities, some by their titles or in the case of the police by their rank.

He then said, 'As you all know, this is the very first official boxing event ever to be held at the Barrowlands.' Then he glanced towards the table I had been invited to join and added, 'But I make a special welcome to some of my friends who have been the unofficial champions of the "Barras".' This broke the ice and everyone then nodded at each other with a grin. It turned out to be another great night in Glasgow.

Jimmy still meets up with some of his old friends from Glasgow when they come down to Blackpool for the 'Scots fortnight'. Jim is able to report on how old mutual friends are doing, now resident on the Costa del Sol – or the Costa del Crime as it is known. That particular part of Spain between Fuengirola and Marbella seems to attract most of the people wanted for various crimes in Britain. Once out there, a lot of the old antagonisms are forgotten out of respect for each other's predicament.

Jimmy is frequently asked to deliver a message to certain of his friends in Spain, to tell them that it is okay to come home as the 'straighteners' have been put in and they are no longer wanted.

I've often sat outside a bar in Los Boliches from about 9 p.m.–6 a.m. with a dozen men and their wives or girlfriends, most of whom are wanted for a variety of crimes in London, Manchester or Glasgow. Anyone passing would think we were a group of businessmen on a break away from the office. No one discusses their crimes. They are common knowledge within the fraternity but the subject is taboo.

There are also one or two phoneys who have managed to ingratiate themselves into the company. These are the kind of people who are always on the fringes, who have gleaned a lot of information about the various underworld figures and can talk about them with apparent inside information. They are one of the reasons I have never wanted to spend much time there. In fact, I have noticed that the men wanted for major crimes keep themselves mainly out of the limelight and socialise at private dinner parties where the conversation is more constructive.

I think that the advent of the Spanish sanctuary for the British criminal has helped forge the links between the underworlds of the major British cities. Crime has become a very big industry and is now a lot more sophisticated. A guy from Glasgow can slip on to the shuttle in the morning, fly to London and plot with his Cockney counterpart, have some lunch and be back home in time for tea.

The difference between London and the other major cities lies in the vast size of the capital which means that there is room for a number of accepted 'governors'. Most of them seem to live without clashing. I think the general public in the more deprived areas of London take a certain pride in their local villains, especially if they are described in the press as 'London crime bosses'. It becomes a talking point and most people realise that when you have some pretty heavy people about, it cuts down on the sort of crime that affects the ordinary hard-working folk. The kind of characters who break in to working-class homes may not realise that they may be breaking in to the house of the mother or relative of the biggest villain on the manor, so in a way their existence has its own policing effect.

Not all the people I have met in Scotland are villains though; quite a lot of my friends have never been involved in any type of skulduggery at all. Most of the guys I know are respected people for numerous reasons, especially for the fact that they are real men. In Edinburgh I have met some pretty tough guys who are mainly businessmen and they are respected because they run bars or clubs that never see any type of trouble because of the people who run them.

My friend, Peter Smith, introduced me to many of the people I was to become friends with in Edinburgh. The Deighans are one of the most respected families in that city as were the Williamsons whom I met back in the 1960s. I was to meet Rab Orr, who ran a few bars, and we became close friends. Rab and his family were very good to me when I stayed in that beautiful city. I would also look forward to seeing Laurence Deighan and his dad, Willie Deighan.

I first heard of the Deighan family many years ago when I was close friends with Ronnie and Reggie Kray. It was when Paddy Deighan had decided to have a period away from Edinburgh and he was a very fearless and respected man in London. While I was visiting Reggie Kray at Blundelstone Prison one day, I mentioned about the boys in Scotland and Reggie said, 'Why don't you invite your mates to a charity evening I'm organising for a very good cause?'

The minute I mentioned this to the boys in Edinburgh, they were full of enthusiasm for a couple of days in London and so it was soon organised. It turned out to be one of the most eventful few days I have had for many a year. Most of the boys who came to that special event, which was attended by a few hundred people who call themselves 'Friends of the Krays', really had a ball and helped raise quite a bit of money for a kid who had had no life at all. Reggie asked me afterwards to convey his thanks to the boys, who had really livened things up at the East End club and within a few days, they had become known as the 'Scotch Friends of the Krays'.

I came to know many villains from all parts of Europe and my own first connections with the Dublin underworld came through a chance meeting with a guy called Michael Gilson in the Brown Bull Hotel in Manchester, owned by Jimmy the Weed. Gilson had started to visit Manchester quite frequently, as did many of the Dublin Underworld figures I would meet on the odd occasion. I found them all very easy to get along with, but little incidents started to occur that made me be on my guard about having any business dealings with them. First there was a police raid on the Brown Bull, looking for a gang from Dublin who were supposed to be operating in the north of England. As a consequence of them being stopped on suspicion of a crime, a police sergeant named Speed was gunned down in the street in Leeds. Subsequently, the Weed and another member of the QSG were arrested on suspicion of harbouring the Dublin Mob and also of trying to involve them in all kinds of misdeeds, including money laundering etc.

I got to know many of the Dublin faces when I went over to Dublin for the funeral of Luke Kelly, the lead singer of the Dubliners. That was a most incredible week. I was to meet up with a lot of my old friends including Paddy Reilly, one of Ireland's greatest singers and a good friend of mine for many years. I also met Charles Haughey, the ex-premier of Eire. We had a drink at Scruffy Murphys along with many legendary people like Pat Jennings, the ex-Arsenal and Ireland goalkeeper.

I started the wake in Dublin and finished it in Waterford – that was some session; only the Irish know how to celebrate the birth or death of someone famous or infamous.

In the 1970s and '80s, there were two major gangland figures who stood head and shoulders above anyone else. There were also many major criminals who would compare equally in every respect with their counterparts across the Irish Sea and in fact even across the Atlantic. I was to meet many of the Irish underworld figures over the years and was always impressed by their coolness and eagerness and the fact that they were very loyal people.

The person who impressed me more than most people was Martin Cahill. He had many nicknames, most commonly, the 'General' and was known to mastermind some of the world's most spectacular robberies – the Thomas O'Connor and Sons Jewellery Manufacturing Plant at Harrold Cross, in which Martin Cahill's gang overpowered more than twenty members of the staff and stole millions of pounds worth of diamonds, gold bars and jewellery. Another infamous caper pulled by the now notorious 'General', was the stealing of the famous Beit collection of paintings that was worth millions. One painting alone, a Vermeer, was worth over £20 million (Queen Elizabeth being the only other private owner of a Vermeer). Sir Albert Beit went to live in Ireland in the early 1950s at Russborough House in Co. Wicklow. He was a wealthy member of a South African diamond-mining family and had been a Conservative MP. After his retirement from Westminster, he decided to settle in the beautiful Irish countryside just outside Dublin. Sir Alfred Beit's name came into prominence when he was first robbed in 1974 by a gang of IRA men led by a woman doctor named Rose Dugdale, the daughter of an English millionaire stockbroker. Rose Dugdale's gang tied up Sir Alfred, his wife and staff and stole paintings worth £8 million.

They were later to demand £500,000 ransom and the transfer of the Price sisters, serving time for car bombing in London, from English prisons to Northern Ireland. They were subsequently transferred to Irish prisons, but Rose Dugdale was arrested before this happened and the paintings were all recovered. She pleaded guilty to receiving the paintings and as a consequence of her plea, other charges relating to the thefts were dropped.

After this escapade, Sir Alfred decided to donate his collection of paintings to the Irish State, under the auspices of the Beit Foundation. Russborough House was opened to the public and attracted many thousands of visitors, one of whom was a man called Paddy Shanaghan, who, on the face of things, was a well-dressed, well-spoken, gentlemanly auctioneer. In fact, Shanaghan had run with some of the most notorious gangsters in the history of the Dublin underworld. He had been a member of the infamous Dunne family, who had run neck-and-neck with the Cahill family for many years, vying as to who were the most notorious villains. It was Henry Dunne who was to introduce Shanaghan to Martin Cahill.

Thereafter, it was only a matter of time before the second, more dramatic robbery of the Beit Collection took place. It was ironic that Cahill had decided to do the Beit robbery after the IRA's attempt had failed, because, as in the case of the Thomas O'Connor jewel robbery, the IRA were alleged to have cased O'Connor's and decided it was nearly impossible to do. They dismissed all thoughts of earning from O'Connor's, until Cahill's gang had in fact struck and been successful. The IRA were informed about the robbery by a member who had been loosely involved with Martin Cahill in its planning and so they decided to put the 'arm' on the Cahill gang for a share of the loot. But they were unsuccessful in their demands, as the 'General' would not be intimidated. When Paddy Shanaghan told Martin Cahill that the Beit Collection would be a doddle for a man like Martin, the plans were soon beginning to come to fruition. Shanaghan had recently been released from prison in England, where he had been involved with two London villains in an armed robbery in the Black Country and on his release from prison he immediately returned his attentions to the Beit art. When he met Cahill and told him that the collection was now the property of the State, Cahill couldn't resist the chance of putting one over on the authorities and so for the next few months, he would make his way every Sunday to

Russborough House in Blessington, where he would glean as much information as he could about the security and also discover what were the best value works to be purloined. Martin knew that four of the works of art were insured for about £30 million, so there would be the chance of a large ransom for their return

The first job would be to set up a legitimate security company to do any bargaining that may arise with the insurance people, for the safe return of the works. The next thing Martin set to work on was the stash for the works. By using only two of his most trusted gang members, he looked for and found, the perfect place in the mountains outside Dublin, where they were to work for several weeks tunnelling, shoring up, lining with plastic sheets and making an air vent with a professionally made entrance. Everything was set and covered with moss and lichen. Now for the job.

First of all, he wanted to get Shanaghan off his back as he did not trust him to keep his mouth shut. He felt that Shanaghan talked too much about his jobs and then when Martin saw Shanaghan with other people picking out various works of art on one of his Sunday jaunts, he decided to let Shanaghan know that he wasn't interested in doing the job. In fact he arranged to have two of his men dress as security guards and pay quite a lot of attention to Shanaghan and his cohorts. This had the desired effect of frightening off Shanaghan and his London friends.

Martin Cahill decided to work fast now. Four motors were stolen, all four-wheel drives to accommodate the terrain they would be traversing, and fitted with other plates. The gang then proceeded to surround Russborough House. Sir Alfred Beit and his wife were in London at this time and in residence were Lt. Colonel Michael O' Shea and the Beit's chauffeur with their families. Cahill's alarm expert made entry and stepped in front of the passive infra red sensors which immediately aroused the local gardai. The alarm men then tampered with the sensor and immobilised it so that it would not set the second alarm off. They then retreated until the gardai arrived to be informed by the Lt. Colonel that everything was in order. Cahill watched the squad car leave, then radioed his men to approach as all was clear. They just strolled in where Martin instructed them to remove a painting. There were the Vermeer, Rubens, Gainsborough and also two or three other famous paintings. The Goya was valued at that time at £30 million.

Then came two months of every scoundrel and con man, fake fence, art expert turned grass and police sting merchant, pitting their brains against one of the coolest crooks ever to walk on someone else's property, culminating in a joint venture between the Dublin police and Scotland Yard, who then decided to bring in the FBI from Washington.

The plan was to introduce two federal agents posing as art dealers. That fell through because of the caginess of Martin Cahill and his uncanny sixth sense. Another guy who is a well-known figure in London, came with an offer of a million pounds to Cahill. But Martin knew that the guy was closely monitored by Dutch and Irish police.

Then came the closest stroke of all. A Dutch fraudster named van Scoiak arranged to buy one of the paintings for £100,000, which was arranged by a major underworld figure in Dublin. A few months went by until van Scoiak got himself in trouble with the Dutch police. Van Scoiak decided to go along with the Dutch and Irish police and set up a sting, the plan being that he was to meet Cahill and produce £100,000 in 'show money'. The asking price was one million pounds for the four major pictures. The set-up by the police was very elaborate, using a specially equipped plane loaned by Scotland Yard, to monitor the meeting in the mountains. The plane was to be in contact with the surveillance team on the ground, 30 or so heavily armed police intending to swoop. Van Scoiak plus two Dutch policemen arrived in Dublin and booked into Jury's Hotel.

The Dublin police had already bugged the hotel room with microphones and cameras, hoping that a meeting would take place between Cahill and van Scoiak. But there was a slight hitch with the police operation when they went to the justice department to get the £100,000 show money. The government officials turned them down as they thought the 'General' was too clever for the police and he would probably 'fly the coop' with the hundred grand. After much discussion between Interpol, the Dutch and Irish police and various government men, it was decided to contact a friendly bank manager and arrange a lodgement slip showing that the money was in Dublin and leave the meeting at Jury's Hotel until the weekend. They had another slight problem after this. The Dutchmen were spending money like water and so they had to find another couple of grand for them to keep the show going until the sting came to fruition. It was left for one of the detectives to go to a publican who owed him a few favours to con a couple of grand to keep the Dutchmen and their new ladies and gentlemen friends all happy. Needless to say, the publican is still screaming for his money back.

Cahill did eventually go on a meet with his three closest friends, but the police who were chosen for the job didn't have an earthly chance of nailing a team of men who had grown up streetwise. Cahill was later to tell them they used the wrong coppers when they had the chance. But unfortunately, Martin Cahill must have upset somebody enough to make them want him out of the way. There have been many conjectures as to who rode up on motorbikes and riddled his car with bullets, but whatever anyone thought of him, they couldn't take away the fact that many people respected the 'General'.

A couple of years after the O'Connor jewel raid, I was to meet a good friend who had handled the 'fencing' of the haul and whilst having a meal in

Bayswater, I was very taken with a ring belonging to the lady who was accompanying my friend. I made a comment about the beauty of the gem and my friend just smiled and said, 'It's just a little gift from our friends in Dublin.'

At the time of writing, I've just spent a weekend in London and I went to Bayswater where I stayed at the Grand Plaza Hotel and in the bar I met one of my oldest friends, Dave Barry, who was also a good friend of the guy who had bought the jewellery from the O'Connor robbery. I asked about our friend and Dave said, 'He must be struggling, he's just sold his missus's diamond ring for a hundred grand.'

It amazes me how some of the women who have been used to living with villains all their lives, go along with their chaps just saying, 'Well, things are not going so well at the moment,' and the lady will just take her most prized possession off her finger and say, 'Easy come, easy go' and think nothing of it! The most wonderful thing about villains' wives and girlfriends is their loyalty to their man. You've only got to spend a few years in prison to see the kind of life that a woman would go through to ensure that her chap has all the comforts that are possible to afford. The staunch ones never miss a visit, as they know what that contact with the outside world means to a guy and it's not very pleasant for women to be searched and subjected to the monitoring and observation when all they want to do is put their arms around someone and tell them that they live for the day it is all over. Believe me, when a judge sentences a man for a crime, he also sentences everyone dependent on the criminal as well.

# 23.

## BACK TO CRIME AND STRANGEWAYS

I had now settled down happily with my girlfriend and was getting on with my business. I had moved my premises to the outskirts of Blackpool and for a while, things seemed to be going quite well. Then a few people started to get behind with payments for the goods they had bought on credit and I was forced to extend my credit facilities with the bank. I struggled on, hoping things would get better, but all the while the bills were mounting. I started to feel that I was a failure – that no matter what I did, nothing would go right for me. To add to my worries, I had just become the father of a son and I felt that I would rather go to prison for a short while than condemn my family to a life of drudgery and debt.

I took the easy way out and decided to get a few quid together and shut up shop. I sold up all my stock and ordered more and then just waited for the inevitable. The police finally came and told me that it was illegal to sell stock for less than it was worth and then not pay the suppliers. I replied that I knew this but customers hadn't paid me what they owed – so I didn't have the money. They started to explain about calling in the receiver when I interrupted. 'I know all about that, but I decided to take the easy way out.'

'You call this the easy way?' They couldn't believe what they were hearing. But I felt a kind of calmness, as if everything would be okay. I ended up back in court, charged with fraud amounting to £300,000.

Although I didn't have very much, I had a bit put by and as I thought I would probably be going back to prison, I decided to take my girl and little son on a holiday before having to face the music. We went off for a couple

THE BRUTAL TRUTH

of weeks to Malaga on the Costa del Sol and it wasn't long before I was bumping into a lot of old friends.

I met Bob Missen and his wife who were running a club in Benelmedina. Then Maurice, who had a nice little bar that was a meeting place for all the chaps. My old mate Curly King turned up there one night looking 20 years younger than he was. Then a pal of mine for many years heard that I was in Los Boliches and came looking for me, with his new wife. This was Ronnie Knight who was wanted in Britain in connection with the £6 million Security Express robbery. At the time, I was quite pleased to see him and we had a couple of days together. I was sorry to have to leave, knowing I was probably facing a bit more time in the nick, but I wouldn't have changed places with any one of the boys who had to live there; they were chancing many years in jail when they got back to this country.

So I came back to face the music and found I still had a few weeks to go before my case came up. I went to London to watch the Bruno v. Bugner fight at White Hart Lane and joined some friends afterwards at George Best's Blondes Club. There was the good old smiling face of Curly King again. We decided to go to Langans Restaurant for a meal. I said to Curly, 'When I saw you in Spain, I thought you were on the run.'

'No,' he said, 'I haven't been in trouble for years and I'm glad to see you've been out of it yourself.'

I didn't have the heart to tell him I was on bail waiting to go up on a fraud charge.

Finally the case started. There was no point in messing around, I was done 'bang to rights', so I pleaded guilty and was sentenced to two and a half years. In the old days that would have meant doing a 20 months with good behaviour. But in the present day, there was a good chance of being out in ten months with parole. So I thought, I've been lucky and it's up to me to get on with it, keep my mouth shut and get home as quickly as I can.

But that was easier said than done. I was sent to Strangeways and the minute I smelt the prison I thought, 'What have you done?' I knew that my wife, Carole, had never experienced the stigma of having a relation in prison – and I knew that she would not get used to it very easily. I was not too happy on my own part either, particularly after trying so hard to go straight.

I was in a prison that had the worst reputation among prisoners. Everyone hated the thought of being sent there and it was common knowledge that if it ever ignited into a riot, it would be one of the worst in the history of prison riots in this country. I remember the stories of the Hull rioters being brought to Strangeways to get the 'treatment'. From the moment they arrived they ran the gauntlet of brutality. People often ask me what causes men to riot and go on a rampage of the kind that happened in Manchester's Strangeways Prison in 1990. There is no easy answer to that question. But I do have a view based upon my own experiences.

The first thing to remember, is that any man who decides to riot knows beforehand that he is going to have to take some lengthy punishment when it is all over. So before he takes up the cudgels, he has to have been brought to a point where he is past caring what the consequences are likely to be.

Therefore, in searching for the causes, one needs to look deep into the whole system. Some of the complaints may appear to be trivial to those who have not had their freedom taken away. But when you add them all together, you will find what it is that ultimately causes a person to snap.

The things that matter most to prisoners are usually food, visits and the ease with which they are able to change cells. One of the greatest causes of personal misery for most prisoners is the guys they are forced to do their time with. There is a considerable amount of bullying as well as the usual tensions you would expect when you have possibly three blokes with very different personalities locked up together in a space ten feet by eight feet for up to twenty-three hours every day.

You try to regulate your bodily functions so as to use the toilet when you are unlocked for exercise or slopping out. However, this becomes nearly impossible, especially in the evening when you are locked up at 7 p.m., following slopping out and then face the prospect of twelve hours before the cell door is opened again. Everyone knows what is going to happen if you ring your bell after you have been locked up for the evening. The first time you ring your bell you will hear the night duty screw shout, 'Use your pot.' The pot is a plastic bucket (in the old days it was a chamber pot). If a new prisoner goes into a cell where the bucket has been used by the previous con for any length of time, the stench which hits him upon lifting the lid immediately starts him wondering what kind of experience he is going to have to get through.

As well as the bucket, you become aware of the smell of body odour the first minute you walk into the cell. There are no such things as hygiene and cleanliness inspections within the prison. It makes me smile when I hear of restaurant owners being fined heavily by the courts for lack of hygiene. Ask any ex-con about the stench of slopping out, the cockroaches and the parcels of shit that are thrown out of the cell windows, to name just a few of the health hazards that exist in any prison.

Then there are the prison officers. There are some reasonably decent blokes among them, but most have their hands tied by the rules and regulations. Prison officers are taught not to trust any prisoner, so suspicion always plays a part in the relationship between officer and con.

Prison officers who are new to the job are given conducted tours round various prisons, wearing their civilian clothes. They look just like anyone's next-door neighbour and I know from many of the conversations I have had with these newcomers, that they either come into the prison service for a secure job with a house provided, or they think they have something to offer the penal system. I really don't think that there are many who arrive with any sadistic thoughts or ideas about running the lives of the people beneath them. But you can tell the type of screw he's going to become by the nature of the screw who shows him the ropes when he first comes into the job. He might well come from his training establishment with all the goodwill in the world, but that can all too easily be forgotten when he starts the job. True, the influences could work the other way, but it only needs one or two bad staff to upset the whole of a prison. This is particularly so if they are senior or principal officers who would normally be expected to stop other screws taking advantage of their position to make things difficult for certain cons. It is easy to see the signs of abuse by the number of complaints, cases such as a bloke smashing up his cell furniture or, in extreme circumstances, the suicide of a prisoner.

Another major problem is boredom, with very little work being done in the prisons. Some cons can get a job where they are paid enough to enable them to buy tobacco to last for a week, whilst the rest are given an allowance to last just a day or so. This creates great resentment and encourages borrowing which results in guys fighting, or worse, prisoners asking to go on rule 43 – complete segregation.

Since most of the mental hospitals have been closed there are thousands of people, who have known no other life except for an institution, being put out into society to fend for themselves. Tragically many of these people have ended up in prison and have been used by some officers to get their own back on certain cons with whom they do not see eye to eye. Moving the poor chap, who may not be able to control his body functions or may have some other unsociable habits, into the cell of a con the screw doesn't like, can have distressing results.

There are also many cases of screws using their pet hardmen to chastise the guys who know their rights and try to exercise them. The landing officers seem to get what is commonly known in prison-speak as 'my No. 1' – generally a recidivist, who takes a pleasure in being the butt of the officers' insults. He's the type who always manages to be in possession of a number of porn magazines so his landing officer, therefore, always has something to read when he has no other work to do. He is always ready to pick a fight with somebody who doesn't see eye to eye with the landing officer. He always ensures that the landing officer has got a cup of tea and is made aware of everything that is going on inside the prison.

It has been an amazing coincidence that while writing about the causes and effect of the Strangeways Prison riot, I happened to visit the licensee of the Dutton Arms, the pub that gave succour to the media and the staff of

Strangeways whilst the riot was being enacted. He had a great deal of memorabilia about the biggest and longest drawn-out riot in the history of the British penal system and he gave me some mementos of that tragic few weeks' protest which was to have such an affect on so many people's lives.

I still don't think many lessons were learned as we still have the enormous amount of suicides going on in our prisons. There are still many mentally sick people being sent to prison. If the authorities think that putting a toilet in the cell will stop people from being disgruntled they are just not addressing a very serious problem. Perhaps when people look at some of the photos that I have in my possession, they might ask if the authorities are proud of the type of system that they run in this country. That if you treat people like animals they will act like animals, as was witnessed in April 1990.

I've since met and spoken to a few people who were involved in that whole catalogue of events from day one to the end. They all say that they got an enormous buzz out of seeing the screws with fear in their eyes – the same screws who would enjoy putting fear into people every day they were at work. So until everyone is educated, there is always a chance of this happening again. The next time, it will have worse consequences.

I have photos of Colin Baker of ITN giving the news to the world about the terrible things 'going on in there', while he celebrated his birthday in the Dutton. But the story really began a couple of days before this, on the exercise yard in Strangeways, where it seemed that the word had gone out that there was going to be trouble in the prison chapel the following Sunday.

Paul Taylor, Alan Lord and a few others had decided there were a few scores to settle and the most certain place for everyone to be able to congregate would be the chapel, as Noel Proctor, the Chaplain, wouldn't allow any discrimination in his church. So there would be Category-A along with all kinds of cons, even child molesters, gathered together in the chapel. And so after Noel Proctor had come to the end of his sermon, it was decided by the leader of the rioters that there would be an additional sermon about the conditions existing in Strangeways. This was a sermon concerning every grievance that was being muttered about daily throughout the prison.

I had met Noel Proctor, when he recommended that I be transferred to another prison to get me away from that madhouse. He had looked at my past record and thought that I deserved better surroundings. He was someone I felt for when I heard that he was the first one to feel the brunt of the anger, but I wasn't surprised to hear 'that he stood his ground. He was a very unusual man and I believe he was later to be recognised for his bravery that day.

I also understood why the riot took place. You would have to experience all the petty grievances, along with the odd act of violence that would take place in the punishment cells and the hospital wards. Strangeways was a cauldron and it was no surprise to anyone who had spent time in there, that it was just waiting to boil over. So when Paul Taylor decided it was time to give his sermon, I knew exactly how he felt. He grabbed the microphone and told the congregation it was time to send a message that 'we have had enough', and then after a few screws had their keys taken from them, the rampage started. Friends in other wings were unlocked, as were a few child molesters, who were on rule 43, for their own protection. One escaped to go up the staircase but he was chased and captured by the mob and thrown over the landing. Every screw in the jail just ran and the prison was left entirely at the hands of a rampaging mob bent on destruction.

In the subsequent days after the hard-core of the rioters had decided to dismantle the prison from the roof to the ground with their bare hands, a task force went in the ground floor to survey what was happening, because by now, the Strangeways Riot was world news. The first thing the task force found was the injured child molester, who was to subsequently die of his injuries. Any other injuries to staff were only superficial but there was a lot made of one screw who died during the siege. He actually died from natural causes.

Paul Taylor and his friends decided, after they had raided the kitchen and victualling store, that they would hold out on the roof, which they did for nearly a month. The rioters spent quite a lot of their time going through the paperwork that they had acquired when breaking into the offices. They were to elicit quite a lot of information about other prisoners and, as a consequence, there have been a few people severely reprimanded. Paul Taylor was eventually sentenced to another ten years' imprisonment for his part in the Strangeways Riot, but I believe he is out now. Good luck to him.

Up until the industrial troubles when the Prison Officers' Association (POA) came through their fight with management and succeeded in becoming more powerful, a prisoner could always make an application to see the governor. He didn't have to explain the nature of his application and was immediately in the governor's office after adjudication able to make his request or complaint. If it was a normal request that fell within the rules of the prison it was usually granted. If, however, it was a complaint against a prison officer or dissatisfaction with the food or something outside the rules, he would be warned immediately of the consequences of not proving his complaint. It was up to him to either pursue his complaint or let the governor deal with it.

But now you make your application and are then brought in front of the senior officer to state your complaint. He then decides whether it warrants going in front of the chief officer or assistant governor. You very rarely get to see the governor himself and in the meantime the word has gone around that you are a troublemaker. Then your problems really start. In the case of a guy who is not able to take the pressure, he is likely to do something silly like smash up his cell furniture. He will then at least see the governor at adjudication, but the chances are that he will be manhandled on the way to the punishment block. The sounds of cell furniture being smashed and the subsequent beating/ create a very strained atmosphere throughout the prison. It then only takes the smallest spark to ignite a very serious situation.

It is quite obvious to me that the prison authorities felt that they dealt wrongly with the Strangeways mutiny and that they should have been allowed to storm the place the day after it started. I think that would have resulted in a larger loss of life. I know that people will say that there were some very serious injuries inflicted in the Strangeways riot but there were many injuries in that place – and in other prisons – long before April 1990 and I believe that there will be many more injuries sustained on both sides unless the whole penal system is looked at critically.

I had already been moved from Strangeways Prison a couple of years before the riot started. I had been released and settled with my family in a new house and had started to write about my experiences in the penal system, when the news came on to say that a serious riot had broken out at Strangeways. After a few days, it began to dawn on me that this was serious and it didn't surprise me one bit, as I watched the news bulletins with interest. I knew that certain things would be more dramatised than they really were, but I also got the feeling that this was something different to the ordinary prison disturbances.

The person who led the riot had obviously been a victim of the violent penal system. He had just had enough. It was obvious that he was a person of strong personality to keep so many people in reasonable control and to exert authority to ensure that violence was kept to a minimum. After all, we're talking about dangerous men here. But humans they were and as humans they should have been treated. They made a statement for the whole world to witness. They exposed the type of penal system that this country runs.

I have come across many things since the day that Paul Taylor decided it was time someone did something about the way people in positions of authority were allowed to treat prisoners. This had been going on for so many years without any redress whatsoever and I had years of the type of treatment that had made me want to riot and fight back. Many times I let visiting magistrates know my feelings and I wrote numerous petitions to the Home Office, which I am pretty certain never reached their intended destination. The stock answer to most petitions was always the same, 'The Home Office can find no reason to investigate your recent complaint about your treatment and warns you of your future disruptive conduct.'

I have read of so many prison officers who were treated for stress after the

Strangeways riot and I have even met one who told me he had a leg amputated because of the stress, though he was never assaulted in the riot. But the worst thing I heard of was that a group of screws had a tie made to signify that the wearer was on duty at the time of the riot and they all kept a piece of slate with the inscription: 'Strangeways Riot 1.4.1990'. I happen to be in possession of one of these so-called trophies that they earned while sitting in a pub all day and night giving interviews to the media about the terrible convicts whom they had to control.

After the Strangeways affair, there were several flashpoints in various prisons around the country and it became the policy for these small uprisings or defiant rebellions to be brought under control swiftly, regardless of what force was used. This has given the POA the idea that it can carry on as usual. Well, I can assure them that if they don't use the strength of their union to ensure that there is a complete overhaul of the whole penal system, there will be an uprising which will make the Strangeways affair look like a playground fight.

There is a vital need to try to reduce the prison population and to start resettlement courses as well as doing something about the hygiene and getting prisoners out of their cells into some kind of work, where they are able to earn enough money to pay for some of the small luxuries of life. I am aware that there is a certain element of prisoners who must be kept in secure prisons and there are also a considerable number who must be shown that other law-abiding people have to be protected. There is, however, one very obvious way to begin to reduce the prison population – by stopping the practice of sending people with mental illnesses to jail. Treat them for who they are – sick people who have no place in prison.

I knew exactly what to do the minute I got in to Strangeways. I was put into D-Wing and, as soon as I got to the cell, I saw it was fitted out for three prisoners. I had never had to experience this overcrowding before and I didn't know how I was going to react to it. But the gods were on my side. There was just one guy in the cell when I got there and he'd only arrived the day before me. He'd never been inside before and was pretty scared about what was going on. So he was pleased to meet someone who knew the ropes. The very next day, we received another cell mate, a boxer, who had got himself into a fight outside the ring and had been sentenced to two months'. They were both clean and we made the place as habitable as possible.

After a couple of days the prison officer called me to his office and said, 'I've been looking at your record and I don't see the point of keeping you here. Would you like to go to Kirkham Open Prison?' He got an immediate affirmative from me and I settled down to wait the couple of weeks before going to the open nick. A few days later, I was walking in the exercise yard when a guy came over and said, 'Are you Eric Mason?'

'Yes,' I replied.

'You may remember me, I'm Billy Cox,' he said.

I remembered Billy as a kid. He was an adopted son of Connie Whitehead and had been convicted with the Kray twins for helping Freddie Foreman to dispose of the body of Jack the Hat and was sentenced to ten years' imprisonment.

'What are you doing up here?' I asked.

Then he told me all about a scam he'd been involved in.

'Seeing as you've only got twelve months, put down for Kirkham. You'll be better off,' I suggested.

He did this immediately and a couple of days later the PO called me up again and said, 'We've got to put you back a bit for Kirkham as there's a new bloke who's just applied for the open nick. As he's a first offender, he's going in your place, but you're top of the list for next month.'

I don't have to tell you who it was who went in my place! But I knew that I had more chance than Billy of getting through that extra month as he was nearly cracking up with all the things that were happening to him. He was dying to knock the No. 1 out and, as I knew Billy was a good boxer, he would have done the business on the guy and got himself a lot of grief. Also, all the screams and shouts that were coming from the punishment block below our cells were a bit unsettling, particularly for newcomers. It was a relief to be going to Kirkham the following month.

As soon as I arrived at Kirkham Prison, I met Billy Cox, who had settled in and made a few mates. Although Kirkham was a pretty easy place as prisons go, it had many petty little rules that were more irritating than intimidating. Most of the staff I came into contact with were pretty decent people, but there was still the odd one or two who would take advantage of the little bit of authority that they had. Overall, however, it was the type of con who was in there that made life in Kirkham difficult to take.

I can never understand people who need to take drugs, and prisons all over the country are rife with the stuff. But as you can imagine, it is a lot easier to smuggle anything into an open prison than into a more secure institution. Consequently, as you are in dormitory-type cubicles in an open prison, you are constantly seeing people abuse themselves with drugs. You would have to put up with stupid, inane laughter for hours during the night from some halfwit who had got a bit of false courage through taking some substance or other.

This, together with the constant spitting that seems to be part of being one of the boys, disgusted me. I remember a very charming lady who was on the Board of Visitors saying to me one day, 'Eric, why don't you take your meals in the dining-room?' I replied that on the few occasions I had walked into the dining-room, I had seen a continual stream of saliva the whole way. I would then have to sit opposite some character who had never heard of the word manners, let alone possessed any. I found it easier to live on what I could get from the shop.

I went to the gym every day to work out. So with the exercise and meagre diet, I went from 16 stone down to 13 in about eight months. By the time I came out I was very fit indeed.

At last I came to that most dreadful of times – waiting for a possible parole. I knew that if I got it, I would be very lucky as I would have done only ten months of my sentence. When the day came, I was sent for and told that I was being let out on my first available parole date. I was overjoyed. I phoned my wife to tell her the good news and then I was able to thank all of the people who had helped me get through that time without too many problems.

I had just three weeks left to do: I thought, at last I know where my happiness was going to lie. I knew I was never going to do anything again to risk losing my liberty. When the morning came and I walked out of that place and saw my wife standing by the car, I was the happiest bloke on earth. Back at home I was greeted by my little son who was playing with a neighbour's kids. On seeing me again he said, 'My dad's back from work!'

The one thing that I knew I was leaving behind was an entirely different type of criminal from the men I had suffered with years before. I just could not believe the conversations I had had to listen to night after night in the dormitory of Kirkham Prison. I was disgusted by the complete disregard shown by the majority of inmates for the misery that they had caused their victims and the pleasure they got from regaling stories showing the despicable habits of common housebreakers like themselves. Stories of excreting in people's beds – that always got a laugh from the other morons who enjoyed that type of behaviour – and the amount of vandalism that they had inflicted on their victims. The amazing thing to me was that such people would strut around the prison as though they were the bee's knees. I would remember my first years in prison when the common housebreakers, muggers of old people and ponces who lived off the immoral earnings of prostitution, were only considered to be just one step above the child molesters. They knew it and were loathed to talk about their crimes. When I watch elderly crime victims being interviewed on TV nowadays and realise that there are so many people totally confined to their homes, living in constant fear of some kind of assault on their person or property and then I hear politicians saying that the only thing they can do is to try to contain it at its present level, I become angry. I can't help thinking there is only one end to it all – and that is anarchy. God help the future generation.

# 24.

## RESETTLEMENT

**W**hilst in Kirkham, I'd done some serious thinking and made up my mind to write a book. I knew that I would have difficulty writing in prison, for various reasons, but I started to make notes of the different periods of my life. It was then that I began to realise what a strange life I had led. The principles that I had reluctantly adopted in prison were not really principles at all. The principles that I had been taught as a kid, by my parents and at school, the normal rules of living – they were the real principles.

I found it all so strange when I started to think back. I remembered that as a kid, I was proud I could stand on my own two feet and tackle a bully and would never dream of hitting a man when he was down. As I got older and accustomed to the people who could only win if they were mob-handed, I thought, well at least I've got something about me that they don't have. It's funny how certain people can take pleasure out of saying, 'We beat him' and think that they had done something really good. That's the one good thing that has come out of all my violent past. I can only ever remember one guy beating me on my own and he was a guy from Stockport when I was about 19 in Portland Borstal. And when I think of that day, he's one of the few people who I've really respected. I've seen and known guys who I've respected over the years because of the way they conducted themselves, although most people wouldn't have given them a second thought. I've seen and known men who have established reputations as tough guys, but when it came to proving themselves, they had no substance. I found I was now thinking more about the people who had been or were 'real' people, even though some of their stories may not be as exciting or as glamorous as those of the more notorious characters.

It wasn't very long after my release from Kirkham that I met Connie Whitehead and Billy Cox once more. I naturally asked Connie about the stuff I'd read concerning the disposal of Jack the Hat's body and he said the whole affair was conjecture. This made more sense to me than all the rubbish I'd read.

Meeting Connie also made me realise how lucky I am, particularly when I think how many years my life has spanned and realise that the Kray twins have been locked up for nearly half that time. Many people I meet pose the question, 'Why do they keep them still locked up after all these years?' It always starts a debate and the usual comparisons arise. 'They let out child killers after a comparatively short time.' This is not strictly true as the notorious child killers always do long stretches in jail. But many people sentenced to life imprisonment are released in a lot less time than the Kray twins. To the ordinary man in the street it is difficult to see the reasoning behind this.

I have my own opinions about why the Krays have spent so long in prison and it is a simple question of the judiciary wanting to have the last word. When the Krays were tried nobody was interested in the actual killings or the people who were killed. The men standing in the dock and the victims were all villains who had come from the back streets of the city. They had had squabbles that resulted in the deaths of a couple of people no one would ever miss. But then came the trial, at that time the longest murder trial in British penal history, and it caught the imagination of the public. Every word in the case was followed diligently and the myth of the Krays was born. When Ronnie Kray's famous outburst to the prosecution counsel, accusing him of being a 'fat slob', was reported in every newspaper in the country, it ensured that the architect of the remark would do the longest sentence for contempt of court that has ever been delivered.

I have spent many years inside and believe that I understand the amount of damage prison can do to an individual. One can only admire the way that Ronnie Kray did a quarter of a century and Reggie has done 31 years in various prisons with dignity. I have recently received a number of letters from Reggie Kray and it amazes me that he still has his sense of humour. I sent him some photos of my family taken whilst on picnic trips and in the garden. His next letter was so poignant. He thought I was lucky to have come through all of my problems and to have such a lovely family. He went on to talk of people who he thinks are less fortunate than himself, such as the kids who have been born with no chance of having a full life because of certain illnesses. I offered to write to people who would have some say in his release, telling them about the help he gives these kids, but he said, 'No, under no circumstances do I want to be released because of a few gestures that I have made.' But I know that what he desires most is to be able to finish his life in the type of surroundings that I have been lucky enough to find myself.

One afternoon I was in Los Boliches on the Costa Del Sol having a drink with an old pal of mine, Neil Robertson. Neil and his brother, Gordon, are two guys who enjoyed life, were good company and seemed to know everyone and anyone. On this particular day, Neil said to me, 'You're an old friend of Jack the Hat McVitie?' I nodded. He said, 'I'd like you to meet Jack's son this evening and he would like to thank you for what you wrote about his dad.' I asked Neil if Jack's wife Anne was about and he informed me that she was, but very ill with cancer. Neil had a couple of sons himself who had grown up with Jack the Hat's son and it was their habit to always end the evening in the Melody Bar in Los Boliches. I agreed to stay over, as I was staying a few miles down the coast from there. I was so glad I did, as it ended up being one of those nights that you remember for a long time.

As soon as we arrived at the Melody Bar, I met so many people whom I had known for many years and I also met some new friends. I was particularly happy to meet the Hat's son, as I hadn't seen him since the days when Jack and I worked together as part of a bank-raid team. Jack and Anne, who had been childhood sweethearts, had been very good friends of mine for many years, so it became a pretty nostalgic night. I remember going over the many things that we had been up to in the old days.

When I next saw Reggie Kray on a prison visit, I felt I had to bring up the many rumours that were beginning to circulate about the fact that there were so many people in the room in Evering Road when Jack was murdered and that no one was certain who dealt the final blow to Jack the Hat. It doesn't seem to matter now, as just about everyone in that room received a life sentence for the murder, whether they took part or not. But the fact is that the Lambrianous were sentenced to life imprisonment and so was Reggie Kray. The Lambrianous have been out well over fourteen years, good luck to them, but Reggie Kray is still inside. He will have been in for 31 years in a few months from the time of writing this.

Whilst talking to Ronnie Kray just prior to his death, he told me that Reggie wasn't to blame for Jack the Hat's death and he was very sincere when he spoke to me about it. Ronnie was very emotional about his brother doing all that time and he mentioned that it must have been because, 'We all decided to stick together and deny everything.' That's obviously what they all did and as a consequence, there were a few miscarriages of justice in that case that have never been challenged. I've just been following the Charlie Kray 'fit up' and Charlie must be wondering what he's done to deserve this, especially after the way he was fitted up with ten years after the Jack the Hat affair.

I've asked Reggie on numerous occasions to speak up for himself and apply for his licence for parole, but he said, 'I'll never ask anyone for any favours. I've sat in these places for years and I've watched hundreds of child killers go free in less time than I've done and if they think that I'm worse than those "nonces", well there's nothing I can do about that.'

I've done many after-dinner talks where I speak briefly about my own life and then open the floor to the various questions that the audience think I may be able to talk about. One of the main questions I am asked is why Reggie Kray is still in after all these years? It is a difficult question to answer. It's one that I would like to ask the Home Secretary. I am sure that the question puzzles many members of the prison staff who have had anything to do with Reg whilst he has been in prison.

No one has ever explained how Jack the Hat was murdered in Evering Road. Any criminal will tell you that the police, especially in the '50s and '60s, were quite confident that if they were to state in court that black was white, they would be believed. Everyone was also aware that the police would lock as many people in the cells and then concoct a story that would sound plausible then set about getting enough circumstantial evidence to support the verbals. Verbal evidence was the strongest method of ensuring a conviction. First the police knew that most solicitors would advise their clients not to dispute the evidence in court because if you were to attempt to discredit the police, you would run the risk of having your own background disclosed to the jury. So whatever went on in the flat the evening that Jack the Hat died would only be told to the jury in the way the police wanted it told, made up of stories that had been told to them by people who had been there at the time. And it was also in the interest of some people who had been there not to tell the truth. It suited the Old Bill, as all they had to do was see that Reggie Kray was found guilty of the murder of Jack the Hat and some of the rest of the people who were assembled at the scene of the crime would go down with him. The fact is, though, that Reggie Kray is still in prison after doing 31 years [at the time of writing] and the others have been out over fifteen years. Also some people who were there did no time inside at all. I can confirm that in all the years I knew Reggie Kray, I never saw him in possession of a knife, let alone use one. I also know that at least one of the people who were in the flat that evening has told lies about other aspects relating to Jack's death and where his body was disposed. Perhaps one day some person in a position to undertake such an investigation into the real story of Jack the Hat's death may unfold one of the biggest miscarriages of justice we've ever known.

Life and death seem to figure much in my own life since I've written the previous chapter. Neil Robertson, who had been responsible for my reunion with the Hat's son, has died in tragic circumstances. His wife phoned me whilst I was having dinner to inform me that Neil had fallen from the top of a block of flats in London.

Neil had lived a very flamboyant life. He had to go to Spain as he was being investigated over a scam to do with VAT evasion of £2 million. Neil and his friend arrived on the Costa del Sol with a large amount of money. The word soon got round and every con man on the coast was scheming to take a few quid off the new philanthropists who had just arrived. It didn't take long before Neil and his friend were involved in a deal with a Welshman who was soon to disappear with nearly £1 million. However, the Welshman didn't realise that Neil was quite well connected and, as a consequence, the Welshman was kidnapped from his new villa and his new Rolls Royce apprehended from the driveway. He was lucky, however; he was set free with no more than a few 'slaps' after telling Neil and his friends where the other £500,000 was hidden. Neil was arrested for this and, after greasing a few palms, he was released on bail. He then purchased the El Gorabo Tennis Club on the Mijas Road, Fuengirola, Costa del Sol. This became a favourite meeting place for every Costa del Villain and a few celebrities who would rub shoulders with the faces from Britain's underworld. It was there that I was to renew the acquaintance of an old friend of mine from the past, the talented Polly Perkins, who was to star in the ill-fated soap, *Eldorado*.

It would be interesting to see under the new proposed rules regarding the parole system, how the Parole Board would look at the case of Reggie Kray. I could not visualise any person who was in a responsible position and who looked at his case dispassionately would fail to recognise that enough was enough. I remember well the reputation that the twins had in the late '50s and early '60s. Every local villain knew that you didn't mess about with the twins, but at the same time every local trader and man on the street knew he was safe from being molested or mugged. A very different world from today. People who had hard times knew that they could always go to see the twins and receive a helping hand.

I often think back to the days when I knew the Kray twins well and I think I am intelligent enough to know the difference between good and evil. I have met many evil people in my life, but although the Kray brothers were typical, tough products of wartime East End London, they had more principles than many people with a privileged upbringing. The type of gangland incident that they were involved in was just a natural progression of the only way of life that they had ever known. So in that sense they were not evil, unlike people who prey on the misery of others. I can assure you the Krays would have been welcomed into the houses of some of the victims of horrible crimes more readily than some criminals who have not received half the punishment that the Krays have.

I think Reggie has got a lot to offer. I'm sure if people could hear Reggie talking today, they would realise that he has not wasted his time. Unfortunately, Ronnie died whilst still doing his sentence.

I knew the victims that the Krays were sent to prison for killing and one of them was once my best friend. I am sure that if Jack McVitie could speak now, he would say, 'They've done their bird like men, let them go now.'

Shortly after Ronnie's funeral, my wife and I decided to part and I was fortunate enough to meet Maxine Doyle, the landlady of the Hare and Hounds. I then decided to settle back in Manchester. I think I have met just about every 'face' in Manchester and quite a few from other northern cities and towns and, invariably over a drink, the conversation comes up about Britain's hard men.

I've known most of the tough guys at some time or other in my life and some of the genuine hard men are the quietest people you would ever be likely to meet. It would be wrong of me to judge the hardest, but in every town there are a few who would impress anyone with their manliness. But it is very hard for me to answer a question I've often been asked, 'Who is the toughest guy you've ever met?' One thing I do know is that the bully will never impress anyone.

I've met many tough guys in Manchester, Liverpool, Blackpool, Leeds and many other towns, but I don't like to compare people. I have met many fighting men who would compare favourably in any company. Four or five come immediately to mind from London, Cliff Field, Lennie McLean, Roy Shaw, Jimmy Smith and Billy Williams.

Billy was a great fighter. He turned professional when he was a youngster and Angelo Dundee took him to the States where he was to have a dozen or so fights undefeated. When he came home, he got into a bit of trouble and got eight years in prison, where he was to spend a lot of time in the punishment block and suffered greatly at the hands of people who wouldn't have stood a chance with him man to man.

Manchester has always had its hard men and I've met them all and admired them as a comparison to any tough guys I've ever met. Ronnie Camileri was one tough, gentle giant, yet he was once charged with killing a man in a fight. He was fortunately acquitted of that but it would have been a tragedy had he been found guilty, as he was a true gentleman. I am proud to know his son, Steve, who has grown into a 'chip off the old block'.

Jimmy Swords has always been a respected man in Manchester and was a good professional middleweight. I saw him fight a few times, but Jimmy, like many good pros, learned his trade in the back streets, or as a guest of Her Majesty. As a consequence, you'll find a street fighter very hard to beat and I'm very pleased to call Jimmy one of my friends. He is now a very wealthy business man and I look forward to our little chinwags now and again.

Whenever anyone talks of hard men in the north of England, the name of Mixie Walsh from Blackpool comes up. I've known Mixie many years, ever since we were the two youngest prisoners in Dartmoor when we were there together. Now, Mixie wasn't only a good street-fighter, he was a powerful, strong keep-fit specialist and at the time we were working together, he would help me to get my quota of rocks smashed in the stone quarry. The one thing I can say about Mixie is that he was a true hard man and a sound fellow. I have seen Mixie quite a lot over the years since I was released from prison and we've had a few drinks together. Also I've visited the gym with him and it makes me sweat just to watch him work out. The last time I saw Mixie was in Liverpool at the funeral of another tough guy, Billy Grimwood. Billy was also respected all over the country and I met some very tough men at Billy's funeral.

But when I think of all-round hard men, I've got to put Roy Shaw up with the best of them. I first became friends with Roy, who had been a professional middleweight boxer in the early '60s. We'd have a few drinks in the Log Cabin Club in Wardour Street, Soho, which was owned jointly by the two well-known boxing families, the Walkers and McCarthys. Roy and myself were getting a living as armed robbers, but Roy was caught after a series of successful robberies and sentenced to 15 years' imprisonment. He had already done a smaller sentence in Wandsworth where he worked in the laundry. I would see him in the punishment block quite frequently, where we both spent a lot of our time. Roy was to go on to Parkhurst on the Isle of Wight and after this he was transferred to Broadmoor Mental Hospital after being acquitted of causing the death of a guy called Brown. I went to visit Roy in Broadmoor just prior to being sentenced to 10 years myself for bank robbery. I visited Roy with a guy called Ray Mills and I couldn't believe my eyes at how well and fit Roy looked. His muscles were bulging and he was literally bouncing with energy. I remarked about this and Roy said, if you had to put up with half the nutters he had to put up with in that place, you'd be fit!

I'm pleased to know that Roy is doing well in life. I believe he's retired now. I'm positive, though, that Roy would admit that one of the greatest of all of the street and prize-fighters was Cliff Field. I could name plenty of guys who were the business in the fighting game, such as George Cooper, Terry Coombes (who was sentenced with me to ten years for doing the bank in Cardiff) and in Manchester there is Dave Ward, who has just finished a 12-year sentence for doing two geezers in a fight. Dave was a good professional boxer but he is also one of the best street fighters I've ever seen. I used to visit Dave in Full Sutton top security prison and he looked very fit and powerful, but he assures me that he never wants to fight again. He now spends a lot of time reading the classics: he quotes Shakespeare and many famous authors. I'm also glad to see he's made friends with another nice guy in the nick, Rab Carruthers, another very tough guy from Glasgow. I saw Rab last week in the visiting room and he looks very well. Nearly every day of my life I meet guys who are very tough characters and the ones with real ability to fight are normally the quietest there are.

A good mate of mine at the moment, Dean Brennan, voted in Manchester as one of the best all-round fighters in town, is very quiet with an incredible sense of humour. He's a good guy to be in company with and he's got all the good traits that make a real man; he's sound, trustworthy and generous. He's respected by all the people who are respected themselves.

In Manchester, I get invited to go to many functions, whether they be charity dos, boxing dinners, football matches – both at Old Trafford or Maine Road – ex-boxers' meetings, or racing days. The invitations will come from many respected people in Manchester or Salford. The Pollard family from Salford are some of the most respected people I have ever met and they match up with the respect that I had with Reggie and Ronnie Kray when I was a youngster.

When I talk of hard men, I always think of Jimmy Smith from Paddington, who looked as if he'd been chiselled from a granite block. Jimmy was well respected by the Downes family. Terry Downes, who became the professional middleweight champion of the world, had a few uncles. 'Chirpy' Downes was a real character and a few times Jimmy Smith got the 'hump' with Chirpy. It became a battle of wits. Chirpy could always win the verbal battles but everyone knew who would have won the physical combat.

Manchester has its own fighting men. One who comes to mind was Hughie Burton – a good travelling man, whom Dave Barry from Bayswater and myself brought to the Epsom Derby meeting in 1964 to fight Jimmy Smith from Paddington. I believe there is a very good travelling man whom I have met recently who would give anyone a few problems – that is Pat Dougherty. Paddy Dougherty is a very respected man in Manchester, not only for his fighting prowess, but for his fairness. He has, for many years, fought all of the famed prize-fighters, with a great degree of success. So great is his reputation that he is now asked to be the referee at all of the money fights. He is also a fine man to socialise with.

Whenever anyone talks of boxing in Manchester, you will invariably find that one of the 'locals' will like to differentiate between Manchester and Salford because they are a very proud people and it means a lot to them to let you know where they were born. I must say I can sympathise with this feeling as it is something I have grown up with, being from London. There is also the same need to let someone know that you are from a particular area, either north, south, east or west London, so when the knowledgeable Salfordians talk of boxing, they will tell you that the first bare-knuckle world champion at lightweight was from Salford. This was Arthur Chambers. He beat Billy Edwards in the 27th round in Canada. Arthur Chambers also helped as a consultant to the famous Marquis of Queensbury to formulate the well-known rules. Another famous fighter from Salford was the legendary Joe Bowker. Joe learned his trade at Billy Hughes' famous boxing booth. He went on to become the bantamweight champion of the world in 1904, when he beat American, Frankie Neil. He was the first Salford fighter to box at the National Sporting Club where he was to beat another legend, London's own Pedlar Palmer. He was later to go up in weight to have two gruelling 20-round contests with 'peerless' Jim Driscoll. Joe was in the Army all through the First World War and he was still boxing and winning fights 14 years after he won the world title.

Many fighters learned the trade with Joe after he retired and Salford had many fighting heroes, none more so than the Marchant family. Billy was the eldest of six brothers from Lower Broughton and joined Hague's boxing booth at the age of 15 and travelled all over the north of England, Lancashire, Yorkshire and Cheshire. Billy had a fallout with Gall Hague over money a year or so after he had become a star attraction and left the booth and walked all the way home to Salford from Castleford in Yorkshire. His dad was soon to see how capable his son was and so he sent him to London where Joe Bowker had set up a gym. Billy came back to Salford after a few months and was by this time a very hard man, so his father decided to open his own gym in Pendleton. This gym was to attract many Salford fighters, notably the good heavyweight, Jack Curphy. Curphy was very popular before the First World War and he was to go on to fight Joe Beckett, Bombadier Billy Wells, Bandsman Blake and he fought Frank Goddard for the British heavyweight title where he was to be knocked out in the tenth round after a very thrilling contest. Billy Marchant went on to attain great acclaim beating all of the leading featherweights in Britain, but Jim Driscoll evaded the Salford boy. Billy started to become rather disillusioned and decided to try his luck in America. He was soon to make a name for himself by fighting and beating seven American fighters in the four weeks that he was there. He was acclaimed by all of the American writers and he so impressed the great boxing pundit Bat Masterson, the sheriff of Carson City, that he headlined Marchant as the future world champion. Billy wasn't very popular with the establishment and he was sidetracked over and over again. But Billy was earning good money as a fighter. He was very confident and would back himself against all comers, consequently doubling his purse.

Many London fighters came north to get a share of the spoils and Billy

Marchant was the star attraction at all of Jack Smith's shows. Smith had been the local promoter and, as a consequence of his popularity, he moved into the City Athletic Club and then to the Grand Theatre in Peter Street, which later became the Free Trade Hall. Collyhurst and Hulme were great nurseries for promising Manchester fighters and the first time the British heavyweight title was contested by a Mancunian was 'Boy' McCormick and Joe Bleckett. McCormick lost that fight, but he was remembered more as the cruiserweight champion at the age of 19. He immediately made his way to the States looking for fame and fortune and became a credit to the city. He was to travel right across America challenging all of the great heavyweights of the day and he recorded victories over Gunboat Smith, Battling Levinsky, Fireman Flynn, (the same Flynn who had once knocked out Jack Dempsey in one round). He also fought Tommy Gibbons who was to fight Dempsey for the heavyweight championship of the world. McCormick became a good friend of Dempsey and joined Dempsey's camp as a sparring partner when Dempsey fought in the first celebrated million dollar gate against Georges Carpentier. Boy McCormick was a great warrior and, on his return to England, he was to fight one of the greatest fighters ever to come from this country – the great Ted Kid Lewis. The London fight crowd loved McCormick. He gave a man who had fought over twenty times for championship of the world one hell of a fight, but eventually succumbed in the 14th round.

But they didn't all come from Salford. Tell me one boxing *aficionado* who has never heard of Jock McAvoy (the Rochdale Thunderbolt), Johnny King of Collyhurst, the home of many great warriors, plus Jackie Brown, the flyweight champion of the world, also from Collyhurst. All three of the aforementioned fighters were managed by a great man of the boxing world, Harry Fleming. The Fleming family have been associated with boxing in Manchester for many years and one of Harry Fleming's sons, John, was a good friend of mine. John was a great champion of the Manchester ex-boxers and worked tirelessly, helping to raise funds for the more unfortunate members of the MEBA.

I was saddened a few weeks ago to meet a friend at the monthly ex-boxers' meeting whose health had really deteriorated. Peter King had fought Peter Waterman for the British welterweight title. I thought, 'Thank God' for the likes of John Fleming and Jack Edwards, that great manager of many Manchester fighters, who still always attends every meeting of the Manchester ex-boxers. I see the same old faces whenever I attend, especially that great Manchester warrior Tommy Proffit.

I was recently invited to go to the Poet's Corner pub in Atherton to honour Peter King. I attended with my partner, Maxine and we were thrilled to meet Peter's grandson, Adam, who is boxing for England as a schoolboy representative. We watched a couple of his fights on video and he looks a good prospect. In presenting him with a dressing-gown I said, 'If you can emulate your grandfather, you will become wealthy and famous.' Unfortunately, Peter fought in the days before the present-day fight purses, so let us hope that Adam can do well for his lovely family and friends.

I have just received the terrible news that my friend, John Fleming, has died after a short illness. John will be sadly missed by all who ever had the pleasure of knowing him and I met so many of John's family and friends at the funeral.

One thing which saddened me was that John hadn't lived to see his expectation of the future champions who have recently brought such excitement to the Manchester boxing scene. I shared John's forecast that Manchester will have at least three world boxing champions in the very near future. There are so many dynamic prospects and I've been privileged to get to know most of them and have been happy to watch their progress through the professional ranks.

There is Ricky Hatton, whom I have been telling people about for over two years. He is a class act and on the Tyson–Francis undercard, he was close to stealing the thunder with his devastating body punches. We have Antony Farnell and Michael Gomez, who are both trained by Collyhurst's second sporting MBE, Brian Hughes, along with that other star middleweight Robin Reid. Manchester has more rising stars of the boxing world than any other city, including Michael Brodie and another young prospect whom I met at a surprise party to celebrate Brian Hughes' 60th birthday – that was Thomas McDonach. I am really looking forward to seeing all of my predictions come to fruition. Good luck to them all.

I am really settled in Manchester now, but I am always being reminded that there are two different cities that make up Greater Manchester: Salford and Manchester itself. Every city has its characters and in most of my friends in the north, I am reminded of someone from my own part of the world.

There are many reliable and trustworthy people who have a lot of respect and good principles. Walk through the centre of Manchester and you will see the down-and-outs who are just unfortunate people, but mingling with them you will see the bums and professional beggars and winos. But as you pass them, you are probably on your way to meet people who have fought against all the odds and made something of their lives. I get quite a few laughs and I suppose I can say that I'm pretty lucky to find myself at the turn of the century, a very happy and contented man.

One of my very good friends is a guy called Alan Ramsden whom I've known for the best part of 30 years. He's been a publican for 27 years, and runs one of the best known pubs in what has come to be referred to as the 'Gay Village'. In the Village, though, you can get more than gay people.

There are quite a few scoundrels, and Alan is fair but firm with everybody. As a consequence, a lot of people come to Alan's bar with their own problems, and no matter how serious or trivial the problem may be, he will listen attentively and give an honest solution. Invariably, his advice results in another happy face walking around the Village.

I've watched, over a long period, the gay scene develop in Manchester, and I think I know just about every character who has made the Village what it has become today. It is a place that is unique, many parts of the world will try to copy it, but no one will ever capture the thing that makes the Village. The people are the real characters, and through their talents comes a wonderful feeling of togetherness. There are the great icons like Frank Pearson, world renowned as Foo Foo Lamarr. Foo Foo is everything to the village – a very talented and strong willed person, his Foo Foo's Palace is just an illustration of what can be done to bring all types of people together. Frank in drag looks flamboyant and glamorous, but start heckling and slagging his friends, and you will soon realise that Frank comes from a tough and respected family who have made it through some pretty hard times. Frank has all the trappings of success: the Rolls-Royce with personalised number plates, and he owns various excellent bars and restaurants. But you will still see him having a butty with the boys and girls in Churchill's Bar. His friends are many, but all wonderful people in their own right. His personal manager, Michael, is a gentleman to his fingertips, married to Frank's beautiful niece, and they have a very exciting hotel and bar, Monroe's. Frank's friends could be named in any *Who's Who* of Manchester. His personal set of Colin Rigby, John Trotter and Alan Owen to mention but a few, are all examples of what makes Manchester a vibrant, exciting city centre.

# 25.

## REFLECTIONS

I often sit and think about my past life after having a few drinks with friends. Many people have a fascination with the underworld scene of the '50s and '60s and so the odd questions come up, such as who were the most impressive people from the various gangs? It's when I get asked questions like that I think back and I find that I'm remembering quite a lot of people who never made a name for themselves, or people who strove to make a name, but didn't quite make it – and it's not only gangsters and villains. I think of people like Burt Wickstead, the so called 'gang-buster' who used whatever method he could to enhance his progress in the police force. A case in point would be the hounding of people like the Dixon brothers, the Tibbs family and so many other people. It was blatant misuse of power and, of course, the myths had begun already after the Kray twins' trial. 'Nipper' Read had become the 'knight in shining armour' because he had arrested the Krays. The Dixon brothers had been no threat to anyone but they looked the part, well over six feet tall and pretty powerful looking. They liked a drink and a bit of fun. Alan Dixon would sing a song or two, George looked a bit fearsome with a few scars around his face and the mere fact that one or two publicans had asked them to pop in now and again to keep a bit of peace and quiet was the green light for the Old Bill to nick them for the old protection game, which would be described as 'demanding money with menaces'. And because their publican friend Phil Jacobs refused to co-operate with the Wickstead method of policing he, too, was nicked as the leader of a bunch of evil people preying on honest publicans. Nothing could be further from the truth. They had a few battles with old enemies in opposition pubs but no more than that. As with the Tibbs family, no innocent people were ever hurt because their problems were with fighting people like themselves. The Tibbs family were sentenced to terms of 12 years and ten years and the Dixons were given terms similar to Jimmy Tibbs. In those days, if a policeman was to tell a juror that black was white, he would be believed, but now I think the average man in the street knows that perjury is not alien to the copper who takes the case as a personal vendetta. But it is very difficult today for the police to fit people up without a lot of forethought and planning, as with cases like Charlie Kray's conviction for conspiracy to smuggle drugs. There is always the chance that another look at the case might unearth a very different picture of what happened in the Elbow Room nightclub in Birmingham.

The sad thing about life is that so many genuine people are brought together through death. It is the one time that people seem to realise how much a person has contributed to the lives of others through the many attributes that that person has bestowed on his or her many friends. It also brings together so many people who would only meet at funerals.

I met so many lovely people at John Fleming's funeral whom I consider my genuine friends, like Bobby Johnson, Eddie Cartwright, Tommy O'Neil, many more ex-boxers and other people who had great regard for John because he was just a good guy.

I was just coming to the end of my book when I received a phone call from Johnny Nash telling me that Charlie Kray had died. I wasn't surprised at the sad news as I knew that Charlie hadn't been well for some time since he had been sentenced to 12 years imprisonment for a most contrived case of conspiracy as I have ever seen.

John kept me informed of the details of the funeral and I travelled down to London the day before with Jimmy the Weed. My pal, David Barry, organised transport for a couple of days as there were so many people to see who would not normally be in one place at the same time.

I met Johnny Nash and we went to the chapel of rest in Bethnal Green Road. The crowd was huge and there were many old faces I hadn't seen for years. I had mixed feelings about certain people I had good cause to feel angry about, but out of respect for the occasion, I just tried to remember where I was and why I was there.

The service was at St Matthew's Church and although I didn't know any of the security firm, they were all very polite and respectful. I liked the woman's touch of 'Flanagan' the model, organising the arrangements at the church.

The reaction from the crowds of people lining the streets was overwhelming when Reggie Kray arrived. The clapping and cheers were spontaneous and the comments of the stallholders, 'Let him out now – they let the IRA bombers out and those so-and-so paedophiles,' rang in my ears.

Once Reggie was escorted to the front row of the church, still cuffed to a prison officer, those of us who were allowed inside had the chance to have a few words with him. I waited till everyone had sat down, then went and greeted him and gave my condolences and a message from all my Manchester friends – which he really appreciated. He put his arm round my shoulder and with a choked look, asked me to come and visit him again. I was really choked myself and I'm hoping that the next time I go to see him, he will have got his release date.

I was to meet up with most of the old faces after the burial, either at The Blind Beggars pub or The Horn of Plenty and I had time to speak to many of the people who have affected my life in one way or another. Some I didn't wish to speak to, but it was reassuring to learn from some of the more respected people how our feelings about things are mutual. Many things were revealed to me that day about which I had been totally unaware, but they will all remain a secret with me as long as I live.

It was the same at Ronnie Kray's funeral. I had a call from Spain to tell me that Ronnie had died and to ask if I would see that a wreath was sent to the chapel of rest in Bethnal Green from the Barnham family from Fulham. This I obviously arranged for the family that I had been closely associated with for quite some time.

When I walked into the churchyard of St Matthew's, I was again stunned at the amount of people who were there to pay their respects – some of whom I hadn't seen for years.

I had travelled to London the day before the funeral from the north of England with a pal of mine, Denis Crolla, a hotelier from Blackpool. Denis had always been associated with many London underworld figures and there was always a bed and a bite to eat for any of the chaps who were passing through. I thought it would be right for Denis to come with me, so we booked into the Tower Hotel and that night we met many people who had come from all over Britain to attend the funeral.

The BBC approached me and asked me to say a few words about Ronnie for their news bulletin, which I did on the morning of the funeral. Quite a lot of people heard that broadcast on their way to the East End and complimented me on what I had to say. That was the first time I met Dave Courtney, who has become a bit of a celebrity himself. Good luck, Dave. He did a good job of organising the funeral arrangements for the most amazing day I'd had for many a year.

The congregation split into two groups on that day after the burial, one group went to the Blind Beggars pub and the others went to the Governors pub where Lennie McLean had erected a marquee to accommodate everyone.

The thought that I took home with me that evening was how quiet and respectful everyone seemed to be towards each other, even the chief

221

inspector of the police who were there to control the crowd and to make sure that only people who had been invited to the service were allowed into the church. As I walked up to the door where Dave Courtney was directing his men, the inspector came forward and Dave said, 'It's okay, guv, he's one of the old firm,' and the inspector said in reply, 'Yes, I know, I was just going to remark how well he looks.'

There were so many people who turned up that day who I thought looked very well: Albert Reading and Roy Shaw, Freddie Foreman, Johnny and Ronnie Nash, Dave Barry, Arthur Suttie, the Dixon Brothers, Patsy Manning and so many others who I was happy to see.

Then Frank Fraser turned up waving at the TV cameras – all the memories came flooding back to that dreadful day in 1964 when I almost died – and *my* memory is crystal clear on the events of that day.

He infers that he bundled me into a motor single-handed and took me off to do me in. He always makes the same lying remark that I mentioned the Kray twins not liking what he was up to.

Well, the truth is that he and more than half a dozen of his friends were standing outside the Astor Club when I came out, including Eddie Richardson, Billie Stayton, Tommy Harris and a little weasel called Larry something-or-other. I jumped into the motor next to Eddie Richardson and challenged any two of them to come with me and fight like men. Their answer was to all jump in and immediately start to use 'tools' on me because none of them could fight. They tried to give themselves some kind of excuse to have a go at someone who could have enhanced their reputation above all the other liberties they had taken in the past.

I've seen some of them in the nick over the years and they are nothing but 'yes men'.

That little mob and the rest of them who pulled up in the other car to add their weight – they know and I know what was said that night and I'll remind them next time I happen to bump into any of them.

People say that truth is stranger than fiction and in my case that is so. Who would believe, looking at me today, that most of my seventy years have been dominated by a sinister underworld of crime, corruption and murder? A gangland world where the famous and infamous – celebrities, politicians, socialites and the most notorious criminals in British history – not only rubbed shoulders, but also did business together.

In recent years, my life has taken a different direction and I have now settled in Manchester at the Hare and Hounds pub with my partner, Maxine Doyle. I now feel able to sit back and reflect on my time as a first-division criminal and my life in the heyday of the gangster in the '50s and '60s. This sub-world was my life for many years. I know every notorious criminal and many celebrities who are part of the glamour that goes hand in hand with the not so glamorous.

I have told my story as it happened – a startling and shocking account of the underworld. A world which – though seemingly removed from normal everyday life on the surface – was in fact lurking around any corner if you just knew where to look. It could suck you in and put you on the slippery road to a life of crime.

Do I have any regrets? Am I angry at the hand life's dealt me? Have I got it all off my chest? Different days bring different answers, but one thing's for sure – it's the brutal truth. And there's no going back on it.